You
Don't
Know
Me

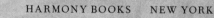

Reflections of

My Father,

Ray Charles

✳

HARMONY BOOKS   NEW YORK

Ray Charles Robinson Jr.

with MARY JANE ROSS

You Don't Know Me

Copyright © 2010 by Ray Charles Robinson Jr.

Published in the United States by Harmony Books, an imprint of
the Crown Publishing Group, a division of Random House, Inc., New York.
www.crownpublishing.com

Harmony Books is a registered trademark and the Harmony Books
colophon is a trademark of Random House, Inc.

Frontispiece photo: Phil Hewsmith

Library of Congress Cataloging-in-Publication Data

Robinson, Ray Charles, Jr.
You don't know me : Reflections of my father, Ray Charles / Ray Charles
Robinson Jr. with Mary Jane Ross.—1st ed.
p. cm.
1. Charles, Ray, 1930–2004.   2. Singers—United States—Biography.
3. Robinson, Ray Charles, Jr.   I. Ross, Mary Jane.   II. Title.
ML420.C46R63 2010
782.42164092—dc22
[B]   2009048177

ISBN 978-0-307-46293-0

Printed in the United States of America

Design by Ellen Cipriano

10 9 8 7 6 5 4 3 2 1

First Edition

To the memory of my father, Ray Charles Robinson, and all that you
were to me and all that you dreamed you wanted to be.
I love you come rain or come shine.

To my loving mother, Della B. Robinson.

To my daughters, Erin Brianne and Blair Alayne.

My prayer for all of you is that God continues to bless you,
heal your hearts, and answer your prayers.
I am so blessed to have you in my life.

I love you.

CONTENTS

FOREWORD

I FIRST MET Ray Charles Robinson Jr. on the first anniversary of his father's death, June 10, 2005. At that time I was working on the series "Silhouettes & Shadows," and I welcomed the opportunity to paint Ray Jr. Nearly fifteen years earlier I was introduced to his father, who had shown an interest in my art. I had developed a relief style of painting, and Ray Charles was fascinated with the textural surface of the canvas and artwork he could feel with his fingertips. It was ironic that a blind man would take to my work—using senses other than sight. Ray Charles responded to my paintings with insights that were astonishing.

That Friday afternoon, Ray Jr. was calm and focused as I traced his silhouette on the paper taped to the wall behind him. We spoke about my encounter with his father, and soon we were taking on deeper issues that connected our lives—like drug addiction and sobriety. Ray Jr. had been struggling to stay clean, and I shared my similar struggles with drugs and how they nearly cost me my life. My nexus to father and son was as much about breaking the chains of addiction as it was about the creative process. When we were done with the sitting, Ray Jr. left for the cemetery to visit his father.

You Don't Know Me is an extraordinary personal story full of heart, heartbreak, and healing. Ray Jr. shares his dreams, his struggles, and a dysfunction inherited, in part, from his father. It is also a shocking and gripping story of Ray Charles that could only be told through the autobiographical lens of his namesake. This is a family history that is conveyed with honesty and tenderness. This is also the chronicle of a man who overcomes despair, and it renders all of the other biographies, films, and accounts of Ray Charles's personal life and public persona meaningless. Ray Jr. is fearless in his frankness about his humbling journey and a forgiveness he finally adopts.

You Don't Know Me is an elegy delivered by the prodigal son of a prodigal father.

Andrew Lakey, Artist

CHAPTER 1

Mother

My mother told me . . .

There'll be hard times.

—RAY CHARLES

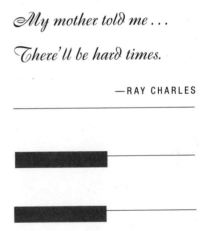

DELICIOUS AROMAS FILLED THE HOUSE. MY MOTHER HAD been cooking all day. Barbecued chicken, sweet potatoes, biscuits and gravy, food for the body and the soul. My brothers and I were squirming with excitement, trying unsuccessfully to concentrate on the toy soldiers scattered across the den floor. The sound of a car door slamming brought us running past the living room toward the front door, and I heard my mother call out, "You slow down, you hear me? You all are going to break your necks!"

I skidded to a halt in the entrance hall, my younger brothers piling up behind me like train cars on a railroad track. We heard the rattle of a key ring and the door opened. The man who walked into the foyer wore a white shirt, black suit, and dark sunglasses. I glanced back at my mother, who had come up behind us, and she smiled and nodded at me. "Go on, now."

As I ran toward the open door, the man's dark face split wide with a brilliant grin. "Baby," he murmured, as he knelt down to meet me. His fingers sought my head, feeling its shape, then moved gently over my eyes and down my face. He gripped my shoulders, running his hands down my arms, squeezing my wrists, feeling the shape and the height of me. He nodded, saying, "All right, then. You're gettin' big." Only then did I throw myself into his arms, his silk shirt liquid against my face, his cheek rough as he turned to kiss me. I breathed him in, that trademark blend of Brut and cigarettes that was my father. Daddy was home. Nothing else mattered.

I spent most of my childhood waiting for my dad to come home from the road. It always felt like he was never coming back. It has been six years since he passed away, but I still feel as though I'm waiting. Not a day goes by that I don't think of him—each time I look in a mirror, each time I introduce myself, each time I remember who he was, each time I wonder who I am. My father was Ray Charles, and I have the honor and the burden of carrying his name. I have never been certain what I was supposed to do with that name. When he left us for good, I knew it was time to figure it out. If I am to have a future, I must begin by understanding the past.

MY FATHER WAS BORN in Albany, Georgia, on September 23, 1930. His mother, Aretha Williams, was only fourteen when he was born, and she had been sent away to relatives to have her baby, where the gossiping neighbors couldn't reach her. She returned to her hometown of Greenville, Florida, a few weeks later with my father in her arms. She named her tiny son Ray Charles Robinson. My grandfather, Bailey Robinson, had given his son a last name but little else. He was already married to another woman named Mary Jane, and there would be other women and other children as well. I don't know much about my paternal grandfather. My father never spoke to me about him unless my brothers and I asked questions. I'm not sure how much he even remembered. My grandfather had passed by the time my father was ten. He remained in my father's memory as a shadowy figure, a tall presence that showed up in my grandmother's tiny home every now and then to be with her, leaving before the sun rose the next day.

Greenville was no more than a speck on the map when my father was growing up there. The entire town was less than a mile and a half wide, and everyone was poor. It was just a question of how poor. My father's family was at the bottom of the economic ladder. As he put it, there was nothing between him and the bottom but dirt. Still there were blessings. A year after my father was born, my grandmother gave birth to another son, George. George and RC, as everyone called my father, were inseparable. Wherever my father went, neighbors recall, George was right behind him, a small shadow struggling to keep up with his big brother. And they went everywhere their feet would carry them. My father still had his eyesight then, and he and George loved to explore, running barefoot down the dirt roads, through the fields, and in and out of the small jumble of buildings that made up the town. George was a whiz with numbers, and by three years old had such a remarkable ability in math that people came just to watch him do problems. The brothers had no toys, so George made little cars and gadgets out of scraps of wood and wire. He had a gift, my father said. George could make anything.

Then there were the Pitmans, the couple who owned the Red Wing Café and general store. My father called Wylie Pitman "Mr. Pit." He loved to run through the little town to Mr. Pit's store, sometimes to fetch things for his mother, sometimes just to see Mr. and Mrs. Pit. He still spoke about Mr. Pit when I was growing up. It was Wylie Pitman who taught my father his notes on the old upright piano in the store. I don't know if the Pitmans recognized my father's musical ability or if they just liked him. Either way, it was Mr. Pit who gave my father his start in music when he was just a little boy.

Most important, my father had his mother, and he also had the woman he called his "other mother," Bailey Robinson's wife, Mary Jane. Mary Jane and Aretha could easily have been divided by jealousy, but that was never the case. Mary Jane loved and watched out for young Aretha, and she watched out for my father and George, too. Mary Jane had lost her own son shortly before my father was born, and Aretha's small boy helped fill the hole in her heart. Much older than Aretha, Mary Jane became the only grandmother my father ever knew. She nurtured him, bought him little presents, and was lenient with him. My dad said his mother was the exact opposite of Mary Jane, very strict, always trying to instill discipline in him. He would tell us about his mother if we asked him. He spoke of how strong she was in her spirit, how beautiful she was, how he loved to touch her long, soft hair. It seemed like his mother was my father's world when he was a child. My grandmother didn't have money to buy her sons shoes or much else, but she gave her boys freedom to explore and a safe place to come home to. Those first years were dim in my father's memory, but the memories were all good ones.

When my father was five years old, his small, safe world began to fall apart. The first blow was one he would never recover from—the death of George. My grandmother was working inside the cabin one afternoon while my dad and George played outside. The big tubs she used when she took in washing were next to the cabin, and she had already hauled the water and filled them. The boys loved to splash around in the rinse tubs on a hot day, pretending they were swimming. She had told my father, as she always did, to watch out for his little brother. That afternoon four-year-old George climbed into one of the big tubs to cool off. My father didn't think anything of it at first since they both splashed around in the tubs all the time. Within minutes, though, my father realized something was wrong. George had begun to flail, gasping for air and trying to scream. My father froze in panic for a moment, but then he ran to the tub as fast as he could. By then George was upside down in the water. My father grabbed George's ankles and tried to pull him out. He pulled with all his might, but my father wasn't much bigger than George. The tub was bigger than both of them, and my dad didn't have the strength to pull his brother out. My father began screaming for help, and his mother came running out of the cabin. She pulled George from the tub, laid him on the ground, and tried to breathe life back into him. Sobbing and praying for God to save George, she screamed at my father, "This is your fault! You were supposed to be watching out for your little brother!" The last thing my father remembers about that day is the sight of his mother, her face streaming with tears, carrying George's lifeless body into the cabin.

There was a funeral, a time of mourning, visits from neighbors, but my father was never able to remember any of it. He knew his brother was dead, and his mind went dark. In that inner darkness, his mother's voice echoed endlessly. He could hear her screaming and begging God for help as the words "This is your fault!" burned more deeply into his heart each day. I doubt my grandmother remembered telling him that, and I do not think she really meant it. In a moment of unbearable grief and pain, she had lashed out at him. But the damage was done. My father blamed himself. Decades later, near the end of his own life, he still suffered from the belief that it was his fault his little brother had died.

Not long afterward my father's outer world began to go dark, too, for his eyes started to fail him. He did not lose his sight all at once. First the objects around him blurred. Gradually, it became harder and harder to see into the distance. People in town thought maybe his sight was failing because of George, that watching his brother die had been so painful that my father could no longer look at the world. His eyes would crust over with mucus, and his mother would have to wash them gently with a cloth so he could open them in the morning. Knowing he would not be able to see much longer, he started to memorize colors. When his mother saved the money to take him to a doctor, the doctor shook his head sadly and told her that her son was going blind. There was nothing the doctor could do to help. Soon my father could tell the difference between dark and light but nothing else, and before long, even that distinction seemed to fade. Many years later doctors told my father it was severe glaucoma that had stolen his sight. No matter, for there was nothing that could be done. My father says that except when George drowned, he never knew his mother to cry out against God or weep with despair. Stoically, she accepted the news that her surviving son was losing his sight. She had barely left her teens behind her, and she had already lost one son and now the other one was going blind.

But my grandmother was a remarkable woman. She refused to feel sorry for herself or to let my father give in to self-pity. My grandmother had never been strong physically. Her health was already failing, and I think she knew that she might not be there to see my father through to manhood. She knew for certain that he was not going to have a father around. There was a job to be done. If her son was to go through life sightless, she was going to make sure he was well prepared.

So despite having no education herself, she taught him what little math she knew, and, most important, how to truly take care of himself, how to be self-reliant. Long after his sight was gone, he continued to do chores—to clean the house, to chop wood, to cook, to run errands, to bathe and dress himself. People in town criticized my grandmother, thinking she expected too much of her poor blind boy. She ignored them. In a time and place where the most a blind man could aspire to was a banjo and a tin cup, she wanted more for her son. I don't know if she realized how gifted he really was. I do know that whatever his gifts were, she wanted him to use them.

It was because she loved her son that she made the hardest decision of her life. She knew that she could never teach my father all the things he needed to learn. So she enrolled him in the Colored Department of the Florida School for the Deaf and Blind in St. Augustine, Florida. It was funded by the state, which would pay all the expenses. My father was seven years old, and he didn't want to go, didn't want to leave his mother and Mary Jane and Mr. Pit and everything he knew and loved. He begged his mother not to send him away, but she stood firm. When fall came, my grandmother put him on the train and watched as he was carried far from home, alone and terrified. It was the best thing she could have done for him, and it gave him a life, but I am not certain he ever forgave her. My mother believes the hurt of that separation stayed with him for the rest of his life.

It was at this school that my father learned to read and write and make music, to do all the things that he would need to live his life. He was there for seven years, coming home only for summers. And it was while he was there that he suffered two more significant losses.

The first loss occurred during his first year there. By the end of winter, the pain in his right eye had intensified. The doctors couldn't find a way to relieve the pain, and eventually his suffering became unbearable. The school doctor told my father that the only way to stop the pain was to remove his eye. He was terrified, but there was no help for it. Eight years old and all alone, my father was admitted to the hospital, where doctors removed his right eyeball. No one even told his mother about the surgery.

The second loss was the one that transformed his life, even more than blindness. My father was fifteen years old when one of his teachers came into class one day and told him he was going home. His mother was dead. With no warning, he was informed that his mother had died. My father never spoke to us of that moment, not even to my mother, but years later I read about it in his own words. He said that in that moment, the world became a series of shadows, of silhouettes, and he sank into a sort of trance. He could not comprehend his mother's passing. It was unthinkable that she was no longer there to stroke his face, to soothe him, to hold him when he was afraid. The last thing he remembered was the school putting him on the train for home. He had no memory of the remainder of that week. He could neither speak nor eat nor respond to anything around him. Modern psychologists would say that he was in deep emotional shock, but he simply said that for a while he went crazy, and he almost didn't come back from the darkness. It was a Christian lady in town named Ma Beck whom my father credits with saving him. She came to him and spoke of his mother, reminded him of all the things his mother had taught him, had hoped for him. She admonished him, reminding him of what his mother would say to him if she were there—that he had to carry on. Ma Beck was somehow able to get through to him. He collapsed into her arms and sobbed for hours, and afterward he went with her to his mother's funeral to see her one last time, stroking her face and her long, soft hair.

I wish I could have known my grandmother. She probably never knew that she had birthed a prodigy in Ray Charles Robinson, but she did know that he was special and that she probably would not be there with him for long. She never had the chance to get an education herself, but she showed her own genius in the way she raised him. She only had him with her for seven years, but somehow my grandmother knew she could shape his life at an early age. She taught him to be independent, not to rely on others to help him through life. She taught a blind son how to succeed in a seeing world. She taught him everything he needed to know—except how to say good-bye to her.

Two years before he died, facing his own mortality, my father wrote a song about his mother. He also spoke of Ma Beck, for he firmly believed that God had sent her to save his life in the midst of unbearable loss. I have no doubt that she did save his life that day, but the truth is that my father had been given a death blow nonetheless. He never recovered from the emotional trauma of that loss. He never recovered spiritually, either. Everyone told him that Jesus had taken his mother away. He hated Jesus for taking her, but he feared Jesus, too. Who was this Jesus that he would take a boy's mother? And why? People at church said one should not love the things of the world too much. Is that why Jesus took her? Because he loved her too much? At the end of his life, he told Mable John, a close spiritual adviser and friend, that he was afraid of loving anyone that much again. If he did, Jesus might take them, too. When his mother died, she took a part of him with her that we never got back.

God understood the kind of mother my father needed, and He gave him that mother for fifteen years. God also understood that it would take another special woman to love a man who was so wounded. That woman was my mother. If my dad had not met my mother, there might never have been a Ray Charles.

MY MOTHER, Della Beatrice Antwine, was born two years before my father, a fact she still hates to admit. Her family lived in Richmond, Texas, a town fifteen miles southwest of Houston that boasted fewer than 1,500 people when my mother was born. Richmond was cotton and oil country, and it wasn't hit as hard as most of the country during the Depression. Visitors from those days described the town as a surviving piece of the old South, with residential streets still lined with fine white plantation-style houses with large verandas. Richmond had been a refuge for emancipated slaves after the Civil War, but by the time my mother was born, the train tracks running through the middle of town was a racial divide as absolute as a razor-wire-topped wall.

The colored section of town, as it was called then, was about three blocks long. It consisted mainly of barbecue places and beer joints where people could dance on a Saturday night. Our family owned about eighty acres of land, divided among the various households. My mother lived in a one-bedroom frame house on ten acres of farm land with her grandmother Mama Lee and her uncle George. They raised cotton, corn, peanuts, and potatoes, and kept a truck garden for vegetables, which they canned. There were many fruit trees and wild blackberries and dewberries to pick, and the fruit and berries were made into cobblers and pies. There were horses to pull the wagons and cows for milk. And with hogs and chickens, ducks and geese, there was no need to buy meat. There were snakes, too, and they scared me to death when we went to visit Mama Lee and Uncle George years later. There was little money for extras, but there was always plenty to eat. My mother could eat as much as she wanted and never left anything on her plate. If she wanted ten biscuits, she could have them, but she could only take one at a time. It was ingrained in her that nothing was ever wasted. Everyone worked the land, and during planting and harvest time, the children stayed home from school to help out. If a family finished their harvest first, they helped the neighbors with theirs.

If things got rough, the younger women sometimes moved to the city looking for work. When my mother was young, her mother and two aunts moved to Houston and took jobs as live-in housekeepers. Every two weeks they would come home to Richmond and bring Mama Lee money and clothes for my mother and cousins. Families stuck together, and they shared. Everyone was expected to do their part.

Children went to school when they weren't needed at home, but school wasn't a priority for country children in those days. The colored school was a two-room building. The younger children went from primer (kindergarten) to the sixth grade in one room. The older children went from the seventh to the twelfth grade in the other. The school was eight miles from the colored section of Richmond, which meant the children had to walk sixteen miles each day. They were expected to study hard when they were there, but the teachers were lenient about tardiness and absences, especially during harvest time. Not all children were able to finish school, though many did. My mother attended school there until the fourth grade, when she moved to Houston.

My mother's family was very religious. They had built a small church called Zion Watchtower on the family property. The congregation's faithful were made up almost entirely of relatives. There was praying and Bible reading at home as well. As a child, I was fascinated by the fact that Mama Lee and Uncle George had never learned to read, yet they could read the Bible. I still don't know how they did that. I guess they must have memorized the passages from "lining" them at church. (Lining is a Southern custom where the preacher or church leader reads a line of song or Scripture and the congregation repeats it. It originated as a way to get by in a church where there was no money for books, and most of the worshippers couldn't read.) Mama Lee sang hymns around the house, and she rocked my mother to sleep singing the old Negro spirituals. When my brothers and I went to visit her in later years, she would do the same for us. I no longer remember the names of the songs, but I can still feel her arms around me and hear the sound of her voice and the rocker on the wooden floor.

Not everybody waited to marry before having sex, but if a girl got pregnant, the couple was expected to marry, at gunpoint if necessary. The young couple was not left to survive on their own, though. They would live with the family and help out with whatever was needed. My mother's parents had not married. She never knew why, for it was never spoken of in her presence. Years later my grandfather did marry, but it was to another woman. It bothered my mother that she didn't have a father like other children. She knew who he was, and she carried his name, but he never came around when she was small. He lived in Houston.

When my mother was ten years old, she left Richmond and Mama Lee and went to live with her mother in Houston. The move to Houston was a struggle. Before long, she dropped out of school.

She fought with my grandmother from the beginning. Accustomed to a quieter life with Mama Lee, she disapproved of her mother's late nights and partying after work. Things got worse when she dropped out of school. Now my mother's new responsibility was her new baby brother, James. She was expected to babysit while her mother went out, and like all teenagers, she resented it. James would cry until my grandmother got home; my mother would become angry and frustrated. She started talking back to her mother, something that simply was not tolerated in their home. One day my mother announced that she was moving out on her own. By the next day she already regretted her announcement, but she had too much pride to back down. She moved in with the only person she could think of, her cousin Robert Lee. She cried every night for weeks, but she was determined to make it on her own. To this day she says leaving home so young was one of the worst mistakes of her life.

When I asked my mother how she survived, she answered with one word: "Lying." In those days nobody asked for a birth certificate, and my mother was so tall that she could pass for eighteen. So she got a Social Security card and a health card and went to work waiting tables. Soon she found a second job as well—singing with a gospel group. She saw singing as a way to do something she enjoyed, serve God, and make a little extra money at the same time. My mother moved in with Ella Dooley, one of the older women in her group, staying in the bedroom Mrs. Dooley's daughter had vacated when she got married. The group wore matching dresses and sang at different churches. They were paid with part of the offering. My mother's world of gospel was an innocent one in those days.

There was always an older person to chaperone the young girls, and they worshipped along with the congregations they entertained. None of them smoked, drank, or used drugs, and they maintained a good reputation where men were concerned.

My mother was sixteen when Cecil Shaw came into her life. He heard the gospel group she sang with and immediately recognized their talent. He began to rehearse the girls and prepare them for a professional career. They purchased choir robes and began singing on the radio and in concerts. Once they were under contract, they moved on to concert halls and bigger churches. Soon there was a recording contract and a series of 78s. Some of the records survived to become CDs and are still available. My mother's face appears on the covers, smiling into the camera, looking beautiful and so young. By the time she was out of her teens, my mother was on her way to a successful gospel career.

The worlds of gospel and secular music didn't have that much in common in those days, but though they might not share a stage, gospel and R & B singers shared a common struggle to succeed. My father was in the early stages of his own career at that time, touring the Jim Crow circuit and barely eking out a living with his music. Listening to the radio helped keep him going on the road. Traveling through Texas one day, he happened to hear the Cecil Shaw singers on the radio. The song was "Pray On, My Child," and the lead was sung by the clearest, most beautiful female tenor he had ever heard. He was deeply moved. He had to meet the woman behind that remarkable voice. That woman, of course, was my mother.

CHAPTER 2

I Got a Woman

I got a woman way over

town,

She's good to me.

—RAY CHARLES

I DO NOT BELIEVE IT'S A COINCIDENCE THAT MY PARENTS met the year my father lost his "second mother," Mary Jane. Though he never again lived in Greenville, my dad visited Mary Jane and Mr. Pit over the years and kept in touch with them as best he could. When Mary Jane became ill in 1953, my father helped with the doctor bills. He knew she was very sick, but he was still unprepared for her death. The news came in the middle of a recording session. My dad had recently signed with Atlantic Records, but with a hit still eluding him, each session was important.

When the phone rang in the recording booth in the middle of a song called "Losing Hand," it was someone calling from Greenville to tell him that Mary Jane had passed. My father received the news impassively, silently, as he did all the deepest shocks of his life. And as always, once the pain hit, he immediately escaped into his music. After a moment's silence, he told the others he wanted to keep going. That session became a professional turning point for my father. All the emotion he was suppressing was poured into the music. "Mess Around," his first major hit, came out of that session. When it was over, he went home to Greenville to bury Mary Jane in the tiny church he had attended as a boy. Then he went back on the road and continued as if nothing had happened. But the aching grief he carried with him took him to a new level of loneliness. For the first time, there was no woman in his life who really loved him. Not with the kind of love that abides.

Neither of my parents had had a successful relationship when they met. Both were in their mid-twenties. Both had been married and divorced, and though my father had no difficulty finding a woman, he had never found *the one*. Between them, they had more than their share of emotional baggage.

Some of my father's affairs were as famous as his name. The serious side of his romantic life is less well known. When he was eighteen, he fell in love for the first time with a girl named Louise. The result of that relationship was my half sister Evelyn. Louise's parents objected strongly to their daughter's relationship with an unknown musician, however, and convinced their daughter to come home. My father was heartbroken, and though he supported Evelyn financially while she was growing up, his relationship with Louise came to a painful end. Two years later, tired of meaningless relationships with women on the road, he met and hastily married a woman named Eileen. They hardly knew each other and, inevitably, the marriage ended as quickly as it began. My father was traveling constantly and barely had two dollars to rub together, so meeting a woman he could build a life with was no easy task.

My mother's romantic history was equally dismal. In the early fifties, it was considered unnatural and even scandalous for a woman to remain unmarried past her teens. By the time my mother was twenty, she longed for a home of her own and children. So when she was introduced to a tall, handsome minister's son after a church service one night, she thought she had found the man of her dreams. He certainly looked the part: six feet four, with skin like ebony and thick, curly black hair. The minute things got passionate between them, she did what good girls did in those days: she married him and moved to a house in the country. For a few weeks she was content with a life that consisted of keeping house, going to church, and singing at concerts with her group. Unfortunately, her newfound happiness lasted for what she refers to as a hot five minutes. This good Christian man began to abuse her physically whenever he was unhappy with her. As the man of the house, he expected her to put up with it. Now my mother will put up with a great deal from a man if she feels it's her duty, but she draws the line at physical abuse. Fighting with words is one thing, she will tell you. Fighting with fists is simply unnecessary. No woman should have to put up with being struck. So she divorced him and went home to Houston. Looking back, she recognizes that she really didn't love him the way she should have anyway. She still wanted a home and family, but it would have to be with a man who treated her with respect.

I believe it was inevitable that music first brought my parents together. The most intimate relationships of my father's life, personal or professional, revolved around the music. My dad's professional prospects were just beginning to look up when he stopped in Houston to do a radio commercial advertising his next concert. In those days every up-and-coming musician relied on live radio spots to bring in audiences. In the course of chatting on the air, the disc jockey said, "I understand you're really into gospel."

My father replied, "Yes. I love gospel."

The DJ asked, "Who's your favorite group?"

My father called out my mother's group, the Cecil Shaw Singers. Then he started talking about how much he loved the song "Pray On, My Child" and mentioned that he had bought all the group's records.

My father had no way of knowing that this was a difficult time for the

Cecil Shaw Singers. They had been very successful on the gospel circuit, where churches became accustomed to paying them out of the Sunday offering. But when Cecil Shaw got them a record contract, everything began to change. Being under contract to a recording company meant they could no longer sing for their supper at local churches. They had to charge a fee, and some of their fans resented it. People expected them to carry on like they always had. The criticism and cold shoulders were hard on my mother, so when she heard my father compliment them on the radio, she said to herself, "Well, somebody likes us."

She decided to call the radio station and asked the man who answered to thank my father for his kind words. The man told her she could speak to him herself, and they put him on the phone. She shyly introduced herself, and something about her voice captured his attention. She thanked him for mentioning them on the air and said if he wanted to meet Cecil Shaw while he was in town, she felt certain Cecil would welcome a call.

My father responded, "Well, I know how to get in touch with Cecil Shaw. I'll give him a call." He called Cecil as soon as he got off the phone with my mother.

My father was staying at the Crystal White Hotel in Houston. It was a popular stop for black musicians at a time when Texas hotels were still segregated. The Crystal White was something of a one-stop service: the man who owned the hotel also owned the taxi stand and the restaurant. That night when Cecil met my father at the hotel restaurant for dinner, my dad started asking questions about my mother. Cecil told him that my mother was the one who sang tenor on "Pray On, My Child." My father said, "That's the prettiest, clearest tenor I've ever heard in my life. I'd like to meet that sweet thing. Would you have her come on over?"

Cecil started laughing and said, "Man, she's not comin' over here!" He explained that Della Antwine wasn't the sort of woman who met strange men at hotels. She was a good Christian woman who didn't smoke, drink, use drugs, or meet men at hotels. She was accustomed to meeting eligible men at church. But my father really wanted to meet her, so after thinking about it a minute, Cecil said, "Well, here's what I'll do. If you want to meet here, I'll bring her. She'll come with me." Cecil liked my father, and he didn't see any harm in their meeting. My mother still laughs when she tells the story. She says that it wasn't until much later that Cecil confessed to his part in the plot to get my parents together.

Listening to my mother talk about meeting my father is downright funny. She was not impressed. My father had been through many struggles in his life, but getting women was not one of them. Girls had been falling for him since he was twelve years old. My father's charm usually attracted women powerfully, but it was completely lost on my mother. To begin with, he was too short. At five foot nine, he and my mother were the same height, which meant she towered over him when she put on high heels. And she loved high heels. Besides being short, he had medium brown skin, and my mother liked her men dark—tall, dark, and handsome, with thick, curly black hair. None of this description fit my father. As for his singing, he was still imitating Nat "King" Cole and Charles Brown. She didn't think there was anything special about his style. Worse, he traveled in the world of secular music where people smoked, drank, took drugs, and slept around. My mother did none of those things. And to top it all, he was blind. He would never be able to keep up with her. She liked my father. He seemed nice enough, but he was not at all her type. When she left the hotel that first evening, she never expected to see him again.

So naturally she was baffled when she kept running into him on the road. Both of them were traveling with their groups, and it seemed like every time she turned around, he was there. It was only much later that she found out the frequent meetings were not a coincidence. My father had made a secret agreement with Cecil to keep tabs on my mother, so he always knew what city she was going to next. Cecil would go to the radio station to meet my father, who would be there advertising his current concert. Then Cecil would bring my father back to the hotel where the group was staying, and of course, my mother would be there. Cecil and my father would start talking music, and soon they would be singing and working on arrangements together. My mother came to dread these sessions because the two of them would be up singing gospel all night, and

Cecil made the girls sing backup for them. At first it was a joy, but after a day on the road and a concert, my mother was exhausted and desperate for sleep. She and the other women would beg them to stop so they could go to bed. When Cecil told my father it was time to go home because the girls were too tired, my father would always say, "Hold on just one minute—just one—let's just get this note right here." And they would be at it again. It never occurred to my mother that my dad was keeping them up on purpose so he could have more time with her.

Midnight would pass and become a distant memory, and Mother would turn to the rest of the group and say, "What's wrong with them? Why doesn't that little man just go home and let us sleep?"

Meanwhile, my mother had jumped into a second hasty marriage with another tall, handsome churchgoer. She was twenty-four years old by then, an old maid by her generation's standards, and she was beginning to fear that she would never have a child. She had always dreamed of a husband and family of six children, and this man appeared to be someone to start a family with. From the outside, he seemed ideal. But this marriage failed even faster than the first one. Her second husband was more violent than the first, and she was frightened of him, too frightened to return home when the group's next tour was winding to a close. Instead she left the tour on an impulse and ran away to New York City. It was winter. She had no job, no prospects, and no winter clothes. But she was desperate and afraid, and she didn't know what else to do.

She vividly remembers arriving in New York. There were six inches of snow on the ground, and when she stepped off the bus in her pumps, the snow came up to her ankles and filled her shoes. She went to the only hotel she could think of, the Hotel Theresa. It catered to a black clientele, and its claim to fame in those days was an infamous stay by Fidel Castro. Castro had shown up at the posh Manhattan Shelburne Hotel with his entourage and refused to stay there because of their unacceptable cash demands. Castro and his entourage would then go to the Hotel Theresa and rent out eighty rooms for $800 per day. The story quickly became legend, and when my mother checked in, that was about all she knew about the hotel except that famous black performers often stayed there. She found a job filling in for a sick waitress at the hotel restaurant and tried to figure out what to do next.

After a week of hiding out in the hotel and eating all her meals there, she got sick of it and went down the block to a nearby coffee shop one afternoon. The snow had been cleaned off the sidewalk, which made it easier for her to make her way down the street. She had decided to get a couple of doughnuts and some milk for lunch. When she walked in, she didn't look around. She felt shy and uncomfortable, so she sat down quietly and waited for someone to take her order. No sooner had she given her order than a strange man approached her and asked, "Is your name Della?"

My mother panicked, assuming the man had been sent by her estranged husband, and thought, "Oh my Lord, he found me. He's sent somebody to get me."

She swallowed and replied, "Yes. Why do you ask?"

The man nodded his head toward the lunch counter and said, "Mr. Charles . . ."

She went blank and said, "What? Who?" her mind still on her husband. But then she looked in the direction the man had nodded, and there was my father, sitting there listening and playing with his keys. He had recognized my mother's voice the moment she ordered and sent the man to speak to her. Realizing what had happened, she went over and spoke to him.

My father said, "What you doin' here by yourself, Bea? Where's Cecil and the girls?"

She replied, "Well, I'm not with Cecil right now. I'm here for a while."

He said, "Oh. Where you stayin'?"

She told him, "The Hotel Theresa. Right next door."

And my father said, "You don't say. So am I. Ain't that somethin'?"

My father played it very cool, like he had no idea she was on her own. But he knew. He had kept in regular touch with Cecil about my mother for over a year by then. My father pursued her with the same single-minded determination he used in his music. He would keep after a piece until he got the notes just right, and he kept after my mother long after most men would have given up. He had faith that she would come around one day. He could wait as long as it took. When my mother finally found out that Cecil was helping him, she told my father, "If it was legal, I'd kill both of you." In the coffee shop that afternoon, he told my mother he was in New York doing gigs there and in New Jersey. He had several appearances lined up in the area, so he would be around for a while. He would keep in touch. They talked for a long time that afternoon.

As the weeks went by, my father was true to his word. Every time he got back to town, he checked on her. He worried about my mother. He asked her what she was doing for work. She told him she'd found a job waiting tables, but it wouldn't last long because she was replacing someone who was ill. She was still looking for a more permanent job.

He worried about her getting cold. He told her, "You don't have the clothes to stay here." It was bitter cold, and she couldn't afford the clothes needed for a winter in New York. He wanted her to leave and return to Texas, but she told him she was afraid to. She was still married, so she couldn't return to Houston. It wasn't safe. She had nowhere to go.

He told her, "I'm goin' to Dallas, and I have a place there. Why don't you come on back with me when I leave? You can stay there as long as you want, 'til you find a place of your own."

Mother replied, "No. I don't think so. I can't do that." So they continued to talk, and he continued to ask, and she continued to say no.

Finally he told her, "Well, I've got a couple more gigs around here, and I'll let you know before I leave." A few days later, he left for Texas.

The minute he was gone, the loneliness hit her hard. To make things worse, money was getting really low. She didn't have enough to pay the whole week's rent, and she was scared to death they were going to throw her out in the street. She didn't know a soul in New York, and she kept thinking about how cold it was outside. She pictured herself slipping and sliding in the snow in her flimsy shoes. The day after my father left, she went down to pay what she could toward her rent. Her plan was to pay part of it and let them know she would pay the rest the next day, as soon as she got another paycheck. Her hope was that if they knew she was good for the money, they wouldn't throw her out.

But when she got down to the lobby and began to talk to the desk clerk, he said, "Oh, you're already paid up."

"No, I'm not paid up. Tomorrow, I'll stop by the desk and pay my balance."

He repeated, "No, you're paid up, says so right here."

She didn't know what was going on. She thought he must be new. Maybe he had confused her with someone else. "How long have you been working here?" she asked.

Finally the clerk said, "Well, I guess I better tell you. I wasn't supposed to, but—before Mr. Charles left, he paid for a week for you."

Mother was stunned. She couldn't think of anything to say except, "*Okay.*" Then she slinked out the front door, too embarrassed to even look up. For days afterward, she thought about what had happened. "Why did he do it?" she wondered. She knew he didn't have much money. He couldn't afford to do something like that. And he had never tried to push her into an affair, as she knew he had with other women. He hadn't asked for anything but her company. His departure left her lonely and miserable. She realized that she missed him. She had gotten used to having him around. The Ray she knew wasn't the careless womanizer everyone said he was. The man she knew was kind, patient, always willing to listen. And when he went away, she was lonely without him.

So when he called a few days later and asked if she had thought any more about coming back to Texas, she was torn. He told her, "I tell you what. You go on down to the Western Union. I'm goin' to send you the money to get you a ticket to Dallas. You can stay at my place for a few days, just until you find a place of your own."

She hesitated, debated with herself, and finally found herself saying, "Okay." It was only for a few days. She needed the help, and it really was kind of him to offer.

He told her, "Do not ride the bus, either. I shall send you a ticket to travel by train."

So my mother packed the two little suitcases that contained all her worldly belongings, went down to Western Union, picked up the money, and bought a train ticket for Dallas. She only intended to stay for a few days. But when she saw my father again in Dallas, she realized that she had fallen in love with him. No one was more surprised than she was. Somewhere along the way, during those hours of talking to him, through all the small kindnesses he'd done for her, he had patiently worked his way into her heart. After twenty-five years and two failed marriages, she discovered what it was like to truly love a man. The man who she felt was all wrong for her had captured her heart.

From the very beginning, my father made it clear to my mother that his intentions were serious. And from the beginning, she kept telling herself it would never work between them. They were from different worlds. As she puts it, she was over here, and he was *way* over there. His world was constant travel, one-night stands with women he hardly knew, performances in clubs where anything went, and little in the way of conventional morality. Her world was the church and gospel music, with chaperones to protect the women from men like my father. Dad urged her to sing with him, to come on the road where they could be together and share their musical gifts. My father loved her voice and thought singing would be a good way for their relationship to grow. He was still doing a lot of pickup work in those days, struggling to find his own musical path. Mother refused, believing God would not approve of her becoming part of that world. But my father persisted. He kept telling her that their differences didn't change the way they felt about each other.

The differences between them were not the only problem. My mother was still legally married to her second husband. She was afraid of him, worried he would find out she was back in Texas. She was also painfully discouraged about marriage. She didn't trust men, and more important, she didn't trust herself. She told my dad, "I don't ever want to get married again. I always made the wrong choice in men. I can't make heads or tails of it. It's too hard. I don't want to try that again. And I can't have babies, either. I want children, lots of them, but I can't get pregnant. I'm just not cut out to be married."

The standoff might have gone on indefinitely if it hadn't been for me. Even then, my father almost didn't get her to the altar.

My father knew I was on the way before my mother did. She still doesn't understand how he knew. One day early in 1955, my father called home from San Francisco. He was on the road, and my mother was in Dallas. Almost as soon as my mother picked up the phone, my dad said, "Bea? Are you pregnant?"

At first she thought he had lost his mind. "What are you talking about? I'm not pregnant. I've never been pregnant."

Undeterred, my father persisted. "Bea, you gotta be. I just know it."

Then my mother got angry. She was certain my father had gotten another woman pregnant and mixed up which one it was. She started cussing him out, saying, "You have gotten someone pregnant and then you have the nerve to call me?" But instead of backing down, my father insisted she see a doctor as soon as possible. This made her even angrier. "I am not going to the doctor to be made a fool of again!" All the women on my mother's side of the family had given birth in their teens. She was certain she was barren and determined not to get her hopes up again. The more my father insisted she was pregnant, the madder she got.

Finally she told him, "Get off the phone! I'm not talkin' to you! I'm gettin' out of here!" And she slammed down the phone and started packing. She had no intention of sticking around while my father made a fool of her. She crammed everything she owned into her two small suitcases, including a pair of red high-heeled shoes. She loved those shoes. They were the prettiest ones she had ever owned.

A few minutes later, Dr. Jordan called. Dr. Jordan was my parents' physician and a close family friend. When my mother picked up the phone, she heard Dr. Jordan's voice. "Dell-a?"

This only made my mother angrier. "Oh, my Lord. He's gotten to you, too." Dr. Jordan told her she needed to come in and get a checkup, just to be sure. She flatly refused.

So he asked, "Well then, tell me. Have you had any symptoms?"

She thought about it for a moment. There had been some strange cravings. She couldn't seem to get enough of sardines and biscuits and syrup—together. In fact, she'd eaten so many that the grocery clerk had commented on it. "No, no symptoms," she told Dr. Jordan. "I'm not coming down."

Dr. Jordan replied, "Now come on, Della. You know we're good friends. I'm not taking any sides in this. I just want to be sure you're all right." After a little more gentle prodding from the doctor, she reluctantly agreed to see him.

The examination left no doubt. Dr. Jordan told my mother she was three months pregnant. She argued with him a little while longer, insisting it was a mistake, but finally she gave in. She was pregnant. She couldn't believe it.

Dr. Jordan continued. "Now Ray tells me you're leaving."

Mother replied, "Yes. I got my clothes packed. I'm going back to Houston."

Dr. Jordan pleaded, "No. Don't leave. Just wait. Just for me. I know you're angry with Ray, but are you angry with me?"

"No," she said. "You haven't done anything to me. You're my friend." So she agreed to wait. A couple of weeks later the tests came back, confirming her pregnancy. By then she was too sick to argue. She unpacked her suitcases and was immediately overwhelmed with regret. Her beautiful red shoes were ruined. After days of being crammed into the suitcase, they were twisted and flattened. She was sorry about what she had said to my father, and she certainly wasn't sorry about being pregnant. As far as she could see, it was a miracle from God. But she was very sorry about the shoes. Those shoes were never the same again. Neither was she.

With news of my impending arrival official, my father told my mother they should get married. This presented an immediate problem because my mother had never gotten a divorce. Getting a divorce meant moving back to Houston, her legal place of residence, for thirty days. She was afraid because I was on the way, for she didn't want her estranged husband to find her. A friend recommended a lawyer, and they worked out a plan.

She returned to Houston long enough to see the lawyer and leave some clothes at her aunt's house, to make it look like she was living there. Thirty days later, the divorce was official.

By then her pregnancy was having serious effects on her health. She was very ill, vomiting continually and confined to bed from weakness much of the time. Her resolve, however, was as strong as ever. She thought it was kind of my father to offer, but she didn't really believe he wanted to marry her. She knew he had lived with other women, and with him on the road so much, for all she knew, he still was. Her first responsibility was to take care of the baby, and she was determined to make sure that I would be all right. My father assumed I would take his last name, but she didn't want me to. Her father had never married her mother, and that had really hurt her. Growing up, she had seen too many men give a child their last name, then later claim, "That's not my child." In her view, being disowned was the most hurtful thing that could happen to a child, and she was determined it would not happen to me.

She decided the best thing would be for me to carry her father's name, Antwine. The problem was that legally she still had her married name. The divorce decree meant she was no longer married, but the decree did not give her back her maiden name. So she made an appointment with a lawyer in Dallas to buy her birth name back. My father knew nothing about her decision. He was on the road at the time.

The night before her appointment, however, my father unexpectedly came home. The next morning he slept until past noon, as he always did when he'd been on the road. My mother was dressed and heading out the door to see the lawyer by the time my dad had awoken. When he asked where she was going, she hesitated a little, then told him that she was on her way to a lawyer to get her maiden name back.

Dad sat up and said, "Now wait a minute. Come back in here, and let's talk about this."

My mother explained. "Well, I decided I don't want the baby to wear your name. Things might change, and I do not want the baby to have your name. So I think it's better if he wears my father's name. Then later on, if you decide we can make it and you really want to marry me, you could always adopt him and give him your name."

My father couldn't believe what he was hearing. She wanted him to adopt his own child? He started cursing and said, "What kind of thinkin' is that? Are you crazy, woman?" After a few moments he calmed down a little and said, "I'll tell you what. I have to go back out of town tomorrow. But as soon as I come back, we're goin' to go down and have a blood test, and then we're goin' to get married."

My mother agreed. She didn't believe for a minute that he would actually marry her. But if it calmed him down, she would pretend that she did. She canceled her appointment with the lawyer, and my dad went back on the road. She really did not expect him to return anytime soon, but the next thing she knew, Dad was back at their apartment with a friend to pick her up. When she asked where they were going, my father said, "To get a blood test."

Mother replied, "It's Sunday! What's wrong with you?" In Texas, nothing was open on a Sunday. But my father had found an Asian doctor who did stay open on Sundays, so my parents got their blood test. The doctor told them that if the blood tests were all right, they would have two weeks after the results came in to get married. My father left immediately to go back on the road.

Three days later the doctor called and told my mother the lab results were in and that everything looked fine. My father was calling her every day to make sure she was all right, but she never mentioned the doctor's report when he called. She remained convinced that my father didn't really intend to marry her. Then one afternoon, they had just started their daily phone call when my dad said, "Oh, by the way. It's been almost two weeks. Did you get the doctor's report yet?"

My mother said, "Yeah, he called. The tests are okay."

Dad asked, "So when do the tests expire then?"

Mother replied, "Tomorrow."

She heard him exclaim, "WHAT!" There was a short silence; then he said, "I'll call you back." She hadn't thought to ask him where he was, but the next thing she knew, he was home. Somehow he had managed to catch a flight and come straight back to Dallas. Before she knew what was happening, they were on their way downtown to get a marriage license.

When they got to the Hall of Records, my mother was in for another surprise. They asked her for her age, and she replied, "Twenty-six."

Then they asked my father for his age, and he replied, "Twenty-four."

Mother looked at him and said, "What are you doing? Stop playin' and tell the people your right age."

My father replied, "That is my right age." And then the truth came out. Cecil Shaw knew my mother never dated younger men, so he had advised Dad not to tell her his real age. As they stood there together, though, waiting for their marriage license, my mother didn't have the heart to be angry with either of them.

The clerk told them where they could go to get married. License in hand, my parents went looking for the building the clerk had directed them to. When they found it, the woman there told them that she was a minister. She said she could marry them immediately if they wanted. My parents were doubtful. They had never met this woman before. They weren't even sure she had the legal right to perform the ceremony.

My mother looked at my dad and said, "Ray? What do you think?"

He thought a moment and said to the woman, "Are you really a minister?"

The woman replied, "Well, you can come with me and find out for yourself. There's an attorney right across the street. He lets me marry people in his office. He can tell you I'm a licensed minister."

When they went across the street, the attorney confirmed that the woman was a minister. The ceremony would be perfectly legal. He would serve as their witness. The attorney led them to the back room. His office was very nice, but the room he took them to looked like some sort of storage room, with broken-down furniture and used paint cans. My mother was afraid that at any minute a rat would come nosing its way out of the debris. She looked around at all the junk and said, "Ray?"

My dad heard the anxiety in her voice and was quick to reassure her. "It's all right, Bea. I got to get back so I can catch my flight out and make the job. It'll be all right. Let's just get married."

And they did. In a back room filled with junk, a woman they had never met read them their vows. On the way to the airport afterward, my mother told him, "Lord, Ray, I don't think I'm married. A real minister would not marry people in the middle of that mess. I think those people involved us in some kind of scam. I won't believe we're married 'til I see something with some kind of legal stamp on it." My father reassured her, and then he got on the plane. When the papers arrived a few days later, my mother saw the stamp. The marriage was legal, all right. It was only then that she allowed herself to believe it had really happened.

Looking back now, she believes that the Lord stepped in. God had given her a man she really loved and who loved her back. God had given her a child after all the years of barrenness. That impromptu wedding in a room filled with junk didn't look like much, but it was the real thing. My parents may not have lived happily ever after, but they loved each other.

CHAPTER 3

Hallelujah, I Love Her So

When I'm in trouble and

I have no friends,

I know she'll go with me

until the end.

—RAY CHARLES

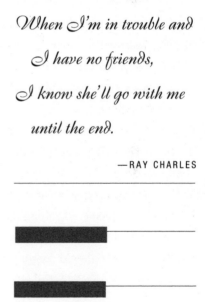

WITH A WIFE AND A CHILD ON THE WAY, MY FATHER FINALLY had a family of his own. The only problem was that he had no idea what a family was, for he had never been part of one. His own father had been absent from his life. When I was old enough to wonder why my dad never mentioned his father, my mother told me that my dad had barely known him. He had been sent away to school when he was seven, and he had lost his mother during his teens. He had been raised in large part by teachers and mentors in an institution. The education he received there enabled him to survive, but it deprived him of the emotional support most children find in their parents. He was afraid to get too close to anyone. As our family grew, it would get harder and harder for him to figure out what to do as a husband and father.

From the time he was sent away to school, most of the people he had to depend on were paid to take care of him. Being blind in the music world meant he had to pay people to do things for him that most people could do for themselves. Many of the musicians he played with during the early years treated him badly. Lowell Fulson, T-Bone Walker, Big Joe Turner, they all laughed at him. They thought he was some kind of joke. Charles Brown didn't like him because my father tried to sing like him. Many people who claimed to be his friends when he became famous had never really been his friends at all. The way they treated my dad hurt my mother deeply. She used to pray that God would help my father rise above them. Their marriage brought my father new hope. With my mother by his side, he could finally do that.

When he was home from the road, my parents would talk for hours about the future. My mother was convinced that my father could make a success of anything he wanted to do. When she saw how gifted he was with electronics, she asked him if he had ever thought of making a career in that field. When he told her he didn't want to go into electronics, she said that was fine, they'd try something else. Like his mother had, she encouraged him to reach his full potential. When she realized he didn't know how to write his name, she told him she would teach him. He became upset and told her, "I can't write!"

She insisted, "Yes, you can. You're going to learn to write your name and initials." And she took his hand and put a pencil in it and showed him how to print the letters in his name. She wanted him to be able to sign things for himself, so he wouldn't have to rely on other people who might not be honest. My mother knew there would come a time when others might try to take advantage of my father.

After that he would practice every chance he got. She would wake up in the middle of the night sometimes and hear him working. She thought he was working on a song with his braille writer, but instead he would be there with a pencil, carefully practicing his letters. When he thought he had done well, he would bring the paper to my mother to show her, like a proud child. It thrilled her to see his effort and his pride.

They talked continually about his music. She encouraged him to get his own style, to stop trying to sound like other artists. He was reluctant, telling her, "I don't like my voice."

She told him, "Well, you're not going to make it singing like Charles Brown or Nat "King" Cole, or singing like anyone else, either. There can only be one somebody like that in a lifetime. Get your own style. You're not ever going to be successful if you continue to pattern yourself after another singer, because you can't walk in another man's shoes. You have to walk on your own and make your own footprints in the sand. You can't go down and say, 'I'm goin' to put my foot here, in this other man's footprint.' If the wind blows, you may miss, you know? 'Cause that footprint may have moved. You have to make your own. I'm willing to stay with you if we have to live in a tent. I'm willing to do that as long as you do something that makes you happy."

Those closest to my father say that was the reason he loved my mother so much. He had nothing when he married her. He was just a blind musician that no one except a few people on the chitlin' circuit had ever heard of. She had fallen in love with him when he had nothing to offer but his name. He knew he could trust her and he loved her.

That first year of marriage was one of the best of my parents' lives. Financially, it was a struggle, but the time they spent together was wonderful. He worked on his music constantly at home, sitting up all night writing out songs and arrangements, punching holes on his braille writer with a stylus. It was slow work. The problem with a braille writer is that you can't erase, so he would go through stacks of paper until the trash can was overflowing. It was time-consuming and expensive, so many times my mother would stay up all night taking notes for him. He would hum some lyrics and say, "Write that down, Bea." It was exhausting for her, especially with me on the way, and she was relieved when he stopped for a while. Yet it remains one of her most precious memories. "There was a lot of enjoyment in that. Lord have mercy," she says to me with that throaty chuckle of hers.

Most of the time, though, my father had to be on the road. My mother still worked while they lived quietly in their small place in Dallas, waiting for my arrival, trying to keep working. They needed the money. My father wanted her to stay home and rest. Always very slim, she had become frighteningly thin. Eventually nature made the decision for them. She passed out at work, and her employer told her to go home and stay there. If she wanted to return to work after the baby came, they would talk about it then. My father said absolutely not. She would stay home and take care of me. He would take care of the family.

Independent as he was, though, the fact remained that my father was blind. He could go only so far by himself, and he found this frustrating. He would always need help on the road. Fortunately, help came in the person of Jeff Brown. Jeff had been a taxi driver before he met my father, and by chance, a friend of a friend had called Jeff to help out when my father needed a driver. By the time my parents were married, Jeff had become my dad's permanent driver, but more important, he had become my father's friend. During their first years on the road together, Jeff watched the small, daily struggles of my father's life and quietly stepped in to help. It was Jeff who made sure my father didn't go onstage with a stain on his suit; it was Jeff who sorted my father's money into ones, fives, tens, and twentys so my father could buy things himself without being cheated. It was Jeff who made sure that my father ate, slept, and made it to the next gig on time along the endless highways he traveled most of the year. Officially, Jeff was just a driver, but in reality, he was my father's eyes on the road, and his vision was clear.

One afternoon while my father was home in Dallas, he, Jeff, and my mother talked over what to do next to gain some momentum for my father's career. My father had many ideas, but he needed help to make them a reality. Dad asked Jeff if he would consider becoming a full-time road manager. It would require a commitment from Jeff that would take him away from his wife and children most of the year, and it also required considerable faith, for there were no guarantees that my father would ever earn enough money to make Jeff's sacrifice worthwhile. Jeff talked it over with his wife, and they agreed to give it a try. Tommy Brown stepped into Jeff's old job as driver, and Jeff took responsibility for the rest. Jeff went on the road with my father full time, and as the old band members remember, if it needed doing, Jeff did it. When I asked my mother what Jeff did for my father in the early days, she replied, "Everything. Drove him, fed him, helped him get dressed, kept the guys in line. He was your father's eyes and hands." His presence enabled my father to survive the lean years, before the four-star hotels and the private planes. For the next ten years, Jeff became a member of our family—our confidant and friend. In all my early memories, Jeff is there in the background, a constant presence, as dependable as the changing of the seasons.

My father was on the road when my mother went into labor with me. It had been a rough pregnancy, and when my mother checked in to the hospital, she still needed a trash can to throw up in. The nausea had never gone away. The small segregated hospital was a clapboard house that had been converted into a maternity hospital for black women. There were only four beds in the tiny nursery, but the medical personnel were well trained, and they took good care of my mother. The labor was long and hard, but I emerged into the world healthy and screaming, with a full head of reddish hair. Within hours, my dad was there. My mother was never sure how he managed it, but for each of us children, he somehow made it home within hours of her giving birth. As soon as he arrived, the nurse took him and Tommy, who had driven Dad from the airport, to the nursery to see me. The nurse had never heard of Ray Charles, and she apparently didn't notice Tommy leading the way for my dad. When she went to tell my mother that my dad had arrived, the nurse was a little indignant.

She said, "Your husband is here, Mrs. Robinson."

And my mother replied, "He is? Oh, bring him in."

The nurse told her irritably, "Well, I don't think he's very happy about the baby."

My mother said, "What do you mean?"

The nurse replied, "Because he hasn't said a thing about the baby. His friend is looking in the nursery, but your husband didn't even go up to the window. Didn't even bother to look at him."

My mother told her calmly, "No, that's because he can't. My husband is blind."

The nurse stood there for a moment, looking like she wanted to go through the floor from embarrassment. Finally, she said, "Oh. I am so sorry. I am so sorry."

My mother reassured her. "You didn't know. Nobody told you." My dad never used a cane, and he didn't carry himself the way most blind people do. With his dark glasses hiding his eyes, he could easily be mistaken for a sighted person.

When my father came in to see my mother a few minutes later, the nurse brought him a chair and then went back to get me. She brought me into the room and then stood there, holding me, not certain what to do next. My father was sitting, his arms out, waiting to hold me. Finally, she said, "Well, uh," and laid me in my mother's arms.

My mother told the nurse, "Give Ray the baby."

The nurse looked doubtfully at my mother. "Give your husband the baby?"

My mother repeated, "Yes. Give him the baby." The nurse took me from my mother and nervously laid me in my father's waiting arms.

My father was more than ready. He immediately began to "look" at me in the way that would become so familiar to me over the years. First he felt my face and then ran his hand over my hair. I had a lot of dark, soft, reddish brown hair, and my eyes were blue, probably from my Creole ancestors. My father pulled the blanket back and counted my fingers. Next he unwrapped me and began to "look" at me all over, down to my toes. When he came to my feet, he said, "Well, he got all his fingers and toes." He felt my arms and legs, and then he said, "But where are the wrinkles?"

"Wrinkles?" my mother said. His first child, Evelyn, had been tiny, and she was covered with wrinkles when she was born.

"Yeah," my dad said. "He's supposed to have wrinkles. Babies have wrinkles when they're born."

My mother replied, "Well, this one is eight pounds, three and a half ounces, and the nurse says there are no wrinkles when a baby's that healthy."

Then she told him she had named me Cedric Durrell. My father was horrified. "No, no, no. My son shall have my name. Ray Charles Robinson Jr."

Thank heaven my father would get his way.

They kept my mother and me in the hospital for three days, and my father had to go back on the road before we came home. But first, he went shopping. My mother didn't feel they could afford real furniture for me, so she had gotten a wicker clothes basket with a pillow to put me in. When my father found out she was planning to have me sleep in a clothes basket, he asked my mother if she was out of her mind. Before they left, he and Tommy bought a crib and a high chair and all the trimmings. It took a couple of days for everything to be delivered. The pillow for the basket had been misplaced while my mother was in the hospital, so while she waited for the crib to arrive, I spent my first two days at home sleeping in a dresser drawer.

For the first couple of months of my life, it was just the two of us in the little house my father had rented on Myrtle Street. My mother was thrilled to finally have the baby she had always dreamed of, but she was nervous, too. When the ambulance brought her home, she was convinced that the attendants were going to drop the gurney and injure us both. She insisted that they help her up the stairs and then carry me up to her. Once upstairs, we stayed inside. It was six weeks before she felt strong enough to go down the steps.

My father had set up an account for us at the corner grocery, and my mother's girlfriend Daisy would get what we needed. My mother wasn't much of a cook in those days, so anything in a can would work for her. Always a finicky eater, I would spit out my mother's breast milk and make a face when she tried to nurse me. After a while she gave up and put me on a bottle, and Daisy would bring milk for me. I was a good baby, I am told, and as long as I was dry and fed, I didn't cause much of a fuss. That didn't stop my mother from fussing over me. The first time I slept all night, she thought I was dead. She had fallen sound asleep herself, and when she woke up in the morning and found me motionless in the corner of the crib, she panicked. She jumped out of bed, screaming, "Oh, God! My baby is dead! My baby is dead!" When she pulled the blanket back, she saw me move a little farther into the corner. My mother would always worry about us. That never really went away.

For most of those early weeks, my father was on the road, but when he did come home, he was determined to take care of me. My mother told me that "anything that was worthwhile and important he was goin' to learn, he was goin' to be at it. 'Now, how you do this?' he'd say. And when you're gone, he's still there at it. He couldn't see, but he did not let that stop him." He already knew how to turn the stove on. He'd listen for the gas, and when he heard the *poof,* he'd strike the match for the burner. He would heat my bottles and test the temperature, and then he would feed me. He even changed my diapers. Babies still wore cloth diapers in those days, so changing me meant he would have to clean me up, then fold the diaper and pin it on without pricking me. If my mother needed to run an errand and I was sleeping, my father would tell her to go ahead. He would babysit me. Just as his own mother had trusted him with chores that other people said a blind child shouldn't do, my mother trusted him with me. She would come home to find me wearing a crooked diaper, but I would be fed and happy and safe.

Other people were astonished by my mother's trust in him. Despite her protective nature, she never doubted his ability to take care of me. When I was six weeks old, we went out on the road with him. We stayed in a two-story hotel. Mother and Dad and I had a room on the first floor, and Tommy Brown and the boys were on the second. My father told my mother, "Bea, I'm goin' up and play some dominoes with Tommy. I'm goin' to take the baby with me so you can get some rest."

My mother said, "Okay. Let me put him in a blanket so if he goes to sleep, you can put this little blanket over him."

My dad said, "Okay." They bundled me up, and my father carried me upstairs to Tommy's room. He had already counted the steps and learned the hotel layout, so getting to Tommy's room was no problem.

My mother thankfully fell into bed. A few minutes later the phone rang. She dragged herself out of bed, thinking, "Oh, my goodness, Ray calling already. I was just falling asleep." She reluctantly picked up the phone, mumbling, "What is it?"

A woman's voice on the other end cried out, "Mrs. Charles! Mrs. Charles!"

Mother said, "Yes, what's the matter?"

The woman identified herself as the clerk at the front desk and said, "Did you know—did you know—oh my God, he's going upstairs! Mrs. Charles! It's your husband. Did you know Ray Charles has your baby?"

My mother replied, "Well, yes. That's his baby, too, you know."

The clerk replied, "Yes, I know, but he's going up the steps, and he's carrying the baby, and . . ."

My mother reassured her. "Yes. But he's not going to harm the baby. It'll be fine."

She heard the clerk say, "Oh, my God," then take a deep breath. "Okay. Okay. If you say so." And the clerk hung up.

My mother was proud of my father's ability to care for me. In a place and time when most fathers would never be seen caring for their children, my father willingly changed diapers and heated bottles. He never felt it made him less of a man. As my mother said, I was his baby, too. I have always wished someone had taken pictures of my father holding me, but my mother says she was never one for taking pictures. Instead, the only pictures that remain are in my mother's mind, as vivid as the day I was born.

It was a happy time for our family, but even then, the troubles that came to haunt us were brewing. My mother was a family girl. She never wanted to be wealthy or famous. The height of her ambition was to find a husband she loved, have children, and have a home of her own to raise them in. That first year of marriage to my father gave her all she wanted and more. But for my father, it wasn't enough. He needed excitement, craved carnal things. He loved my mother, called her his one true love until the end of his life, but his love for her did nothing to lessen his desire for other women, and it certainly did nothing to lessen his craving for drugs. Friends say he tried to be a good husband. He told my mother about his daughter, Evelyn, who was six years old when I was born. He was aware that she knew there were other women, though in his mind, he was in love. While he was on the road the other women fulfilled his sexual appetite, he said. They didn't touch his heart. When he married my mother, he would tell his girlfriends to stay away, and he did his best to put a boundary around his family that no one was allowed to cross. He would cut back on hard drugs and rely more on pot for a while, both because money was scarce and because he knew how my mother felt about heroin. She could tolerate his drinking and smoking pot. But hard-core addiction—that was something else again.

He began his affair with Mary Ann Fisher the same month he married my mother, and within two years he was also involved in ongoing affairs with Margie Hendricks and Mae Mosely Lyles. What a double standard. My mother knew it, and she struggled with the knowledge of the affairs. She thought of leaving him many times. But she came from a generation where marriage was not taken lightly. She did not believe a woman was required to accept physical abuse under any circumstances, but the affairs were another form of abuse. In Sunday school she had learned about the Old Testament patriarchs, about King David and King Solomon and their many wives and concubines. These were men of God, yet God allowed them to have as many women as they wanted. Maybe some men were just made that way, she told herself. She decided her only choice was to accept it, as long as he didn't bring other women around the family. There were boundaries of decency and dignity that could never be violated. Her children had the right to grow up seeing their mother treated with love and respect. What he did on the road, behind closed doors, was his business.

She didn't want to know about it. He understood the rules, and for many years was able to keep his two worlds separate.

He kept his heroin addiction from her as long as he could, but inevitably, she found out about it. He had tried to wean himself from the drug their first year together but had never really succeeded. To keep her from finding out, he used heroin at another friend's home in town. My mother found out what was going on by accident. One day the friend was late getting the drug, so he brought the heroin to their home, knowing Dad would be going into withdrawal by then. It was the first time heroin was brought into my parents' home. The friend expected my dad to be there, and when my mother told him Dad wasn't home, the friend started to get nervous. An addict himself, he always shot up with my father and was getting desperate for a hit of his own. He paced back and forth for a while, saying, "I don't know what to do here. I don't know what to do."

My mother repeated, "Well, he's not here." She wasn't sure what was going on. She thought he was probably there to bring my father some pot.

After a while the friend became very agitated and asked her, "Can I use your restroom?"

A minute or two later my mother went in after him. He had some liquid mixed in a spoon. She asked him, "What are you doing?"

He said, "Well, I brought this for Ray, but I can't be walking around with it. So I'm going to use it here."

Then he took out a hypodermic needle and drew the liquid out of the spoon. My mother was horrified. It was obvious by then what was going on. "You know you can't do that in my house—"

But he cut her off, saying, "I got to use it."

By then he didn't care what she said. He needed his hit. He tied off his arm and was about to inject himself. My mother was panicking and thought, "No, God, no, I can't watch this." And she turned to leave the room.

The friend said, "Hey, don't leave. Come on. Take a hit with me."

She said, "I don't do that."

The friend replied, "Well, Ray says you don't use but come on, try it, you'll see how it feels. It's okay, you'll like it. I won't give you much."

Mother stiffened and said, "I think you better do what you're goin' to do and leave my home. Because I don't appreciate what you're doing." And she left the room.

A few minutes later, the friend left. When he told my father what had happened, my father became very upset. He told the friend, "You shouldn't have done that. You had no business doin' that. I already told you, Bea is not into drugs. She didn't need to know about that."

My mother was very upset with my father. When he got home, she told him she did not appreciate what had happened, and she never wanted to see something like that again. He promised her that she never would. That was the end of the friend. He never came around our house again.

My mother still did not understand how serious the problem was, though, because heroin addiction had never been part of her experience. My father had already been arrested in a heroin bust while he was on the road in Philadelphia, but he managed to get the charges dropped, and the arrest was a well-kept secret. My mother had no idea. The tracks on his arms weren't that visible yet, and he was determined to hide the truth from her. Heroin was still a luxury in those days, and apart from his concern for my mother, my dad couldn't afford to get high very often. For all she knew, the incident with his friend had been a one-time thing. It had happened shortly before I was born, but once they were married, it became impossible to hide the extent of the problem.

Money was more plentiful by then, so for the first time, getting high daily was possible. Even though the tracks were not that deep yet, the effects of the drug were obvious. My mother hated it, and my parents argued, but it was clear that heroin was a permanent part of my father's life. He told her that he loved it, that it gave him pleasure like nothing else ever had, and that he was certain it wasn't hurting him. My father was in denial like most addicts who won't face their addiction; he honestly believed he had it under control. My mother was unwilling to break up the family over it, so she made a grudging agreement. She would live with the drug as long as he kept it away from the family. I was to grow up knowing nothing about it. If he ever crossed that line, that would be the end.

IT WAS DURING those years that my father stopped being Ray Charles Robinson, known by that name to a small group of jazz and R & B fans, and became Ray Charles, household name. After moderate success with "Mess Around" and "Don't You Know, Baby?" in 1953, he began to assemble his own band in 1954, his first year with my mother. About the time she found out she was pregnant with me, he had his breakthrough: his own band, using his own arrangements, recorded his first huge hit, "I Got a Woman." He had finally found his own voice, and the result changed music history. My parents' fortunes rose faster than either of them had dreamed of. In less than two years, my father formed a band and recorded his own arrangements, brought in a girl group called the Cookies (soon renamed the Raelettes) to back him up, bought a station wagon for the band to travel in, promoted Jeff Brown from valet to band manager, and began churning out a series of hits that left the music world breathless. Between the time my mother fell in love with him and my third birthday, my father recorded hit song after hit song: "Hallelujah, I Love Her So," "Drown in My Own Tears," "Lonely Avenue," and "What Would I Do Without You." He had moved from the rural circuit to the epicenter of American music. It was time to move his family from rural America to the big city where he could take his career to the next level.

My mother was reluctant to move. Her roots were in Texas and though she had lived in Houston and Dallas since she was eleven, she remained a small-town girl at heart. Texas was familiar, her family and friends were there, and despite the size of the two cities, she moved within a familiar comfort zone. My parents talked about it repeatedly, and eventually she came to accept the fact that they would have to move. My father told her there were two choices: either New York or Los Angeles. All her memories of

New York were painful, and the most vivid memory of all was the freezing weather. After a lifetime in southeast Texas, she couldn't imagine living in that cold. So she chose Los Angeles.

In 1958, just after my brother David was born, the move was made. Jeff Brown loaded everything he could into the station wagon, and along with my mother's dear friend Bernice, they drove to Los Angeles. The doctor wouldn't allow my mother and David to make the trip yet, so we stayed in Dallas and followed a few weeks later. Meanwhile, my father looked for property, eventually purchasing a piece of land in rural Riverside County and a second property on Hepburn Avenue in an affluent suburb of Los Angeles. He was excited about the Riverside County acreage, already planning to purchase a plane that he could land on his own property. When my mother heard his idea and saw the property, she thought he was out of his mind. She had no intention of living alone with two children in rural California several months a year while my father was on the road; and when she saw where he planned to land a plane, she informed him that if he could see the place, he would know what a crazy idea it was. They agreed that our family would live in the home my father had purchased on Hepburn. Within weeks the four of us had settled in. It was a fresh beginning for our family and my father's career.

My parents had achieved the American dream. They had begun life as a poor girl from segregated small-town Texas and a poverty-stricken blind orphan who seemed destined to make brooms for a living. They grew up in the Jim Crow South and moved to California years before the civil rights movement had achieved any of its major goals. Yet they reached a level of success most Americans only dream of before either of them was thirty years old. It was extraordinary. Though shadows were already lurking in the corners of our beautiful new home, my mother resolutely ignored them. As she puts it, when you grow up, you reach for the stars but you settle for the moon. It was more than we ever dreamed.

CHAPTER 4

Moving to the Outskirts of Town

Let me tell ya, honey,

We gonna move away

from here.

—ROY JACOBS AND WILLIAM WELDON

M Y EARLIEST MEMORIES SWIM INTO FOCUS LIKE IMPRES-
sionist paintings, blurred images of trees and gardens, of blue skies
and children playing. Our street had a movie star's name: Hepburn. It was
beautiful there. It was a place where nothing bad should ever happen.

The house we moved into is in a suburb of Los Angeles called Leimert
Park, a residential neighborhood built in the thirties and forties as one of
the first planned communities in Southern California. Located in the

southern part of the city, Leimert Park is bordered on one side by Martin Luther King Jr. Boulevard (named Santa Barbara Boulevard when we lived there). The boulevard is wide, populated with Los Angeles's iconic palm trees. It leads to one of the first malls in the nation. My mother regularly shopped for our clothing at the May Co. and Broadway half a mile down the road. Today the area is often referred to as the "Black Greenwich Village," a tribute to the richness of the artistic community that thrives there.

When we first moved to Leimert Park in 1958, the neighborhood was racially mixed, a combination of Asian, white, and African American residents. Our neighbors were all successful professionals—doctors, lawyers, judges, entrepreneurs. It was a mecca for upwardly mobile families of all races. Some of the most successful African Americans in the nation lived there when I was growing up. Ella Fitzgerald lived just down the street. Los Angeles mayor Tom Bradley lived nearby. Though the Asian and white populations gradually dwindled during the sixties, our street remained stable. Many of the families I grew up with still live there.

The neighborhood is a mixture of two-story Spanish colonial homes, postwar bungalows, and art deco apartment buildings, many of them built by progressive architects. There is a sense of spaciousness despite the parade of homes lining every block and the numerous businesses only blocks away. The streets are wide and remarkably free of traffic, with plenty of room for children to play. Well-maintained sidewalks run along the blocks, with a grass border dividing them from the street. Girls can play hopscotch or jump rope, and boys can ride their bikes down the long expanses of cement. I spent much of my childhood riding my bike up and down our long block. The yards are large, too, with fifteen-foot lawns fronting most homes and large, grassy backyards with plenty of room to play or barbecue.

Our section of Hepburn Avenue had a personality all its own. The houses are large, nearly all two-story, gracious havens for the families that live in them. Nearly every house contained children. Its two blocks made up my world. What I loved the most about Hepburn, though, were the change of seasons and the color of the trees. Dense rows of mature syca-

more, big-leaf maple, oak, willow, and ash trees lined the street and filled
the yards, providing shade on hot summer days. In the spring jacaranda
trees were covered with lavender blossoms, making the sidewalks slippery
for skaters. Backyards were filled with lemon, avocado, and peach trees,
ripe for the picking every summer. Boxwood hedges framed the houses
and lined the driveways. Perfectly edged buffalo-grass lawns, with their
coarse blades and dense turf, surrounded every house. The grass was perfect for running barefoot and playing ball. Every house had a gardener,
and every housewife took pride in her flowers and manicured lawn.

I was three years old when we moved into the house on Hepburn, and
my brother David was just an infant. It was a world away from the small
house in Dallas, a universe away from the Florida shack where my father
had grown up. Our house was a mild yellow-colored two-story stucco
with a big bay window, white shutters, and ornate white metal trim. A tall
leafy tree leaned over the second-story window facing the front yard. My
father's Pontiac station wagon, and later my mother's lavender Cadillac,
sat in the driveway next to the neatly trimmed front lawn. Like every other
house on the block, ours was immaculate. Fallen leaves did not remain in
the yard for long. Our house did have one unique feature, however. My
mother disliked stepping from her car onto the grass in her high-heeled
shoes, so my father had a strip of lawn bordering the driveway replaced
with cement. My grandfather, who also lived in Southern California and
had reestablished contact with my mother, did the work himself. For reasons that still baffle me, my grandfather painted the new strip of cement
green, to match the grass it replaced. Why he didn't match it to the rest
of the driveway escapes me. That strip of green cement remains, to this
day, a legacy of my grandfather's unfathomable taste. The crack in the
sidewalk from the tree's roots, where I sometimes tripped running with
my friends, is still there, too.

Downstairs the house was divided into roughly two sections: the
entertainment area and the family area. The living room and the dining
room formed the entertainment area. We seldom went in there unless we
had visitors. The living room was where we kept my father's baby-grand

piano. He rarely played unless the band members were there, but he liked to noodle around on it now and then. Behind the kitchen was the maid's quarters, with a room to sleep in and a half bath. The utility area was back there, too. We didn't have a live-in nanny when we first moved there; my mother wanted her privacy.

The family area was on the other side of the foyer. It consisted of the den and the kitchen. The den was where we lived. My mother believed that part of the house should be a space to relax in, where we didn't have to worry about making a mess or damaging the furniture. With active little boys in the house, she knew that keeping the whole house nice would be impossible. She bought a bright blue sofa and sturdy retro furniture for the den that could withstand our play. When neighbors commented that she didn't have nice things in the den, she replied that the den was the family area. We could roughhouse and play there all day without worry if we wanted. The only rule was that at the end of the day, we had to put our toys away.

Outside of the play area, we were expected to keep our house clean and neat, especially when my father was home. My mother helped us understand how important it was to Daddy that we keep everything in its place. We knew that if we left things on the floor, Daddy might trip and fall over them. If we didn't put things back, Daddy might not be able to find them when he needed them.

If we weren't in the den, we were usually in the kitchen, where my mother would read to me there. Dr. Seuss, *Curious George,* and the *Dick and Jane* books were my favorites. As I got older, the kitchen table was where I did my homework. The kitchen was white with a red table and chairs. I had a little red booster seat of my own where I would sit for meals. I was a picky eater, so much of my food would end up hidden under my seat. After a few days the food would mildew and start to smell, and then I would get in trouble.

Upstairs were the bedrooms and my father's office. The master bedroom overlooked the backyard. David and I shared a bedroom across the hall. In the front of the house, overlooking the street, was my father's office.

The view from the office was almost completely blocked by a large tree, but that was not a concern of my father. Those were the days before he had his own studio, so his office was the music and rehearsal room where he wrote and arranged music and worked with the band. I spent countless hours sitting on the carpet by the closed door, listening as he practiced or played cards with band members. His office was where he kept his photographs and awards. Over the years, the carpet and drapes gradually absorbed smoke from my father's cigarettes and the scent of his cologne. If I missed him while he was on the road, I could always sneak into his office to look at his photos, run my hand over his things, and breathe in his scent.

Out back were a garage, a covered patio with a nice set of lawn furniture, and a grassy yard with a big lemon tree. A wall next to the lemon tree divided our yard from our neighbors, the Andersons. Anthony Anderson soon became my best friend. David and I spent countless hours hanging around the backyard, shooting the breeze and talking to our friends across the fence. My mother liked having us in the backyard because at least she knew where we were.

Life on Hepburn Avenue was simple. As I grew up there, our lives followed a regular rhythm orchestrated primarily by my mother. My father came in and out of our lives every few weeks, leaving and returning as his life on the road dictated. But my mother was always there. Everything with my mother had to follow a routine. She cooked breakfast every morning, and we always ate together. If it was a school day, my mother would also pack our lunches in the morning. We never bought our lunch. I didn't want homemade sandwiches; I longed for "kid food," the kind they sold at the local hamburger and hot-dog stands. We used to pass a Pup 'n Tail hot-dog stand on the way home from school, and I always wanted to stop for a chili dog. We never did. Despite our affluence, my mother remained a frugal woman with simple tastes. She didn't believe in wasting money by buying food she could prepare herself. So my brothers and I spent all of our school days eating lunches our mother packed for us in our tin lunch boxes.

When we got home from school, we were expected to do our homework before we could go out to play. I didn't mind. My friends had to do their homework first, too, so there would be no one to play with except my brother if I went straight outside. If *The Mickey Mouse Club* was on, my mother might let us watch it before we went out to play, if we had behaved. Once outside, we could run around as much as we wanted as long as we stayed on the block and out of forbidden areas, which included the garage, the fence, and the neighbors' yards—unless, of course, she knew the neighbor, and we had been invited.

Dinner was always at six o'clock. If we were out playing, my mother would call us to come in. The rule was that we always ate dinner together. Our friends were welcome to join us. My mother would cook a complete dinner of pork chops or smothered chicken, vegetables, banana pudding. Oh, how I loved that banana pudding. If my father was there, he would eat with us. Afterward, there might be more homework to finish. If it was summer, we would go outside to play again after dinner. We liked to play sock ball on the front lawn. Most often, though, we rode our bikes, me on my Schwinn and David behind me on his tricycle, riding up and down the street.

Once it got dark we had to be inside, no matter what the time. During fall and winter, we would play in the den after dinner if our homework was done. We played with Lionel trains that ran around tracks and over toy bridges, Tonka trucks, and whole armies of toy soldiers. None of these toys lasted very long. We never meant to break them, but somehow they didn't survive much more than six months. Our indoor play involved a lot of shouting, jumping, and tumbling. Then it would be time for our bath ritual. Afterward my mother would put us in our pajamas, the kind with feet if it was cold. We always had superhero pajamas with Superman, Spider-Man, or the Green Lantern. If we were really lucky, after our bath we would get to watch television.

Strange as it sounds to many people, I loved *Leave It to Beaver*. It didn't matter to me that none of the people on the show looked like my family. Wally and Beaver weren't much different from me and David, and the way they lived was like our lives on Hepburn. I looked forward to watching each episode. My favorites, though, were the Walt Disney programs. Walt Disney was such a remarkable man. He was a visionary, and had a vision of utopia that in many ways he was able to bring to life. Everything he produced offered glimpses of what the world could be. There was always a lesson to learn, a dream to aspire to, an adventure to imagine.

Bedtime was the rule that could never be broken. Throughout elementary school, I had to be in bed at eight, even in the summer when it was still light outside. On weekends I might be allowed to stay up to nine-thirty, but only if it was a special occasion. Looking back, I'm not sure how much of the bedtime rule was my mother's belief in children getting their sleep and how much was her own exhaustion from dealing with very demanding little boys all day. Whatever the reason, bedtime was not negotiable. David and I would be tucked in our twin mahogany beds, kissed good night, and expected to close our eyes and our mouths as she switched off the light.

The one concession was that she would leave the bedroom door open. I did not want the door shut. I was deathly afraid of the dark, or more accurately, of what I feared was in the dark. In those days horror films were screened on television on most weekends, and we would watch them on rainy afternoons, our eyes glued to the TV. I was terrified of Boris Karloff in *Frankenstein*. Lying in bed at night, I would imagine the monster coming into our room, stalking rigidly toward my bed, his arms extended to grab me. Then there was Karloff in *The Mummy*, with his dragging foot and dirty muslin strips unraveling as he crept along. It was the era of supernatural shows like *The Outer Limits*. The Crawling Eye also lurked in the darkness of our bedroom. *The Day the Earth Stood Still* convinced me that aliens were coming to abduct me or blast our house to smithereens. My mother's reassurances that none of these things were real did nothing to lessen my fears.

I relied on my dog, Mikey, to keep me company whenever I was afraid. Mikey wasn't a guard dog. In fact, Mikey wasn't a real dog at all, but he was real to me. His fur had worn off long ago, and stuffing was coming out of his seams, but I loved him. I had tied a piece of string around his neck, and when I left the house, I often took Mikey with me. I would walk my dog down the street, and when we got to the corner, I would stop and say, "Sit, Mikey!" Since Mikey was already in a sitting position, he was very good at following this command. As a result of our outings, Mikey was filthy and torn. My mother sewed him up repeatedly, but there was nothing she could do about the dirt. If she had scrubbed him, he would have disintegrated. Every now and then she would try to get rid of him without my knowing, but each time I would cry and go search through the garbage can until I found him. There was one firm rule for Mikey, though: he was not allowed to sleep in my bed. My mother flatly refused to let that funky dog in my clean bed. So the best Mikey could do was keep watch by my bedside at night and help to keep the monsters away.

Our mother was the strictest parent in the neighborhood, and sometimes I resented her discipline. One day when I was about six years old, I decided I had had enough of my mother's demands. I informed her that I was going to run away from home and be a hobo. (I loved hoboes because of their freedom. I would usually dress up like one on Halloween.) To my surprise, my mother didn't object. Instead, she continued with our regular routine. It wasn't until years later that I found out she intentionally kept me busy with our usual activities until evening came and the sun started going down.

After dinner I went out front and sat on the porch, thinking about how life on the road would be for me. It seemed to work all right for my father, I mused. As I sat there thinking, my mother came outside. She had made a bundle for me, with some clothes and sandwiches wrapped up in a cloth, and tied the bundle to a stick. She handed it to me and said very solemnly, "Son, I love you, but you've got to do what you've got to do." Then she put my jacket on me and said, "You'll need your jacket on in case it gets cold," as she buttoned me up.

Inside the house, I could hear David crying. He shouted through the open door, "Oh, no! Please don't let my brother go!"

"Now son, I want you to be careful out there, you hear me?" my mother told me. Then she kissed me good-bye, went back inside, and closed the door. I could still hear my brother sobbing on the other side. I stood there for a while, looking out at the street. It was dark by then, with only the porch light illuminating the spot where I stood. As I hesitated, rooted to the porch, my mother turned off the light. I could hear her throw the lock on the door behind me. I was frozen. Finally, I worked up my nerve, picked up the stick with its bundle, and forced my legs to move me off the porch. All around, there was darkness.

I never even made it to the end of the driveway. Halfway there, I dropped the stick and ran back to the front door, pounding on it and screaming, "AHHHHHHH! Let me in! Mommy! Mommy! Let me in!"

A few moments later my mother opened the door and peered down at me. "Back already?" she said calmly.

I threw myself into her arms. "I don't want to go! I'll do whatever you say!"

"Well, that's fine, son," she replied. "Come on in, then."

I never tried to run away again.

At one point, my brother David tried to run away as well, but he too was unsuccessful.

A BIG PART of our lives was church. Our church was Traveler's Rest, a small Baptist church near East Florence and Compton Boulevard on the east side of Los Angeles. Inside there was a gold-leaf ribbon painted across the wall behind where the preacher stood, with blue sky, a piece of Scripture, and the words "Traveler's Rest." Our church was a haven for hardworking people, who went there every Sunday to rest their souls and get energized for the next week. The congregants were all African American, most of them Southerners. They referred to one another as "Brother" and "Sister." At church, my mother was Sister Robinson and my father was Brother Ray. Church was an all-day affair. We were never there less than five hours. There was Sunday school and prayer service and a potluck and then more worship. To a young boy, the services seemed to go on forever. I would sit on the pew in my little suit, snap-on bow tie, and Buster Brown shoes, swinging my feet back and forth and squirming. I was too old to be in a separate room with my little brother, so I had to sit there next to my mother through the entire service. Every now and then she would pinch me to stop my wiggling. The building wasn't air-conditioned, and in summer it was miserable. The hot, dense air was like a whiff of hell bubbling underneath us. The only relief was the hand fans on a stick they handed out at every service. On one side was a picture of Jesus, and on the other was an ad for the local mortuary. Life and death on opposite sides of the cardboard seemed like a paradox as a child. I thought that was an odd combination. My mother was always dressed beautifully in her suit and hat. The hats were sometimes spectacular. I could never understand why the heat didn't seem to bother her as much as it did me.

The pastor, Reverend Durham, became my godfather not long after we moved to California. He was an old-fashioned, pulpit-pounding preacher, and when he got "in the Spirit," he would slap the podium and say, "I *heard*," pausing for dramatic effect. An incurable mimic, I would hit the back of a chair at home—or worse, at church—and say, "I *heard*" just like Reverend Durham, then turn around and stare intently at my listeners.

This was very upsetting to my mother. She would slap me up the side of the head and say, "Don't you mimic Pastor Durham!"

The deacons sat in a row up front. When it was my turn to walk forward and put a dollar in the offering plate, I always noticed their socks. They all wore thin black nylon socks with a red stripe up the side. One Sunday before church, I sneaked into my father's closet and found a pair of thin black nylon socks like the deacons wore and put them on under my Buster Browns, using a rubber band to hold them up. When my mother saw what I'd done, she smacked me on the head and said, "Take your daddy's socks off right this minute!" I don't know if she ever made the connection with the deacons.

When my father was in town, he would sometimes come with us. He was treated like any other member of the congregation. He didn't interact much, just sat there listening and nodding in agreement, twitching occasionally, humming along with the choir director. My mother, on the other hand, would get carried away by the Spirit every Sunday. She would begin to sway and cry, and other ladies from the church would gather around to fan her. It was a jumping, shouting, deliverance kind of church, and when Mother really got into the Spirit, she would sometimes be "laid out" by the Holy Ghost, falling unconscious onto the floor. As a child, I didn't understand what was happening to her, and my mother never explained it to me. Neither did anyone else. She would just say, "Thank you, Jesus." As an adult, I understand the burden she was bearing and her need for spiritual comfort and emotional release, but at the time, her dramatic reaction was very confusing.

There were compensations at church, though. Gospel music was in my blood, and I loved listening as the congregation swayed and sang along. I also liked singing the children's songs like "Jesus Loves Me." And oh, my goodness, the food. Church potlucks made the long, hot services worthwhile. The women brought their soul-food specialties: yams and greens and cabbage, spare ribs and lamb chops and pork chops, and always homemade corn bread. The best food in town.

EARLY IN MY LIFE, school held its own challenges. I wanted to do well, but I was born with what is now called ADHD—attention-deficit/ hyperactivity disorder. This was long before the research, formal diagnosis, or medication options that have become commonplace for children who exhibit the symptoms I did. When I was small, children like me were called hyperactive, told they had "ants in their pants," or more harshly, described as "brats" who simply needed stricter discipline. All I knew was that sitting still for very long was agony, and that no matter how hard I tried, it was impossible for me to stay focused on anything. Luckily, I had two advantages that many ADHD children don't have: a father who could afford to send me to good schools, and a mother who was committed to my education.

My mother was adamant about my brothers and me getting a good education. She had dropped out of school at a young age and learned the hard way what a struggle life was for those without an education. They would spend their lives as maids and waitresses, as she had until she met my father. She demonstrated her belief in education by returning to school after we moved to California, eventually earning her GED. My mother knew that education could open doors, especially for black children, and she wanted us to have every opportunity to build successful lives so we wouldn't have to rely on our famous father's name.

I started kindergarten at the Thirty-ninth Street Elementary, a public school around the corner, just a couple of blocks from our house. Every morning my mother would walk me there and back. My second year I started walking with a group of my friends, carrying the lunch box my mother had packed for me. Every day when I got home from school, my mother would read with me. We read the *Dick and Jane* series, and *The Cat in the Hat* and other Dr. Seuss books. I would sit next to her at the kitchen table, carefully sounding out the words. She was patient with me. She took her time teaching me to read.

When it came time for David to start school, she researched schools to find the best place for us. She enrolled me and David in a Montessori school when I started the second grade. Unfortunately, that only lasted one semester. My brother refused to take naps, and one day he had a tantrum and tore up the whole area. That was the end of Montessori for both of us. Our family friend Dr. Foster told us about a private school on Adams Boulevard called Mary Clay, and that is where we attended next. Our mother continued to look for a school that would give us the safe environment she wanted and the individual attention we needed. Eventually she found Colin McKuen, a private school on Highland, adjacent to the Hollywood Bowl. I remained there throughout elementary school.

I loved Colin McKuen, or more accurately, I loved Mrs. Reynolds. We all did. She was a remarkable woman who was the head of the faculty and our teacher. She strongly believed that Colin McKuen was a place where she could educate children the way they should be educated. She believed that children learned best when they could work at their own pace in a low-pressure environment where they could get the individual attention they needed. Colin McKuen was a three-classroom school, much like the pioneer schools of our ancestors, with all of the grades together. We learned some topics as a group, but for the most part, the curriculum was self-paced. She moved among us throughout the day, explaining, correcting, and encouraging us as we worked on our lessons. It was a racially mixed environment drawn from upper-middle-class families. The majority of the students were white, but it was never a "white" school. Everyone felt welcome.

ON HEPBURN AVENUE, my father built a little cocoon that kept us safe while he was away. Every year we made a pilgrimage to Texas to visit my mother's family and to stay a couple of weeks with Jeff Brown and his family. At least once a year Jeff and his wife came to California to stay with us. There was a steadiness, a security, that came from a strong sense of community and the freedom from financial want. We had everything we needed and more, everything my father had lacked when he was growing up. Our lives on Hepburn were a world away from the life on the road that made the lifestyle he provided for us possible. Two months of the year my father lived with us in the world of Disney. The other ten months he lived in a world he kept rigidly separate. Eventually we would all pay a high price for that separation. When I was little, though, the only thing I knew was that whenever he was gone, I missed my dad.

CHAPTER 5

What Kind of Man Are You?

What kind of man are

you?

Why can't I let you go?

—RAY CHARLES

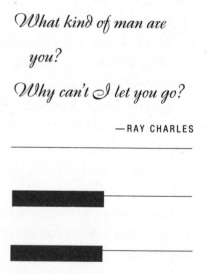

W HEN I WAS A CHILD, MY FATHER WAS LARGER THAN life. He came and went from our lives in a way that seemed myste-rious to me. Every year as February drew to a close, he would leave with the band for a ten-month tour. Except for quick trips home when he had a day off, he was gone almost continually. As each year came to an end, Daddy would return just in time for Christmas. It was an iron-clad rule with my father: he had to be home at Christmas. My mother says he never cared about Christmas until I was born. But once I got old enough to celebrate Christmas, it became the most important day of my father's year.

In the weeks before Christmas, my mother would shop for the practical things for us—clothing and all the things we needed. Then she would pick out some toys and put them on layaway. Getting toys was a big deal for us at Christmas. Toys were for special occasions like birthdays and Christmas. I used to beg my mother to take me to Karl's Toy Store. I would walk around inside and dream about the models and the slot cars and the electric planes. When my dad returned to town right before Christmas, he and the valet would go shopping for us. They would pick up the toys my mother had put on layaway along with a few more that my father thought were really cool, like electric airplanes.

As much as we loved the toys he bought for us, buying toys for my dad at Christmas was even more fun. My father loved toys. Our mom explained that he was too poor to have toys when he was growing up, so toys were special at Christmas. My mother would take us shopping to pick out something for him. Dad loved any toy that made noise, bumped into things, or turned around—tops, gadgets, cars that he could follow by the sound. He especially loved the kind of old-fashioned spinning top that would spin and whistle each time you pushed down on it. He would lean over and put his ear right next to it, to feel the motion and listen to the sound. Stuffed animals and other playthings with interesting textures were also favorites. He saved the toys we gave him for Christmas in his office over the years. I would go in there sometimes and see a toy we had given him years before.

The ritual was always the same. On Christmas Eve, Dad and I would put out the cookies and milk for Santa. Mother would put us to bed on time, though we were usually too excited to fall asleep. My father would always stay up late putting our gifts together after we went to bed. When I was small, of course, I still believed the elves did it. It was important to Dad to assemble them himself, and he was good at it. David and I would sneak downstairs about four in the morning to see what Santa had brought us. We'd peek at the unwrapped gifts, but we never tried to open anything.

No one was allowed to open presents until my father woke up. He loved to open his own toys and to listen as we opened ours. I can still see him sitting on the sofa by the Christmas tree, his glasses off, smiling and running his fingers over his gifts. We would spend the morning together as a family and eat a big Christmas dinner. Sometime in the afternoon, my father would usually go back upstairs. I loved Christmas. It wasn't just the toys. Christmas was a special day for me because it meant we didn't have to share our dad with anyone else.

For two months of every year, we were a family, but at the end of February, he would leave for the road once again. I hated it when he went away. Whenever he left for another trip, I would pepper him with questions. "Where are you going? What are you doing? When are you coming back? Will you bring me something?" Endless questions, all designed to delay the moment when he would walk out the door and be gone again. After he left, I would go in his office and breathe him in.

When he was home with us, I wanted to spend every waking moment with him. I wanted to sit on his lap and touch his face. I loved to feel his face, running my fingers over it the same way he did when he "looked" at us. His skin was like leather, and he had a rough five o'clock shadow that rasped against my fingertips. I especially liked to feel his face without the glasses. The glasses hid him from me, and I wanted to see all of him.

I also liked to sit and watch him get dressed. This was only possible on weekends. He woke up late every morning, so on the weekends I would get a chance to see him shave. Dad had a battered old leather shaving kit that he carried with him everywhere. I thought that kit was the coolest thing ever. He shaved with an old-fashioned soap brush and a straight razor. He would take his glasses off, lather his face with the brush, and shave the stubble off with quick strokes—whoosh, whoosh, whoosh. He didn't miss, and I never saw him cut himself. Then he'd sprinkle aftershave on his hands, rub them together, and pat his face with aftershave. When I was very small, he used Brut. When I was a little older, he started using Cannon. It became his distinctive fragrance. To this day, I remember that smell of Cannon.

His clothes were wonderful. He was particular about them and partial to fabrics with nice textures. He always wore silk boxers and a matching undershirt. I would sit on the bed and watch him put on his nylon socks that came up past his calves. His clothes were tailored for him, so they always fit perfectly. He did not vacillate in weight. I don't think he put on more than twenty pounds in his entire adulthood. If he was staying home, he would wear slacks and a T-shirt and a pair of house shoes. If he was going out, he always wore cool shoes, made out of expensive leathers. I loved to try on his shoes.

On a typical day he would wake up between ten a.m. and noon, get dressed, have breakfast in the kitchen with my mother, and then go up-stairs to his office. A few hours later band members and arrangers would start filtering in, drifting up to my father's office to continue working on his music or rehearse. Sometimes he would emerge long enough to have dinner with us, but not every night. We seldom went out to eat. Dad didn't like to eat in public because he had to use his fingers to locate the food. My dad always came home late, after I'd gone to bed. Otherwise he would be there at bedtime for a hug and a kiss. His schedule was always different from ours because his internal clock was set for life on the road. Long after we were asleep, he would be in the kitchen eating. On the road, midnight was dinnertime, after the last set. He liked to fix his own dinner while my mother slept. His specialty was macaroni and cheese. He would call our friend Herbert Miller in the middle of the night and tell him to come over; they were having mac and cheese. Herbert would tiptoe up to the front door, rapping lightly so he wouldn't wake us, and eat dinner with my dad at the kitchen table while we slept.

My dad used to sing and hum while he puttered around during the day. He would walk around the house singing something like "Hallelujah, I Love Her So" under his breath. He liked to hum and jingle his keys on the way upstairs to his office. He very seldom played the piano in the living room, but every now and then he would just start playing and working out some arrangement in his head or trying to remember a tune. He did play the sax at home, though. The strains of an alto sax became the soundtrack to life at home with Daddy.

He twitched and was fidgety almost all the time. He always carried a big key ring, and he would fidget constantly with his keys. When we asked our mother why he was always fidgeting, she would tell us that was just Daddy's way. He always seemed to be preoccupied. I have an abiding image of him looking like Rodin's *The Thinker*—bent over, head down and resting on one hand. Unlike the statue, though, he always had a cigarette dangling from his lips or at his fingertips. I used to wonder what he was thinking about so intently. I don't know if he was thinking at all, or had just retreated into some deep place where he could escape the world for a little while.

My father wasn't one to talk much at home. I was always wanting to talk to him, but there never seemed to be a good time to do it. I don't think he knew what to talk about with a child. His own childhood had been so fractured that he never learned what fathers and sons were supposed to talk about. Being blind only made things worse because it meant he would never be able to do normal activities with us. Maybe he felt awkward with us. Most of the time, he was preoccupied with his music. Music was not only his work but his comfort zone. In his office with the door closed and his music surrounding him, he was in a world he could navigate like no one else. In that world, he was the genius and those outside his world would try to comprehend.

His office was a magical place for me. I didn't dare knock when he was in there. He would hang a towel on the door to indicate he didn't want to be disturbed. Yet even when I couldn't see him, I would imagine him. If the door was closed, I would listen for him. When he was gone, I would sneak into his office and sit in his chair. His room had a special smell to it. I liked to walk around, looking at all his things and touching them. I would look at his plaques and the photographs of him with the band. I would run my fingers over his reel-to-reel tape deck imagining his music, leaf through his *Cashbox* and *Billboard* magazines looking for his name on the top-100 charts and in the magazine and newspaper articles. He had leather bags that he took on the road, and he always stored them in his office when he was home. I would run my hands over them and breathe in the smell of the leather. And I would look at all the equipment that he had in there. Afterward I would tiptoe out and think to myself, "What does he do when he's in there by himself? What's going on in his head?"

HIS SIGHTLESSNESS FASCINATED ME. I didn't think of it as a handicap so much as a special gift. He never referred to himself as blind. He said he just couldn't see. I knew he had a different way of seeing things. When I wanted to show him something, I would take his hands and run them over it, just as he did when he showed me something. He would bend down so I could reach him, and I would explain: "See, Daddy, this is what it looks like." He would memorize it with his fingers while he listened to me, and I knew he could see it.

Afterward he would nod and say, "You don't say."

Sometimes I would just sit and stare at my dad, wondering what was going on behind his sunglasses. He would take them off at home if only the family was there, and I would stare at his closed eyelids. "What does he see?" I'd wonder. "Why does he always keep his eyes shut? Do his eyes look like mine?" When he heard something, I would see his face turn and his eyebrows move just like a seeing person's. The illusion was that he was witnessing something. Sometimes I wondered if he was. My mother would tell me that he was just listening, but I wondered if he could somehow see through those closed eyelids. Sometimes he would appear to look right at me, and I would wonder, "Can he see me? Is he looking at me?"

Only once did I get a glimpse of my father with his eyes open. When I was very young, my dad was startled by a loud noise and turned his head, raising his eyebrows a fraction higher than usual. His eyelids opened just a little, and for a moment, I could see what lay behind them. There was nothing, just whiteness. I caught my breath. "My daddy's eyes look just like the Invisible Man's!" I thought. It scared me to death. It also made me wonder if I was right about my dad being able to see things. Maybe he was like a superhero.

I already knew he could do things that no one else could. Other kids thought it was easier for me to get away with things with a blind father, but the opposite was true. His sense of hearing was downright uncanny. He knew who everyone was by the way they moved. He could identify all of us by the way we walked, even on a thick carpet. He said he always knew it was me because of the distinctive way I dragged my feet when I walked. There was no sneaking up on him, and there was no way to sneak around him, either. My mother said that when she tied bells on my shoes as a toddler, she did it so she could find me. My dad didn't need bells. He could always find me.

One of the biggest mysteries of my childhood was how he got around without bumping into things. It was like he had sonar. He never used a white cane like most sightless people did, and he didn't need anyone to lead him in familiar surroundings. He did have to reorient himself on occasion. Sometimes when he got home after an extended absence, he would be uncertain where everything was. Things had been added or moved while he was gone. My mother would re-acclimate him, guiding him around the house and showing him where everything was. After that, he had it. He remembered where things were, knew where they were in relation to each other, could construct angles in his head to keep his perspective.

Sometimes he would ask me to get something in the house, and I couldn't find it. "Where?" I would say. "I don't see it."

He would take me by the shoulders, turn me to face whatever it was he wanted, and say, "There. It's right in front of you." And he would be right.

I could never fathom how he did it. My mother explained to me that Daddy had counted the steps to get him everywhere he went and had memorized the location of everything he needed. That didn't explain, though, how he always knew which way he was facing. The only time he ever bumped into things was when he was high or in an unfamiliar place, or in another state of mind. The one exception was the outdoors. Every now and then he would go outside with me and try to pull me around in a wagon or play with me. That was nearly always a disaster, for he had no points of reference to tell him where he was.

He was also better at many everyday tasks than my brothers and I were. I was always spilling my milk, but my dad never did. He would walk to the refrigerator, get out the milk bottle, and fill his glass without spilling a drop. He never poured it over the top of the cereal bowl, and he never knocked over his glass. As I got older, I learned that he could tell how full a glass was by the sound of the liquid as he poured it, and he could tell when the cereal bowl was full by keeping his fingertip on the edge of the bowl.

I also marveled that he could get dressed by himself and that all of his clothes would match perfectly. I needed my mother to help me match my clothes, but my father could do it without anyone's help. It was only much later that I asked my mother how he did it. She explained that whenever he bought a piece of clothing, he would sit down with my mother and go over every inch of it with his hands—buttons, seams, collar, fabric, everything—so he would remember which one it was. Then he would hang it in the closet. He had a specific place for everything. He would also sew braille numbers onto his clothing labels to tell him what color everything was. He could put an outfit together by matching up all the numbers. Dad kept his shoes under the bed until he bought so many that there was no longer enough room. He put a pair of socks in each one according to the color and texture. When it was time to dress in the morning, he already knew where everything was and could locate it quickly. On the road the valet helped dress him before a performance, but at home he didn't need any help. If I complained that my mother expected me to dress myself as well as my father could, she would tell me, "No, I don't expect that. But I expect you to come close. If he can do it, you can learn to do it, too."

It's one thing to feel you don't do things as well as your father. But when your father is blind, the comparison takes on a whole new meaning.

Despite being billed for years as "the Blind Sensation," my father's blindness never defined him. My dad once told our dear friend Herbert

Miller that he really didn't mind being sightless. He was used to it, and his accomplishments proved that. His only regret, he told Herbert, was that he would never see his family. "I'd give anything to see Ray Jr.'s face on Christmas morning," he told Herbert one winter afternoon as they rushed to Los Angeles for the holidays. "Just once, I'd like to see my son's face."

My father had an amazing mechanical ability that baffled most people. He could repair nearly anything with instructions from someone. He was always taking things apart or putting them together—toys, stereo equipment, reel-to-reel tape recorders. He wanted to know how everything worked and why it did what it did. Every time my parents got a new appliance, my father wanted to disassemble it. He would ask my mother to read the directions out loud, and he'd fool with it until he understood how it worked. Afterward, over her objections, he often started breaking it down. She always warned him, "Don't expect me to plug that thing in after you put it back together."

When he purchased one of his reel-to-reels that he used for playback and to compose some of his greatest hits, he was fascinated with the mechanism and needed to know every working part. He made my mother spread a sheet out on the table, and then he took it apart piece by piece. All my mother could think was that the recorder cost a fortune, and they were in deep trouble if he didn't get it put back together correctly. He always did, though. He could lay out two or three hundred pieces of a complicated mechanism on the table, and as long as no one moved any of the pieces, he could come back three days later, remember where each one was, and put them back together perfectly. He had an astonishing memory.

He learned about the engines in the planes he owned over the years and could repair them if he needed to. Herbert Miller told me that one night when Dad's twin-engine Martin 404 was grounded in a storm for engine trouble, Dad completed a repair no one else could manage. The pilot and mechanic had struggled unsuccessfully for an hour in the pouring rain to get the newly repaired engine back into its compartment, but they couldn't get it to clear the cowl flap properly. Finally my dad said, "Let me give it a shot."

The pilot and mechanic gave each other a "Yeah, right" look as my father climbed under the wing and disappeared from view. They could hear him adjusting something, and a few minutes later he asked for a wrench to tighten the bolts, and they were ready for takeoff.

My father loved airplanes, perhaps for the sense of complete freedom they gave him. In the air, he didn't need eyes. One of the most exciting experiences of my life was seeing and flying in my father's airplane. I was five years old at the time. It was a twin-engine Cessna 310 that seated five people. He kept it at the Compton Airport. When he described it enthusiastically to my mother, she didn't exactly react like he'd hoped. In fact, she says, she thought he had taken leave of his senses. She could not understand why he would want a small airplane. When we went to the airport to see it, though, she was pleasantly surprised. The plane was larger than she had expected and much nicer. David and I thought it was the coolest thing we'd ever seen. My father introduced us to the pilot, a young black man named Simon Barry. None of us had ever seen a black pilot. My mother privately wondered if Simon knew how to fly the plane. He seemed far too young to entrust her family with.

After the introductions, my father told us to get in the plane. We were taking a ride. My mother panicked, convinced that if we got in, it would be the end of us all. Eventually, though, my dad convinced her to give it a try. He lifted me into the pilot's seat and then slid into the copilot's seat next to me. He put my small hands on the steering wheel and then placed his hands on top of mine, the way he always did when he showed me things.

"This is the wheel," he explained. "You use it to steer the plane." Then he placed my hands on the throttle, once again covering them with his own. "This is the throttle. It powers the plane. You move it back and forth like this." He proceeded to show me every button on the instrument panel, placing my hands on each one and then explaining the button's function. I was so fascinated!

Then he put me in back where my mother and David were sitting, and Simon got on board and made sure we were all strapped in. By then my mother was starting to panic again. "Lord, have mercy," she was praying.

"Lord, have mercy." I unbuckled my seat belt, stood up, and leaned over Simon's shoulder. "Do you really know how to fly my dad's plane?" I demanded. Everyone burst out laughing, including Simon. I guess we were all a little nervous. He buckled me back in, and we took off. It turned out that Simon really did know what he was doing. We christened the plane by circling Los Angeles for nearly an hour, taking in the shoreline and the buildings below. It was amazing. In 1960 how many black children had a father who owned his own plane and could take them flying over the city whenever he wanted to? How many blind men of any color had the vision to consider it, the talent to make it happen, and the technical knowledge to understand how it worked? There was no one like my dad. No one at all.

My father even learned to fly his planes himself. I loved flying, but it terrified me when my dad took over as pilot. He would sit in the copilot's seat, put on the headphones, adjust the instruments, and talk to the tower like any other pilot. Pilots use the expression "flying blind" to describe flying in thick fog or under bad weather conditions where they can't see where they're going, so I guess what my father was doing was pretty much the same thing. He relied on the instruments on the control panel and Simon, along with the tower, to guide him. He could probably have landed the plane in an emergency, though, thank God, he never had to. Dad's pilot explained to me that as long as you knew what the instruments said, you didn't really need eyes. Maybe so, but flying with my father at the helm was an eye-opening experience.

IT WAS IMPORTANT to my father to teach me some of the things other fathers taught their sons. One of the things he wanted to teach me was how to ride a bike. My dad loved bikes. He had ridden an old beat-up bicycle all over Greenville as a boy, even after going blind. The Christmas before I turned six, he excitedly bought me my first bicycle.

I came downstairs that Christmas morning to find a candy-apple-red Schwinn with streamers and a horn under the Christmas tree. It was beautiful, exactly what I wanted. Unfortunately, in his eagerness to get me the perfect bike, my dad had bought one that was intended for an older child. I couldn't get on it without help. And that wasn't the only problem. My dad had put it together in the basement with Herbert Miller in the middle of the night, but my father's mechanical expertise had failed him on this occasion. He prided himself on his ability to assemble almost anything, but for some reason, he had forgotten the fine details on my bike. The handlebars were crooked, the horn was upside down, and when I climbed onto the seat, it tilted straight up. I was puzzled.

"Mommy, what's wrong with Santa's elves?" I asked. "Were they drunk when they made this for me?"

My mother managed to smother a smile and said, "Son, just go on outside and let your daddy show you how to ride it."

Dad asked what was wrong with the bike, and when I explained, he got out his toolbox and fixed the seat. Then we went outside. He walked my bike down the driveway to the sidewalk so I could climb on. My father didn't seem to notice that the bike was far too big for me, and I was too excited to say anything. There were no training wheels, so my father balanced it while I got on. I struggled to climb on the seat, which was too high for me, and I could only reach the pedals when they were straight up.

Dad gave me a good push and told me to pedal. He trotted beside me, holding me up. I tried, but my legs weren't long enough and my feet slipped off each time I pushed the pedals. I wobbled a few feet, then tumbled onto the grass verge running along the sidewalk.

"That's okay, baby," my dad reassured me. "Just get back on and try again."

My father righted the bicycle and held it while I clambered back on. That Christmas he pushed me up and down the sidewalk for hours, trying to teach me how to ride. He would give me a push, then stand and listen so he could tell where I was. He was the only father playing outside with his child that morning. I fell off again and again, but I didn't care. I savored every minute. I was proud to be with my dad.

After that day, bike riding became one of my favorite activities. I attached playing cards to the spokes with clothespins so I could make my bike sound like a motorcycle and it would be easier for my father to find me. I rode my bicycle everywhere, up and down the street, just like my dad had taught me.

LIKE MOST FATHERS, my dad also spoke to me about how to defend myself. "You have to decide: either you fight or you don't," he told me.

I needed his advice. My mother told me not to get into fights, but the truth was, I couldn't avoid it. As Ray Charles's sons, David and I were targets. Someone was always picking on us. Sometimes they tried to take things from us. It was my job to take care of my little brother. "Don't let anyone jump on your brother," my mother would tell me. I had to defend David all the time. I was always getting into fights, whether I wanted to or not. I tried to avoid it, for after every fight my mother would spank me, and the spanking was often worse than the fight itself. It was a no-win situation. Despite my best intentions, someone would pick on me or my brother again, and I'd be right back in the middle of another fight. I eventually had to stop avoiding the fights and put my father's advice into practice. I had learned my father's lessons well.

I became adept at protecting myself and my brothers from other children, but the dangers of the playground were the least of our worries. During the sixties, racists were still burning crosses on the lawns of black families. Being black and rich could be fatal. Entire neighborhoods of wealthy, prominent African Americans were a new phenomenon in the sixties, so they attracted attention. Newspapers and magazines were publishing articles with titles like "The Richest Negro Neighborhoods in America." My mother was hearing stories on the radio about wealthy people's children being kidnapped. Sometimes the kidnappers would give the children back after getting a ransom, but other times the parents would never see them again. While I was still in elementary school, my father hired a driver whose responsibilities included taking us back and forth from school, but his real job was to protect us. It wasn't until I became a father myself that I understood how hard the situation must have been for my dad. A father's first instinct is to protect his family. He disliked being in public himself, for he was always hyperaware of his surroundings, alert to the possibility of a stranger approaching him unannounced, or being attacked. Hiring a driver as security was my father's way of protecting us. It was the price of his fame.

During those years, my mother had a phobia that someone was going to take us. She never left us alone if she could help it, even with a baby-sitter. For safety she always carried a pearl-handled derringer in her purse. She was prepared to defend us and herself if she had to. Nobody got by my mother. If my father came home unexpectedly in the middle of the night, he sometimes got quite a greeting. Several times I woke up in the middle of the night to hear my mother shouting down at an intruder from the upstairs hall.

"Halt! Don't move!" I could hear someone bumping and fumbling around downstairs. Gun drawn, my mother would shout, "Didn't you hear me? Don't move!"

This would usually be followed by the nervous jingling of a large key ring, and then my father's voice would float up the stairs. "Bea, it's me! It's me!"

Lowering the gun, she'd reply, "How many times do I have to tell you to come in the front door? How am I supposed to know you're not some intruder?"

She had good reason to be vigilant. Sometimes the danger did invade our home. My father had a female visitor who came to our home to give him what my mother called his "daily bread." I saw her coming and going, but I had no idea why she was there. My mother wasn't crazy about having the woman in her home, but it was less dangerous than having someone inject heroin outside our home. As long as the process was safe and none of us saw it, she tolerated it. On one occasion, though, the dosage she gave him was far too high, and my father had a violent reaction.

The next night, when this woman arrived at our home, my mother was waiting for her downstairs. We were already asleep upstairs. My mother says she told the woman she needed to speak with her for a minute. Calmly holding the derringer where the dealer could see it, she said, "I under-stand that my husband is paying you for a service. You are doing what he is asking you to do because that is your business. I understand that. But when you come into my home and almost kill my husband because of your carelessness, that is not acceptable. In the future, you will be more careful about what you do to my husband. Is that clear?"

The word went out that Mrs. Charles was not a woman to be crossed, and where her husband was concerned, anyone who harmed him did so at his or her own risk.

The painful truth, though, was that it was my father who brought the biggest danger into our home. As my mother has said, he was the one who ordered the heroin. He continued to deny that it was harming him, and until he faced the truth, there was nothing my mother or anyone else could do.

CHAPTER 6

Mr. Charles Blues

Well, I finally got a

break, baby,

Easy things are coming my

way.

—RAY CHARLES

THE EARLY YEARS ON HEPBURN AVENUE SHOULD HAVE been an age of innocence for me. My parents worked hard to make it that way. The parts of our lives that I saw could have been episodes of fifties family television programs. The world of our family and the world of the road were as clearly separated as the McCarthy hearings were from *Father Knows Best*. Eventually reality and fantasy would blend, and we would all suffer mightily for it. But when I was very young, the paparazzi were only a distant nightmare, and celebrity families could still live in relative peace. About the only trouble I ever had was the kind I made myself.

Like most little boys, I was fascinated with cars. I was always trying to get hold of my mother's car keys. With no understanding of the consequences, I thought that starting a car would be the most fascinating thing ever. One day my mother put David and me in the car to run an errand and then realized she had left something in the house. She went back inside, and as soon as she left, I jumped into the driver's seat and started playing with the gears. Somehow I managed to put the car into neutral. The emergency brake must not have been on, for to my surprise, the car started rolling back out of the driveway. As the car rolled, David stared at me, his eyes round and wide. Mine were even wider.

"Ooooh!" I said.

"Ooh-wee!" David replied.

The car kept rolling, straight into the middle of the street, and came to a stop. Luckily for us, there was no traffic. By then my mother had come out of the house and seen what was happening. It must have scared her to death, but at the time, all I could think was, "Boy, does she look mad!" She ran down the driveway, straight into the middle of the street, to retrieve us and her Cadillac. She drove her car back into the driveway and I received a good spanking right on the spot.

When it came to trouble, birth order usually ruled. As the oldest, I was given the biggest share of responsibility. I was expected to look after David and, later on, Robert. I had to be careful with David. He would follow me wherever I went and do everything I did. If I headed down the street, I would turn around and see him following me. If I was riding my bike, David would follow on his tricycle half a block behind me. If I went into the street, he went into the street. If I climbed the wall separating our house from the Andersons', he would try to climb it, too. One time he scrambled up on the wall behind me and fell into the kennel next door where the Andersons' boxers were kept. That time David was bitten, and I got into big trouble. But then having younger brothers also meant always having somebody else to blame. If I got into trouble, I would routinely say that David had done it, and when Bobby came along, David and I would say, "Bobby did it, Mommy." Not that she usually believed us, of course. We would blame Bobby for things he couldn't possibly have done, because he was far too little.

I was always going someplace I wasn't supposed to be, seeking adventure. I wasn't supposed to sit on the fence between our backyard and the Andersons', but it was a great vantage point for throwing mud at my best friend. I periodically fell off the fence in the excitement of the moment, landing on Anthony's side, where their dogs were roaming back and forth. The result was usually that I would be chased around the Andersons' yard by their angry boxers.

I even went underneath the street in front of our house to play. My mother would have had a heart attack if she'd known. One time some workers left the manhole in front of our house uncovered, and some of the other boys and me climbed down to see what was under the street. I was uncomfortable going down there, but I didn't want to be a chicken, so I climbed down after them. It turned out to be a great place to play army. After that first time, we moved the manhole ourselves. It took three of us to drag the heavy cover far enough for us to squeeze down inside, but we were so little that we didn't have to drag it far. Jack, Alvin, and I would play army until we got tired, then sit and watch through the grate as cars drove over our heads. Our adventure was sneaky and dangerous. I was terrified that my mother would catch us and give me a whipping.

I really got in trouble for getting into my father's things. I was always poking around in the garage. My father kept a lot of equipment in there, including a trailer that he pulled behind the station wagon when he was on the road. One day I was fooling around in the trailer and closed the doors so I wouldn't be seen if somebody came in the garage. The doors got stuck, and I ended up locked inside. Three hours went by. My parents didn't know where I was, and when they couldn't find me, they panicked. They were about to call the police when they finally found me.

I was always getting in trouble for going into my father's office. I was forbidden to go in there unless he invited me, but the room drew me like a magnet, especially when my father had been gone for a while. It was where he kept his arrangements, expensive recording equipment, valuable memorabilia, awards, and—as I eventually realized—his drug kit. His office was the last place my mother wanted me and my brothers to go, but we did.

Usually my mother was the disciplinarian. On one occasion, though, I went so far—literally and figuratively—that my father spanked me.

When I was seven years old, I decided I wanted to have another adventure. The horn on my Schwinn had rusted through, and I wanted to buy a new one. I also wanted to buy more streamers for the handlebars. I saved my allowance until I had the three dollars I needed. To buy the things I wanted for my bicycle, I would need to go to Pep Boys at Forty-third and Crenshaw, almost ten blocks from our house. It was a long trip that involved crossing several major streets, so I planned it carefully. I would stick to side streets as much as possible to avoid traffic.

One morning, with my money in my pocket, I told my parents, "I'm going out to ride my bike for a while."

Then I went outside and set off like I always did, as if I were just going to the end of the street. This time, though, I kept going. On the major streets, I rode on the sidewalk. At each corner I got off my bike, walked it across the street, then got back on and rode to the next corner. I was very careful but in a hurry. I made it safely to Pep Boys, went inside, bought my horn and streamers, and then made the return trip home. I laid my bike on the porch and knocked on the door for my mother to let me in like I always did.

While I was gone, my mother had begun to wonder where I was. She was keeping an eye out the window, and she didn't see me going up and down the block as I usually did. When I didn't come back after a few minutes, she sent my brother David out to see where I was. I hadn't realized it, but when I set off, my little brother Bobby had decided to follow me. He was just a toddler at the time, but he had gotten on his tricycle and followed me down the block. What made her realize that I had left the block was that Bobby was sitting on his tricycle at the end of the block pointing, wondering where I'd gone. When she saw that, she became hysterical, convinced that someone had kidnapped me. My father, who was home that day, was also frightened. He sent Duke Wade, his valet, out in the car to look for me. Then he and my mother walked up and down the streets for blocks, looking for me. The neighbors helped them search. Forty-five minutes went by, and there was no trace of me. They were just calling the police when I knocked on the front door.

I had no idea what was going on, of course, so I was surprised to see that my mother was crying when she opened the front door. She pulled me inside, clutched me tightly, and swatted me on the behind.

"Where have you been?" she asked me.

"I was just riding my bike," I told her.

She shouted upstairs, "Ray, he's here! He's all right." I heard my father's voice rumble in response. Turning back to me, she said, "Where did you go?" While I tried to think of something to say, she noticed the Pep Boys bag in my hand.

Uh-oh. I decided to play dumb. "What did I do? I just went to Pep Boys," I told her.

She was having none of that. She replied, "You know what you did."

Then she went upstairs to talk to my father. I could hear raised voices. By the time she came back down, I knew I was in real trouble. "Your father wants to see you upstairs," she told me.

Oh, boy. Reluctantly I dragged myself upstairs to my parents' bedroom, where my father sat on the side of the bed waiting for me, fiddling with his keys. He looked very upset. As soon as he heard me come in the room, he said, "Son, you scared us all—you scared your mother nearly to death. Now, young man, why did you scare your mother like that?"

I stared at my feet. I didn't know what to say. My dad kept turning his key ring over and over. "Your mama wants me to spank you because she's too angry to do it." My father had never spanked me before.

"But I didn't mean to do anything, Daddy."

"I know, son, and I don't want to, but I have to spank you. You are never to leave this house without tellin' your mother where you're going, and you never cross a major street by yourself again. You could have been killed." Then he said the dreaded words: "Son, this is going to hurt me more than it's going to hurt you."

Grown-ups always said that when they were about to do something awful to you. The reality of what was about to happen began to sink in. "Oh, yeah? How's it going to hurt *you*?" I replied. It was the wrong thing to say.

"Man, I have to do it," he told me, taking off his belt and folding it in his hand. Then he grabbed me by the collar and wedged my head between his legs so I couldn't get away. He felt for my behind to orient himself, then pulled his arm back and BAM! Then he did it again—BAM! He spanked me hard, and he didn't stop for what must have been ten minutes. Every now and then I would wiggle out of his grip, and he would have to grab me and grope around to find my backside again.

I couldn't believe what was happening. My mother spanked me all the time, but my father had never laid a hand on me. I cried, begging him to stop: "Please, Daddy! Please, Daddy!"

He kept on striking my backside until he was tired. Finally he told me, "I'm goin' to take a break. Then I'll be right back, and I'm goin' to spank you again." By then he had warmed to his task. He was angry, and so was I.

The minute he let go of me, I crawled as far as I could under my parents' bed. I was furious. I already had blisters on my behind, and now he was telling me he was going to come back and do it again.

My father got down and felt under the bed, but it was a king-size bed, and I had scooted back where he couldn't reach me. "You come out from under there!" he shouted at me.

"I'm not coming out! I'm never coming out!"

I don't know how long I hid under that bed while my father shouted at me. Exhausted and frustrated, he eventually gave up and left the room. Silence fell. I stayed under the bed a good three hours. It was dark and stuffy and hard to breathe. Finally I heard my mother's footsteps approaching.

"Son, come out now," she said to me. "Come on out from under there.

It's time for dinner. You're on punishment. I was going to let you go. I was going to have your father spank you and write it off, but you're on punishment now." Reluctantly I crawled out from under the bed.

For the next week, I had to stay in my room. No TV. Couldn't go outside. Couldn't talk to my friends. I was busted. It was one of the most miserable weeks of my life as a child. It was also the only time my father ever spanked me.

I got into plenty of trouble of my own, but nothing I did came close to my brother David's exploits. He nearly burned down the house.

David loved playing with matches. Sometimes when I opened our bedroom closet to get something out, I would find matchbooks with burned matches. David would swipe the matchbooks from my parents and sit in the closet watching them burn. He was always playing around with matches when my mother wasn't looking. I kept telling him he was going to get in trouble.

One evening my mother and I were sitting in the den when we smelled smoke coming down the stairs. We ran upstairs to find my bedroom closet on fire and black smoke billowing through the room. David stood watching the fire with his mouth open, going "Ooooh!" My mother grabbed David and hauled him out of the room while I ran next door for help. I pounded frantically on the Andersons' front door, shouting, "Help! Help! Fire!" Our bedroom window faced the Andersons' house, so they had already seen the fire and called the fire department. I could hear the sirens of the approaching fire trucks. My mother was frantic by the time I got back. She had David, but she didn't know where I was because I had taken off running to the Andersons' without telling her.

By the time the firefighters put out the flames, the fire had burned through our closet into the next room. The ceiling and walls of our room were black. From what the firefighters could tell, David had been burning paper in our closet, and the clothes had caught on fire. That night was taken up with getting the fire out, talking with the firefighters, and preparing someplace for me and David to sleep. Most of our clothes, along with our bedding, had been lost. My mother put us in the bed in the guest room, where we slept together for months afterward while our bedroom was being repaired and painted. The second level of our house smelled like fire and mildewed carpet for six months.

The next morning was a day of reckoning for my brother. I'm not sure he was sorry about setting the fire, but he was very sorry about the punishment he knew was coming. Our mother gave him the worst whipping he ever received. It wasn't so much a punishment for the fire he'd set as her attempt to make him understand the seriousness of what he had done. He could have maimed or killed all of us. She made it clear to David that he could never, ever play with matches again. I think she put the fear of God in him, because it cured him of playing with matches. I don't know if he was afraid of playing with matches or just afraid of what my mother would do to him if he did.

WHEN IT CAME TO MISCHIEF, the apple didn't fall far from the tree. My father was incurably mischievous, and he loved anything that made a cool sound and went fast. He loved cars so much that he wasn't going to let a little thing like blindness stop him from driving. My mother used to tell us how Jeff Brown would take Dad driving on the turnpike in Texas at night when there were no other cars on the road. My father would take the wheel, flooring the car and laughing as they roared down the road with Jeff directing him. They loved it. They thought it was the best thing ever.

When my father got the itch to drive our car, we would usually go to the Los Angeles Coliseum. All of us would pile into the station wagon, and my mother would drive us to the Coliseum parking lot. Unless there was an event that day, the big parking lot would be empty. Dad would sit in the driver's seat, and Mom would sit in the back to guide him. She didn't have to do much, since the lot was huge and there was nothing for him to hit unless he got too near the perimeter. We didn't mind driving with my dad in the parking lot with no one around. David and I would tumble around in the back, laughing and shouting, "Daddy's driving! Daddy's driving! Oh, noooo!" as he cruised and swooped in big circles.

It was one thing to drive in an empty parking lot, but it was another thing entirely to drive on a city street. One night as we were coming home, my father decided he wanted to drive the rest of the way. We were coming down Hepburn with my mother at the wheel and my father in the shotgun seat when Dad announced, "I want to drive."

There was no traffic on the street right then, so my mother stopped the car and got out while Dad slid into the driver's seat. David and I looked at each other, petrified. My mom got into the backseat directly behind my father, looked around to make sure no cars were approaching, and told him he could go. She put her hands on his shoulders as he eased onto the accelerator. As we rolled down the street, she used his shoulders to guide him if he drifted out of the lane and told him when there was a stop sign. After what felt like an eternity, he came to a stop in front of our house. My mother got back behind the steering wheel and pulled the car into the driveway. Both of my parents were perfectly calm. It was obvious they had done this many times before.

When I was about seven years old, my father purchased a sports car. Dad and Duke were on the way home from a Dodgers game one afternoon when Duke noticed a beautiful Corvette. When he mentioned it to my father, my father wanted to see it, too. My dad got out and ran his hands over the car, feeling the sleek lines. He liked it so much that he went out and bought one the next day. He claimed the car was for my mother, though he had already bought her a lavender-and-white Cadillac. The problem was that my mother could not drive the Corvette with its manual shift. I still laugh when I remember the first and last time she tried. She took me with her to the grocery store in the Corvette, and we jerked the whole way there because she couldn't get the car out of first gear. I thought it was hilarious. After jerking her way back home, she vowed she would never drive it again. After that, the car belonged to my dad. Duke would drive him around in it.

Inevitably, Dad couldn't resist trying to drive the Corvette himself. One evening he and Duke were coming home when Dad decided he wanted to drive. I'm not sure if they were both absent of their senses, but

Duke agreed. Duke was directing him, but Dad wasn't really listening when they came to the intersection. Dad hadn't had much practice with a stick shift, either, and he released the clutch. Two hundred feet from our house, he shot out into the middle of the intersection and hit another car.

My mother and brothers and I were eating dinner in the kitchen when it happened, and we heard the crash. We had no idea it was Dad's car. A few minutes later, when we heard emergency sirens, we all trooped out on the front lawn to see what was going on. About fifty yards away, we could see my father's Corvette, totaled, in the intersection of 39th and Hepburn. Corvettes were pure fiberglass, and they shattered like a tortilla chip if you hit them at a certain angle. All of us took off running down the street, with Bobby in my mother's arms. We were scared to death. When we got a little closer, I could see my father leaning on a police car, talking to the officer. He was bruised and a little dizzy, but otherwise fine. The people in the other car also looked pretty shook up, but no one was seriously injured. Duke was talking earnestly to another officer. By the time we got there, the officer was putting handcuffs on Duke. They were arresting him for reckless driving.

I could hear Duke pleading with the policemen. "But it wasn't me. Mr. Charles was driving. Mr. Charles."

The officers exchanged a look. Yeah, right, it was the blind guy. They thought Duke was either drunk or lying. The people in the other car never saw who was behind the wheel, so they were unable to identify the driver. My father stood quietly by with his head down, listening while Duke pleaded. The police did not believe he could drive. He waited until the officers started to put Duke in the squad car before confessing the truth. My dad finally admitted that he was the driver.

I'm still not sure whether or not they believed him, but after a while, the police took the cuffs off Duke. No one had been hurt, and they thought the whole situation was peculiar. They were probably imagining the headlines: "Ray Charles Arrested for Reckless Driving." It would make them look pretty silly. There was some more conversation, and I think my father arranged to pay any medical expenses and buy a new car for the people he'd hit. Whatever the exact nature of the arrangement was, I do know that the police let everyone go. I can only imagine what my mother had to say to my father when she got him in private, but whatever she said, it was better than going to jail.

My father's favorite thing to drive, though, was the Vespa given to him by Hugh Hefner. The Vespa was his prized possession. It arrived in a giant crate. Dad and Herbert Miller assembled it in the backyard while we kids watched.

Dad liked nothing better than cruising down Hepburn on his Vespa with the wind in his face. He would get on it and ask us to tell him when it was clear. Then he'd pull out into the middle of the street while we kept watch. Sometimes he would just go in circles. Other times I would run alongside him down our block, and he would follow the sound of my footsteps. If David and I didn't pay attention and went back up on the curb, Dad would hit the curb and fall down. That never lasted for too long, because Mom didn't like me being in the street.

Other times Herbert would get on the back and guide him while Dad drove around the neighborhood. We would beg my dad to get on the back and ride with him, too, but he always said no to that because it wasn't safe for us. Some people in the neighborhood were convinced that my father could see because they saw him riding up and down the street on his Vespa. Everyone in the neighborhood remembers that Vespa. Mrs. Anderson simply smiles when she speaks of it.

I ALWAYS KNEW my father wasn't like other fathers. It wasn't just that he was blind. My father was internationally famous. He seemed to be larger than life.

The move to Hepburn had been followed by a career-changing deal. My father left Atlantic Records and signed a deal with ABC-Paramount. In addition to receiving an unheard-of percentage of royalties, my father was able to keep 75 percent of the profit his records earned whenever he produced his own songs. Most amazing, he demanded and got ownership of his own masters—the original recordings of his songs. Record labels rarely gave up control of their master recordings of an artist. The revenue from a successful song is endless, as those from my father's master recordings proved to be for over twenty-five years. My father demanded—and got—a contract that was the envy of the music industry.

In the small office upstairs in our house, musical history was made. I was too young to understand the significance of the procession of great musicians who graced our home. The men who gathered upstairs to compose, arrange, and play that remarkable music with my father were great musicians. During my most formative years, my life was enriched by their presence. There were so many of them—Marcus Belgrave, Leroy Cooper, James Clay, Henderson Chambers, Edgar Willis, Clifford Solomon, Gerald Wilson, Billy Brooks, Quincy Jones, and Sid Feller—each with a unique musical gift.

Among all of them, David "Fathead" Newman and Hank Crawford are the two who stand out the most in my memories from those years. The memories are as vivid in my mind today as they were fifty years ago when I played on the other side of the door in our home on Hepburn Avenue. My father used to describe Hank and Fathead as the heart of his sound. The bond my father's early band shared was strong. These men respected and trusted one another musically. Fathead was Dad's star tenor, and my father made sure Fathead's distinctive sax was featured on *Fathead: Ray Charles Presents "Fathead"* in 1959. I was only four years old at the time. Hank composed and arranged my father's music as well as directing his band. I remember the soft sound of Hank's alto sax drifting into the upstairs hallway and whispering through the house. When I was five, Hank would put his saxophone around my neck and say, "Little Ray, maybe." It made me burst into a big smile.

And I vividly remember Sid Feller. Sid was not only an arranger for ABC-Paramount but a close friend of my father's as well. Sid had a gift for knowing what my father wanted and needed to hear. Even though my father had come into his own as a composer and vocalist while at Atlantic Records, his collaboration with Sid and ABC-Paramount would change the course of his career creatively and financially. The music created by Ray Charles and Sid Feller during those years was woven into the fiber of American music, and it secured their place in musical history. Though Sid initially opposed my father's idea of fusing his signature voice with the string-laden sound coming out of Nashville, their collaboration was one of the most fruitful of my father's career. Together they created a remarkable musical synergy. During these intensely creative periods, my father would be holed up in his office with Sid for days at a time. The musicians would come and go, and my mother would climb up and down the stairs several times a day to keep them supplied with food.

The fruit of their labors speaks for itself. During the first four years we lived on Hepburn, my father put out a breathtaking procession of hits: "Night Time Is the Right Time," "What'd I Say," "Georgia on My Mind," "Hit the Road, Jack," "I've Got News for You," "One Mint Julep," "Unchain My Heart," "I Can't Stop Loving You," "You Are My Sunshine," and the tracks that made up the album *The Genius of Ray Charles.* All of them made the top 10 on both the pop and R & B charts. In 1962, "I Can't Stop Loving You" was number one on the pop, R & B, country, and British charts all at the same time.

I spent countless hours between the ages of four and eight listening to my father's music while sitting on the stairs or in the hall by his office door. Sometimes I walked back and forth as I listened. Cigarette smoke drifted under the door, and the towel hanging on the knob warned me and my brothers not to knock. All day and night when my father was not on the road, music would flow from his office. The distinct sound of my father's early arrangements would fill the hall, and I would hear him singing. There would be the sound of one finger hitting a piano—bink, bink, bop. I would hear snatches of conversation through the door, my father saying, "Listen to this, man. See how this goes. What do you think about this, Hank?" Every so often my mother would come up the stairs with trays of food and take it inside. As she opened the door to carry in food and drinks, I would catch glimpses of my father next to his reel-to-reel recorder. If I was really lucky, they would rehearse in the living room. He'd have his whole band crammed in there around the piano. I would watch them play, mesmerized, the music vibrating through me. It was moving. It was magical.

Some days he would be in his office alone, playing new pieces on his reel-to-reel, trying to decide if he had the arrangement right. At night I would knock on his door, but the only answer would be the music emanating from the room. I would wake in the middle of the night to hear strange sounds coming from his Ampex recorder, something between a whir and a squeak as it was rewound over and over.

I heard my father's music many other places as well. He would bring my mother copies of his recordings as they were released. In the beginning the recordings were the old 78s, and later they were 33s. My brothers and I heard him on the radio while riding in my mother's car, and we'd shout "Daddy!" and sing along. I would see his face on the covers of record albums he brought home. My mother kept magazines around the house, and I would leaf through them. She would read the articles in *Life, Ebony, Billboard, The Saturday Evening Post,* and *Jet,* but I would focus on the pictures of my dad and wonder what the captions said. Sometimes he would be on the cover, and other times he was the featured story.

It was especially exciting to see him on television. Those were the rare occasions that my mother would let us stay up. I saw him on *The Dinah Shore Show* when I was seven, and later I watched him co-host *The Mike Douglas Show.*

I also became very good at mimicking my father when he was performing. We would put on talent shows with my cousins and some of our friends from the neighborhood to entertain our parents and relatives. I, of course, was always "the great Ray Charles." I loved to do "Hit the Road, Jack." I knew it cold and performed it complete with all my father's inflections and mannerisms, including the trademark twitch. I loved to sing along with his records by myself, too.

Of all the songs my father composed and performed during those years, "You Don't Know Me" is the one that remains burned into my soul. I was six years old when my father composed it, and it was the first time he let me into his private musical world, inside his office where he composed those great songs. I stood between his legs as he sat in his favorite chair working on the song. He explained the different instruments to me as each played. I stood there, captivated, as he took my fingers and ran them over the controls on the reel-to-reel recorder to stop and rewind while we listened over and over again. I remember the cigarette he held with his thumb and two fingers and the scent of the smoke as it swirled around us. He sat there in his white T-shirt, with his glasses off and his face vulnerable, as I leaned against him and felt the music vibrate through my body and fill my soul. I knew even then that his music was something special, a gift from God illuminating the darkness in which my father lived each day.

My father's music remains embedded in my mind and soul. At a very early age, I knew his music was influential, that it was moving, that it was important. I knew it from the way people spoke about him. And I knew it at a young age when I watched him in concerts. Chills would run through me as I closed my eyes and listened to his music fill the concert halls. My father gave me a great gift. He shared his music with me and taught me how to listen. I learned to listen to everything, the richness of the violins and horns, the arrangement itself, and the notes that change the mood of the song. I did not know at the time how my father's music was shaping me. I did not inherit his musical gift, but I did inherit some part of his musical soul. I still have melodic dreams of orchestrations that are complete in my mind. But I still wake up longing to write on paper what I hear in my head, and I am left with a feeling of profound emptiness, as though there were a hole in my life. I still listen to music the way my father taught me, just as my granddaughter listens to his music the way I did as a child. My father is still with us, alive in our hearts and his music.

These are the memories, the images that I lived with when I was growing up. All the famous photos and album covers that lined the walls of his office remain clear in my mind. My father playing his sax with Fathead, *Ray Charles at Newport, Ray Charles and Betty Carter, The Genius Hits the Road, Genius + Soul = Jazz, Ingredients in a Recipe for Soul,* and

Modern Sounds in Country and Western Music. A photo of Frank Sinatra and my father together. My dad practicing with the band, laughing, his head thrown back and his arms wrapped around his body. And my favorite, Daddy in his white silk undershirt, without his glasses, smoke curling up from his cigarette and a pensive smile on his lips. I spent hours looking at those photos and album covers. I knew he was more than just our father; he was Ray Charles.

CHAPTER 7

Pray On, My Child

Pray on, my child,

I need Jesus to carry me

home.

—THE CECIL SHAW SINGERS, LEAD
TENOR, DELLA BEATRICE ANTWINE

WHEN I CLOSE MY EYES AND REMEMBER HEPBURN AVENUE, I see a burst of color—trees, flowers, beautiful homes. But my memory is selective, for behind every tree and house a shadow loomed. When we began filming the scenes set at Hepburn for the movie *Ray*, I expected to be flooded with happy memories. Instead I was overwhelmed with panic as the reality of those years started coming back. Chills ran through my body, and I would have to check my emotions. Hepburn was not the idyllic place I wanted to remember. The year I turned six, the fearful apparitions haunting my imagination at night started to become real. It began when I found out in the worst possible way that the father I worshipped was mortal.

WHENEVER MY FATHER was in town, we would always hug and kiss him before we went to bed. I would not go to sleep unless I had kissed my father good night. But one night my mother wouldn't let me go to his office to kiss him at bedtime. My dad's twitching and scratching had been much worse than usual that afternoon and evening. My mother had sent him to his office hours earlier and told him to stay there until he felt better. When bedtime came and I wanted to kiss him good night, my mom said no. She said Daddy wasn't feeling well, but I could have two hugs and two kisses in the morning to make up for it. David and I were already in our pajamas, and she took us upstairs, tucked us in, and kissed us good night.

But I couldn't sleep. I still wanted to see my dad. As I lay in bed thinking about it, I started to hear a banging noise coming from his office. There was a steady knocking, as though he were hitting the wall. I was curious, so I decided to disobey my mother and see what he was doing. I got out of bed and crept down the hall. I knocked, and when there was no response, I opened the door a crack and peered in. When I saw my father, I froze in fear.

There was blood everywhere. The walls were splattered with blood like someone had fired a paint gun, there was blood all over his glass desk top, and there was a big puddle of blood on the floor. Across the room my father stood, leaning against the wall and twitching violently. Blood streamed from his wrist. His white shirt sleeve and cuff were completely soaked. He was slinging his arm back and forth like he was trying to shake something off, and every time he slung his arm, blood flew everywhere. He was completely unaware that he was bleeding. I yelled, "Daddy! Daddy! Daddy!" but he showed no awareness that I was there.

I took off running downstairs to the den where my mother was watching television. She was eight months pregnant with Bobby at the time. I was yelling incoherently about Daddy and the office, and at first my mother thought I was having a tantrum because she hadn't let me kiss my dad. She took my hand and pulled me up the stairs, scolding and telling me I was going right back to bed. Meanwhile, I was screaming hysterically, "Daddy! Daddy! Blood, Mommy, blood!"

By the time we got upstairs, blood was beginning to seep under the office door. My mother let go of my hand and ran to the door, pushing it all the way open. When she saw my father, she shouted, "Ray! Ray!" and ran to him, but he was too high, and he didn't hear her. She rushed into the bathroom, grabbed two towels, and returned. Shouting at him to keep his arm still, she applied pressure to try and stop the bleeding. She called to me to go to my bedroom and wake David. We were both to put on our slippers and jackets. She must have phoned Dr. Foster from Dad's office after I left. She could not call for an ambulance because my dad was home out on bail, awaiting his pending court date. With the heroin in his system, he would have been taken to jail.

When I emerged in the hall a couple of minutes later, dragging my confused brother behind me, my mother hurried us down the stairs to the front door. I could still hear my father banging around in his office. My mom said we were taking Daddy to the doctor. She got us settled in the backseat of the Cadillac and then rushed back into the house. A few minutes later she came outside with my father. He was still thrashing aimlessly as my mother struggled with him and tried to keep two blood-soaked towels pressed against his wrist. She was so pregnant that she could barely walk, and I do not know how she got my father down the stairs. She later told me that she'd had to fight him, alternately pulling and punching him to make him move. Without realizing it, he had elbowed her in the stomach several times as they struggled.

She forced Dad into the front seat and closed the door just as Hank Crawford and Milt Turner drove up. They had come to bring my father some arrangements. My mother spoke with them briefly, then got into the driver's seat and backed out of the driveway. Hank and Milt followed us in their car.

My father was still bleeding, twitching, and flailing around as we drove. My mom kept pressing the bloody towels back against his wrist every time he threw them off. It took fifteen or twenty minutes to get to Dr. Foster's office, but it seemed like an eternity. David and I were huddled fearfully in the backseat.

When we finally got to the doctor's office, Hank and Milt came in with us. Dr. Foster and his nurse were waiting. We went through the reception area and into Dr. Foster's office. Dr. Foster pulled up chairs for us as he instructed his nurse to take my father into an examining room. He was talking to my mother when he caught sight of Hank and Milt. They had finally gotten a good look at my father's wound in the light. He was soaked with blood. Dr. Foster saw their faces and said, "Uh-oh."

We all turned to look at them. Hank and Milt were as white as a sheet. My mother said, "Sweet Lord, they're going to faint."

Dr. Foster quickly took them into another examination room and told them to sit down and put their heads between their knees. Then he called the nurse and told her to stay with them until they felt better. Unfortunately, every time they tried to sit up straight, they began to pass out again. The nurse didn't dare leave them alone. Meanwhile, Dr. Foster was struggling with my father in the examining room, trying to get a good look at the wound. When my mother went to see what was happening, he told her that he was having trouble examining my dad's arm without the nurse to hold it down. My mother immediately said she would take the nurse's place if he would tell her what to do.

Dr. Foster replied, "Absolutely not, Della. You cannot handle all this blood. You're eight months pregnant. Now get out of here."

My mother replied, "That's my husband, and I can stay if I want to. Now tell me what to do."

Dr. Foster could not sedate my father while he had so much heroin in his system, and he could not risk surgery, either. My father had severed a tendon and artery, and the operating procedure was delicate. If it wasn't done properly, my father could lose the use of his hand. The best Dr. Foster could do right then was to stop the bleeding and prevent further injury until the drugs wore off. In the morning, when my dad had come down, he could be admitted to the hospital for surgery. My mother held my father's arm still while Dr. Foster sterilized the wound and closed the gash temporarily. Then he wrapped the wound tightly in several layers of gauze and told my mother she would have to keep my father still to prevent more bleeding. My father had already lost a dangerous amount of blood.

Meanwhile, my brother and I waited in Dr. Foster's office. It was eerie being in the deserted building at night. I could hear Dr. Foster's voice behind the door, and every now and then I would hear the nurse minister to Hank and Milt. David had fallen asleep in the chair. At three years old, he was too little to understand what was happening. There was a lot that I didn't understand, either, but I was old enough to know that something was seriously wrong with my dad, and I was scared to death.

Finally Dr. Foster came out of the office with my father. Dad was holding his bandaged wrist up, the way you do to stop bleeding. He was still wearing his bloody clothing, and there was blood on my mother's clothes, too. I stared wordlessly at my father, hoping for some reassurance from him, but there was nothing. He just stood there still twitching, in another world.

My mother held out her arms to comfort me as I went to her. "Your father's going to be okay, baby. He's okay."

No one said a word on the ride home. My mother reached over and stilled my father's arm whenever he tried to move it. At some point, I fell asleep. It was well past midnight by then. It had been hours since I had first gone to bed. When we finally got home, my mother waved off Hank and Milt, who had recovered enough to follow us home. They drove away, and my mother shook us gently awake and guided me up the stairs with David sound asleep on her shoulder. "Your father's going to be all right. I need you to go to bed now," she told me softly. I crawled under the covers and immediately fell into a deep sleep. My mother was up all night with my father, watching over him and holding his arm still whenever he began to thrash, but this time, I didn't hear a thing.

The next day my father was admitted to the hospital for the delicate surgery. He had to wear a cast on his wrist for several weeks afterward.

The hospital was told it was an accident resulting from my father stumbling into the glass-top desk in his office. The injury was played down in the press. When my dad wanted to go back on the road, Dr. Foster cautioned him against it, but Dad was worried about the effect of a hiatus on his career. He didn't want people to think he couldn't play anymore. They ultimately compromised: Dr. Foster would agree to let him go as long as my father had continuing medical care. My dad would hire Dr. Foster to accompany him on the road for a few weeks. Dr. Foster was able to find someone to sub for him at his practice, and shortly thereafter he met my father on the road. For several weeks, he traveled with my father, changing casts and treating him until the wrist was completely healed. My father's wrist would be all right. His wrist healed and he was able to play the piano as well as ever.

Gradually the house returned to normal. The blood stain remained, an ugly reminder of what had happened that evening. Once my mother had the carpet replaced and the wall cleaned, no visible traces of the accident remained. But the horror of that night never completely left me. Whenever my mother or I opened the office door, I felt myself flinch, afraid to look for fear I would find my father dead of an overdose. His music was no longer the only reason I listened at the door. After that terrible night, I listened for my father whenever he was in there alone, creeping to the door and putting my ear to it to make sure he was moving around. I wondered if my father understood what had happened. Did he know I had saved his life that night? Did he know God had given him another chance at life?

IF MY FATHER was the center of our world, my mother was the one who held our world together. She was so incredibly strong, and she endured more pain than most people could survive.

Looking back, I cannot begin to imagine how she coped with it all. The husband she loved so deeply was blind, a serious heroin addict, and a womanizer. Between my birth and our departure from Hepburn Avenue nine years later, my father was arrested for drug possession four times, each arrest more serious than the one before. My father's affairs caused her tremendous pain and were a strain on our family. Not only did she have to endure the knowledge that there were other women; she had to live with reports of his other children as well. A few months after my brother David was born, Margie Hendricks, one of the Raelettes, gave birth to my father's third son, Charles Wayne Hendricks. Within weeks of my brother Bobby's birth, Mae Mosely Lyles gave birth to my half sister Raenee. Two years later Sandra Jean Betts gave birth to my half sister Sheila, naming Ray Charles as the father. Both Mae and Sandra Jean filed suits asking for child support. My mother endured the humiliation of my father being dragged through two very public, seamy paternity claims. Both times she found the courage to attend the court hearings to show public support for my father. I don't know how in the world she was able to face it. Both times he lost after graphic testimony about his sexual behavior and tearful claims by the women that he had told them he loved them more than he loved my mother.

In 1963 Sandra Jean Betts showed up at our home on Hepburn with her lawyer before her suit went to trial. My father was out of town at the time. Miss Betts and her attorney made themselves at home in our living room and essentially offered my mother a deal. If she would give my father a divorce, they would drop the paternity suit and keep matters private. As Miss Betts explained, "We all know you're married in name only. Your husband doesn't love you. Why don't you just give him a divorce and make it easy on everyone?"

My mother responded to Sandra, "If you both leave quietly, everything will be fine. Then you can try to convince my husband to divorce me and marry you, and if he does, it will be your turn to be married in name only."

When my father returned home a few days later, he found all of his clothes on the front lawn. My mother had thrown them out of the upstairs window. She informed him that he would not be staying at Hepburn. She would let him know if and when he could return. She allowed him to gather a few things and then told him it was his job to explain his departure to me.

I was eight years old, but I still remember it. When my father came into my room and sat down next to me on my bed, he was very nervous.

"Um, son," he stuttered nervously. "Baby, Daddy has to go away for a while."

I couldn't understand why he was telling me this. He was always going away, but he had never done this before.

"Okay, Daddy," I said. "When are you coming back?"

My father brushed nervously at his ear. He couldn't look at me. "Well, son, I just don't know. That will be up to your mother. You be good now, baby, and give your daddy a hug and a kiss."

When I look back on it now, the wonder isn't that my mother threw everything she could find of my father's onto the front lawn; the wonder is that my mother didn't shoot him.

With my father gone ten months of the year, the loneliness must have been crushing for her at times. I missed my father terribly when he was gone, but she must have missed him more. I used to watch my mother sometimes when she was in the den listening and singing to some music alone. She often played the Temptations, B. B. King, Marvin Gaye, and other gospel groups. She loved Marvin Gaye's song "Ain't That Peculiar": "Honey, you do me wrong but still I'm crazy about you, stay away too long and I can't do without you." Today I find some irony in those lyrics. Like the rest of us, my mother found comfort and a sanctuary in music.

One form of entertainment in my father's absence was card parties with her friends. They used to come over and play bid whist with her. Bernice, Birdie, Norman, and Herbert were her closest friends. They had come to California or followed from Texas with my parents and settled into homes of their own. My mother's family came out to visit regularly, too, and some of her cousins stayed in California. Despite her recent wealth and celebrity, my mother remained very private, and she was always more comfortable with her old friends.

People who knew about my father's womanizing sometimes wondered why my mother stayed with him. Some of them thought she was naïve about the other women; others thought she put up with it because of my father's celebrity. Some people just thought she was a fool. She knew exactly what was going on, but she stayed with him anyway, and it had nothing to do with money or fame. My mother is deeply religious, and she grew up believing that God expects a woman to remain faithful to her husband through good times and bad. When she married my father, she married him for life. She also had three children to think about. We adored our father, and the last thing she wanted was to break up our family. She and my dad had both grown up without fathers in their lives, and she didn't want us to grow up the same way. Most of all, she loved my father deeply, and she knew him well. Despite the pain and humiliation she endured, she never stopped loving him.

I began getting glimpses of what my mother was going through very young. When I started school, I heard rumors about my father's philandering. Other kids would say nasty things about my dad. I remember her reading copies of *Jet* and *Ebony* at home; I would hear her talking about Margie Hendricks and Mae Mosely Lyles. My mother had no idea I knew. Sometimes at night, I would hear her crying. I wanted to comfort her, but I didn't know how. Yet as much as I loved my mother, I didn't fully understand how much she meant to us until we nearly lost her.

One of the most painful episodes of our lives began on New Year's Eve 1961. I was six years old, David was three, and Bobby was just eight months old. Dad's band and some friends had come to the house on New Year's Eve for a party. My mother was cooking for everyone when her stomach began to hurt and she felt hot. She mentioned to my father that she wasn't feeling well, but she kept going, so no one thought too much about it. The next day she continued to complain of stomach pain, but she did not contact Dr. Foster.

On January 2nd my father woke up at ten. He usually slept until the afternoon, but he woke up early that day, sensing that something was wrong. My mother was burning up in the bed next to him and barely seemed aware of her surroundings. Dad called Dr. Foster, who told him to call the paramedics, and said he would meet them at University Hospital. By then my mother was incoherent and unable to walk. My brothers and I huddled fearfully with Myrtle, our nanny, as four paramedics carried her down the stairs. They carried her out to the waiting ambulance. Myrtle stayed with us while my father went to the hospital with my mother.

Dr. Foster admitted her to the hospital, and they ran some tests. At first they thought she might have a virus that was causing the high fever and stomach pain, but she kept getting worse. The doctors reassured my father that she would be all right but that they needed to run some additional tests. Dad had a performance scheduled that week, and they told him he should go ahead with it.

When a specialist was called in, the diagnosis was devastating. New tests revealed that my mother's appendix had ruptured. The poison had already spread through most of her system, and she was suffering from severe peritonitis. Her abdominal cavity was flooded with toxic fluids. The situation was grave. Her only hope of survival was immediate surgery, but the specialist refused to perform the procedure. He told Dr. Foster that my mother was in such serious condition that if he attempted the surgery, she might die on the table. He did not want to be sued for killing Ray Charles's wife. He knew that without the surgery, my mother would die, but he did not want to be responsible.

Dr. Foster was angry and disgusted with the specialist. Dr. Foster had never performed this particular surgery, but he had no intention of standing by while my mother died. He said that he would take the responsibility and then called Dr. Beck to assist him with the surgery. When he was warned about the potential legal consequences if my mother died during surgery, Dr. Foster said, "Fine, let them sue me." He knew my father would never do that, but at that moment, his only concern was my mother.

As she was prepped for surgery, the hospital tried desperately to get in touch with my father. The doctors could not operate without consent, and my mother was unconscious and unable to give consent herself. They were told that my father was on stage, rehearsing his band, and the hospital managed to contact someone backstage, but no one would connect them with my father. The hospital was told that Mr. Charles was preparing to go onstage and could not be disturbed. Someone took a message and said they would let him know after the show. Finally someone at the hospital thought to contact my uncle James. He gave consent, and they were able to proceed with the operation. Together Dr. Beck and Dr. Foster performed the surgery that saved my mother's life. They opened up her abdominal cavity and removed the liters of toxic waste, then inserted a tube in her abdomen that would continue to pump the toxic waste out of her system.

Once the performance ended, my father was given the message. He and Herbert Miller rushed to the hospital and waited there as the surgery was completed. Afterward Dr. Foster told my father that my mother had survived the surgery, but that she was gravely ill and still might die. It would be weeks before they would know if she was going to make it.

Despite having the toxins pumped out of her twenty-four hours a day and continual intravenous antibiotics, my mother's fever continued to rage, and for weeks her body literally cooked. Her skin turned black. She remained unconscious, hovering between life and death. My father explained to us that Mommy was very sick and would have to stay at the hospital for a while so the doctors could make her better. He did not tell us that she might die, but we sensed his fear. I was terrified. My mom was going to die, and nobody would let me see her. In those days children weren't allowed in hospital rooms.

For weeks we all lived in terror. My father was with her every day. He had Myrtle move in to take care of us and hired extra help on weekends to give her some rest. Our lives went into suspended animation as we waited.

Weeks after entering the hospital, my mother finally regained consciousness. She had no memory of entering the hospital and didn't know where she was. Dr. Foster warned my father that she might have sustained permanent brain damage from the high fever. Children could survive a fever of that magnitude without permanent effects, but adults seldom did. Gradually, to everyone's overwhelming relief, my mother began to return to herself. Reverend Durham and his wife had been coming to see her almost every day, holding her hand and praying for her recovery. Their excitement and relief when my mother was finally able to respond to them was palpable. As the days passed, the reactions of those around her helped her understand how near she had come to death. Doctors, nurses, staff members, even the people who did the cleaning, came by to say they had been praying for her. A long succession of kind strangers stopped by her room to smile at her and say, "Hi! It's so good to see you doing better." She was touched and encouraged by their concern.

The first thing she asked for when she woke up was us. The second thing she wanted was 7-UP, because she felt like she was burning up inside. She drank it eagerly, but a few moments later she could feel the cold liquid running through her body and out into the tube. Food was an even bigger problem. It was a long time before she could eat anything. First there was clear broth, then Jell-O, and eventually tiny bits of soft food. Everything tasted terrible, but Dr. Foster was happy that she felt well enough to complain. Meanwhile, he had figured out a way for us to visit her.

We were not allowed to go to her room, and she wasn't allowed to go outside. She could not have direct contact with anyone besides the hospital staff because she was too vulnerable to infection. So Dr. Foster arranged for us to come to the patio downstairs where visitors could congregate. He then had my mother brought down in a wheelchair and rolled up to the patio entrance to the hospital. The glass door remained closed to guard my mother against infection. That way we could see each other through the glass and hear a little bit, but we couldn't hug or kiss her. She was connected to a portable machine and IV pump. We stared at her through the glass, and we all cried. Then they wheeled her upstairs to her room. Once a week we could go back to visit her, always standing on the patio on the other side of the glass.

My mother desperately wanted to come home. She was worried sick about us and missed us terribly. My father had to leave for the road again any day, and she wanted to be with us. Against Dr. Foster's better judgment, they brought her home. Nine weeks had passed since the paramedics carried her downstairs unconscious. Now she was carried upstairs to her room. We barely recognized the woman they carried in. When she went into the hospital, she weighed 125 pounds. When she came home to us, she weighed 106 pounds. At five foot nine, she was skin and bones. Her skin was black and shriveled. The toxins in her system were extremely damaging to her body.

She was home, but she was still far too sick to be our mom. We were afraid to touch her. Her skin was so fragile that she could barely touch the sheet without pain. Dr. Foster had released her on the understanding that she would remain on bed rest with full-time nursing care. She hated the loss of privacy and argued with the nurses. They explained that it wasn't safe for her to do these things on her own yet. Apart from the weakness, pain from the adhesions and scar tissue could hit without warning. When the pain did start, she had a better understanding of her condition. The pain was so intense that it caused her to collapse. In the years that followed, she would undergo ten surgeries to relieve the pain from the adhesions and the intestinal blockage caused by the scar tissue. Almost fifty years later, the severity of that illness continues to affect her health. She copes with the painful complications by reminding herself that without the surgery and its consequences, she wouldn't be alive to complain.

For our family, 1962 became a year lost to trauma. We lost the first half to my mother's illness and near death. My mom missed nearly most of Bobby's infancy, and she had to surrender the care to Myrtle. The only good thing to be said about that year is that when summer came, our mother was still with us. It was one of the roughest years of our lives. What we couldn't know was that her illness was just the beginning of seemingly endless fear and loss.

IN THE MONTHS FOLLOWING my mother's return, she needed a lot of rest. This was a challenge with two young sons and a baby boy crawling around the house. Bobby was eleven months old when my mother came home from the hospital. He had inherited my father's curiosity, and he was fascinated with electrical cords like all babies. He would crawl around looking for something to get into, plugs and cords to play with. If we saw him in time, we would grab him before he got hold of a cord. If we didn't get there fast enough, he would start chewing on the cord. He scared us to death more than once, but we had always been able to stop him before he got hurt.

One afternoon, a month or so after my mother came home from the hospital, David and I were running around the house while Bobby, who was only a year old, crawled after us. While we were playing in the next room, my mother called out to me to keep an eye on Bobby. Meanwhile, Bobby had crawled into Myrtle's room and reached up to grab a lamp cord that was plugged into the wall behind her nightstand. I found him just in time to see him bite down on the cord. I screamed "Bobby!" but it was too late. This time he bit all the way through the cord. There were sparks and an explosion, the kind of loud popping sound it makes when two live wires touch, and Bobby convulsed. The side of his mouth was burned, and I could smell his flesh, like a steak too close to the broiler. Bobby's whole body became rigid, and he fell flat on his back, his arms thrown out to the sides. I ran into the room screaming his name. His tiny body was completely still, and he was not breathing. The right side of his mouth was black where he had burned it. Myrtle jumped off the bed, and I heard her exclaim, "Oh my sweet Lord, the baby's dead!"

I ran into the den where my mother was watching TV, screaming, "MOMMY! MOMMY!"

My mother moved slowly to where Bobby lay and picked him up in her arms. She shook him and shook him, then pounded him on the back, trying to force air back into him. The seconds went by. My mother was praying out loud as I screamed and sobbed. After an eternity, Bobby took a shuddering breath and began to whimper. My mother and Myrtle bundled him into the car immediately with the rest of us and we raced to the hospital.

In the waiting area, I sobbed. No one could comfort me. I was sure my brother was dead, and it was all my fault. My mother had asked me to keep an eye on Bobby, and I was responsible for his accident. Years later I realized that when Bobby was electrocuted, I had experienced some of the same trauma my father went through when his brother George drowned.

Thank God, the doctors were able to stabilize Bobby. He was legally dead for a brief period of time, but my mother's efforts had revived him.

Bobby was going to be all right. My mother was not going to lose her child, and I would not have to live with the same burden of guilt my father had carried all his life for George's death. God had shown us mercy.

Bobby had suffered a severe burn on the side of his mouth. The doctors told my mother he would need plastic surgery when he was older. But eventually his mouth healed, and fortunately, the skin did not keloid. He was not left with the ugly raised tissue many burn victims suffer. But the burn affected him. His mouth looked misshapen, and the burned side didn't move, leaving him with a speech impediment. The other kids teased him about it. It always made me feel really bad. Even today, you can hear a slight slur when he pronounces certain words. My parents waited for him to get older before having plastic surgery, but when the time came, Bobby decided he didn't want it. The small deformity was hardly noticeable anymore, and besides, it had become a part of his face. "This has become a part of me," he told me. "It's just part of who I am."

I DON'T KNOW how we could have gotten through my mother's illness without Myrtle. Next to my mother, I never loved any other woman so much when I was a child. She was more than our housekeeper or nanny. She was family who was there to nurture and love us as children.

The year before my mother went into the hospital, my dad had hired Myrtle to help my mother with the housework and to keep her company and help with us. Myrtle was an African American woman in her forties. She was a sweet, gentle, loving woman. Myrtle was a schoolteacher by training, and she would sing little songs and play games with us. She was wonderful with me and my brothers, attentive and protective. During the long months my mother was in the hospital, Myrtle kept us together mind, body, and soul.

I thought of Myrtle as a grandmother. She had a soft voice that was the perfect counterpoint to my mother's voice. Myrtle was gentle, and we would listen to her without her ever having to raise her voice.

When she first came to work for us, Myrtle went home every night, but when my mother became so ill, Myrtle moved into our home to take care of us. While our mom was in the hospital, her absence was made bearable by having Myrtle in the house. None of us knew what we would have done during those frightening months without her. We loved her so. We wanted her to live with us forever.

Months after my mother came home from the hospital, Myrtle began to feel sick herself. When she went to the doctor, he told her there was nothing wrong with her. She had nothing to worry about. But she kept feeling worse. Finally she went to see Dr. Foster. By the time she saw him, it was too late. Dr. Foster diagnosed Myrtle with terminal cancer. My mother told us that Myrtle was sick and had to go into the hospital. She took us to see Myrtle one time. It was the last time we would see her. A few weeks later Myrtle passed away.

I was stunned. Why wasn't Myrtle coming home from the hospital like Mommy did? In those days, cancer was kept secret. No one talked about it. And no one talked to children about death. My mother tried to explain to us what had happened, but I couldn't understand. Why had Myrtle died? David and I were confused and heartbroken. We begged my mother to take us to see Myrtle. Finally she agreed to take us to the mortuary to say good-bye. Myrtle was so still in the casket. We were too young to understand what death meant, only that Myrtle was not with us anymore. We didn't want to leave Myrtle all alone there. We wanted her to come home with us where we could take care of her and make her better. My brothers and I cried inconsolably as my mother forced us to leave. For weeks afterward I kept asking my mother when Myrtle was coming home.

Myrtle was the first person I loved who passed away. It was a bitter irony. Our mother had lived to come home to us, but Myrtle had been taken from us forever. Losing Myrtle hurt me deeply. It was my first glimpse of what my father must have gone through when his mother passed away.

A YEAR LATER, President Kennedy was assassinated. Like millions of other Americans, I sat with my mother in the den and watched his funeral on television as his coffin was borne to its final resting place. Caroline Kennedy, only a year younger than I was, stood with her mother and her small brother, John. Like the rest of America, we cried at the senseless death of our president. Like most African Americans, we mourned the passing of a man who believed in equality for all Americans. We wanted change, and it was difficult for me to understand the complexity of President Kennedy's assassination. If the president wasn't safe, no one was. We had seen him killed in front of our own eyes.

Hepburn Avenue, once a haven of innocence, seemed permeated with death. Darkness had seeped into every corner of our home. I didn't feel safe there anymore.

ONLY ONE BLESSING emerged from all that pain: my grandmother. A year after coming home from the hospital, my mother had to return for what would be the second of ten surgeries, all resulting from her original illness. Although she had survived, she was left with scar tissue throughout her torso, and over the years she suffered repeated intestinal blockages as a result. She wasn't certain she would be able to continue taking care of us. Her worry was made worse because my father was gone most of the time and her family was still in Texas. Every year since I could remember, we had gone to Houston for a visit, and one of the purposes of those visits was to check on my grandmother. Her drinking had worsened, deepening into increasingly serious alcoholism, though I was too young to understand what was wrong with her. My mother could not rest easy until she saw for herself that Grams was all right. So a year and a half after she was first hospitalized, Mother convinced Grams to move to California. With Grams nearby, my mother could check on her more easily. More important, we would be able to see her more often, and Grams would be able to step in if my mother's illness worsened.

Grams was reluctant to leave Houston, but once she settled into an apartment in Los Angeles, she adjusted quickly. Grams was a free-spirited woman with the most beautiful smile. She loved life and us dearly. Within a short time, she had surrounded herself with a new group of friends and was back to enjoying herself in the evening and playing cards with her new friends on the weekends. When our next-door neighbors, the Kimballs, needed someone to clean their house and help care for their two young children, Grams went to work for them. If my brothers and I wanted to see her, she was next door. The next year Uncle James moved his family to California and became an important part of our lives as well. My mother was relieved to know that she didn't have to worry about David, Bobby, and me being alone, even with our father on the road much of the time. For his part, my father welcomed his in-laws. He had lost his brother and mother at such a young age, and in Grams and Uncle James, he found another mother and brother to help fill the void. He loved them as his own.

A FEW MONTHS after my ninth birthday, my father took us all for a flight in his Cessna. Tommy McGarrity was piloting the plane as we flew over Baldwin Hills and View Park.

Pointing down below, my father said, "You see down there?"

Tommy banked the plane, and we all looked. We saw tracks of houses, and in the middle of them, on three large dirt lots, our new house was being built.

"See where the construction is going on?" my dad asked. "That's where we are going to live."

We circled for several minutes before Tommy leveled off and headed back toward the airport. It was thrilling. Even though a new house meant leaving Anthony Anderson and all my other friends behind, it also meant a new beginning. I was ready to leave behind Hepburn and the pain that lingered there.

CHAPTER 8

In the Heat of the Night

Seems like a cold sweat

Creeping cross my brow.

—QUINCY JONES

BY THE TIME I WAS NINE, I KNEW MY FATHER WAS AN ADDICT, though I didn't really understand what that meant. We never talked about it in the family. My mother always explained away my father's strange behavior as nerves or "just the way Daddy is." But I knew from reading *Jet* and other gossip magazines I found around the house. I knew what people were saying about him, and I had put together most of the pieces. The year we left Hepburn for View Park, a series of events forced our family to face the problem together. Years of addiction finally caught up to my dad.

My father had started using heroin in his teens, and as his success grew, so did his heroin use. Heroin was expensive, and in the early years, he couldn't afford to use very often. Poverty had limited his access to heroin. Once his records started hitting the top of the charts, though, he could have all the drugs he wanted.

Most of the time when my dad was around, he would be in withdrawal—twitching, jumping, and sweating. It was a cycle. When the drug was first administered, he would be violently agitated, but then he would gradually mellow out. Band members joked that if you wanted a raise from my father, the time to ask him was when he was mellow. The mellow mood didn't last long, however. Soon he would be craving another hit. Sometimes I would see him standing in the hall at home, sweating, barely aware of his surroundings. It was frightening because I didn't know what was wrong with him. When I was older and my friends would see him that way, it was embarrassing. I didn't want people to know. Sometimes he reacted violently, and when that happened, I was terrified.

My mother dealt with the situation as best she could. She and my father had talked about his addiction many times, and since it was clear he wasn't going to quit using heroin, she did what she could to protect us from it. When we asked her, "What's wrong with Daddy?" she would give us various explanations and change the subject. Sometimes she would say he was hyper, other times that it was his nerves. Whatever she said, the message was always the same: Daddy's just like that. If he started jumping and sweating, my mother would tell him, "Stop it, Ray! Stop it! Go upstairs. The kids are down here." As my mother later told me, it was the only way she could prevent him from going completely out of control. Part of the agreement he made with my mother before they married was that the family was never to see any drugs or paraphernalia. I never witnessed him getting high, nor did I ever see his "works"—he was supposed to keep them where we couldn't find them. If Bobby, David, or I had ever stumbled across his works, I think my mother would have lost her patience and respect for him. She did everything in her power to protect us from the effects of my father's addiction, and coping with it every day took a tremendous toll on her. She saw the magazine articles, too, and she knew the neighbors talked about my father when she wasn't around. Her reaction was to withdraw into our family and socialize less and less. Always a woman who lived quietly, she became increasingly isolated in our home on Hepburn.

My father never believed heroin was harming him. He continued to make music and deal with the demands of the road more successfully, so it was easy for him to convince himself that there was no real problem. But he respected those close to him who did not use drugs. He kept the drugs away from my mother as much as he could, and he did not ask friends to carry the stuff or shoot him up if they didn't use it themselves. My father's drug use was a normal part of life for everyone around him, and they accepted it. There was nothing they could do about it. Every once in a while, though, something would go very wrong.

Occasionally, he would overdose. After he would receive his daily bread, he sometimes used more if he thought he wouldn't be able to use for a couple of days while he was on the road. Then he would insist on a second hit to carry him over. This often meant having too much in his system at once. When he ingested too much, he would become violent at first and would have to be restrained until he calmed down. Once the initial agitation passed, he would start to slip into unconsciousness. When this happened, his friends would have to get him up and keep him moving until the drug began to work its way out of his system. They would put him in a cold shower and then walk him around. They couldn't let him sit down, for if the drug stopped moving through his system and went to his heart, it would kill him. One of his friends would tell him, "Put your arm around my neck. Don't let go. Put your arm around my neck." Another friend would put an arm around my father's waist on the other side, and together they would keep him moving. Sometimes they would have to keep him walking for hours, until he finally started to come down. Herbert Miller had to do this more than once. He said it was terrifying. He was always afraid that this time my father wouldn't make it.

Another time, on a Pan Am flight to Hong Kong, my father overdosed in the restroom. He tried to use all of the drugs before he went through customs. When Dad came out of the bathroom and started down the aisle, thrashing violently, unaware of where he was, the other passengers were terrified. When the plane landed in Hong Kong, the entire band was detained and interrogated at length. By that time the effects of the drug were wearing off, and since no one was carrying any heroin, the authorities finally let them go. Another time my mother found my dad on the upstairs landing at Hepburn, thrashing so violently that he kicked out the stair railing. My mother had to have it rebuilt.

I learned that the biggest danger came from other addicts who were on the road with him. The dealers were careful not to overdose him, but other guys who used would get so anxious to shoot up themselves that they'd give my father as much as he wanted. In their eagerness to get the drugs into their own bodies, they would inject my father too quickly and accidentally butcher him. He would have blood streaming down his arm, and they wouldn't even notice. Neither would my father. Afterward his friends would find him high and bleeding heavily. They would have to put a tourniquet on his arm and hold a cold compress on the wound until he stopped bleeding. I don't think my father ever realized how many times the people who loved him saved his life.

By the time I was six, I knew the danger as well as any of the adults, for I had witnessed it firsthand. If I hadn't found my father bleeding in his office, he would have died. After that night my mother and I shared a terrible secret and the fear that went with it. We worried constantly that he would overdose again. I cannot remember a time in my childhood after that when I wasn't afraid my father was going to die.

And then there were the arrests. I didn't know until I was an adult how often my father was arrested on drug charges. Even now, I'm not sure I know about all the incidents. I know he was picked up in Philadelphia the year I was born. Jeff Brown bailed him out and found a lawyer who got the charges dropped. Even then the arrest made the papers. The Associated Negro Press (ANP) ran some articles, and there was a mention of it in *Jet*. In those days, though, my father was first striking out on his own, so he wasn't well-known enough for the arrest to be picked up on the major national wires.

Four months after I found him bleeding to death at home, he was arrested in Chicago. Once again, the charges were dropped. Drug use was
so widespread in the music industry that musicians often got by with little
more than a slap on the hand as long as they weren't selling or carrying
large amounts. This time, though, the arrest was reported far beyond the
ANP. My father was hugely successful by then, and the news found its
way into papers nationwide. There were photos of him looking frightened
and depressed, and graphic descriptions of the needle tracks on his arms.
One police officer said the tracks were the worst he had ever seen. My
father was still in denial, but it was clear to everyone else that the situation
was spiraling out of control. Magazine articles described his addiction and
speculated that my father was on the brink of a terrible fall.

Within months he was arrested again. This time my mother was on
the road with him. In November 1961 my parents had just checked into a
hotel in Indianapolis with the band when my mother decided she wanted
to go back to Chicago. She had seen something there she wanted to buy
for my father, and when she mentioned it, my father told her to go on back
and finish her shopping if she wanted to. Jeff Brown made a reservation for
her, and she went to the airport. She remembers noticing something odd as
she walked through the hotel lobby on her way out. Two men in dark suits
were sitting in the lobby, holding newspapers open and watching people
walk by from behind the cover of the paper. She remembers thinking that
they looked like detectives from an old movie, doing surveillance at a
hotel. It didn't occur to her until later that the detectives were watching
my father.

Not long after she left, two men knocked on the door of my father's
hotel room, claiming to be from Western Union. When my father opened
it, still half asleep, the detectives rushed in and confiscated his drug paraphernalia. The detectives later reported that when they arrested him, he
began to weep and told them that he used heroin because "a blind man has
to have something." During questioning at police headquarters, he told
the officers that he was very worried about what the arrests were doing to
his wife and kids. My mother didn't find out about the arrest until she got

back to the hotel in Indianapolis. Jeff called to tell her what was going on, and she spent a long night in the hotel room wondering what to do next, whether to stay in Indianapolis and wait for my father to get out or to come home to us.

News of the arrest raced through the city and around the country. The next morning fans mobbed the courthouse as my father's attorney led him in. The paper described the scene as "pure bedlam." My father refused all questions. The judge set an arraignment date for January 8, 1962, and released my father on bail. Jeff called my mother to let her know that Dad was being released. Exhausted and silent, my dad was brought back to the hotel room. Neither of my parents talked about what had happened. My mother was confused and upset, angry with my father but afraid for him as well, knowing that things were becoming increasingly serious. More than anything, though, my mother was worried about us. So was my father. What would happen to us if our father went to prison? How would we get by if he couldn't make a living?

Newspapers and gossip magazines had a field day with the arrest. *Time* magazine ran an article about my father's drug addiction and personal problems. Some radio stations began banning his records. His appearance on *The Ed Sullivan Show*, scheduled for one week after the Indianapolis arrest, was abruptly canceled. His image as "the great blind musician" was gradually being overshadowed by the publicity surrounding his drug use.

My father's luck held for one last time. The search of the hotel room turned out to be illegal, so the charges were dropped once again. If the arraignment on January 8 had proceeded as scheduled, my father might have been in custody in Indiana while my mother was in the hospital with a burst appendix, hovering near death. It wasn't until years later that I found out how close my brothers and I came to losing both of our parents in the same week. I don't want to think about what might have happened to us if we had. By God's grace, my mother survived and my father was released to his family once again. But it was only a matter of time until the long legal trail caught up to him. I was nine years old when it finally happened.

It was late 1964, and my father had just finished a tour of Canada. He flew with the band on his private plane from Montreal, landing in Boston. His pilot, Tom McGarrity, needed to do some maintenance on the plane, so the band was going to take a couple of days off while the airplane was serviced. My dad and the band went through customs and then drove to White Castle for burgers. Afterward they all went to the hotel. Everyone was relaxing, drifting back and forth across the hallway from room to room, talking and laughing. The radio was on in the background. No one paid much attention to the broadcast until someone heard the announcer mentioning my father's name. A few seconds later the phone rang, and Herbert Miller answered. It was Jeff Brown.

Jeff said, "Herb, did you go somewhere with Ray? Did he want you to go with him someplace tonight?"

Herbert replied, "No."

Jeff said, "Then how did he leave the hotel?"

"Is he gone?" Herbert asked. For a minute his mind went blank. Then it suddenly dawned on him that he hadn't seen my father for a while. He had assumed my dad was in one of the other rooms. The first inkling of panic started to set in. When Herbert asked the other guys, it quickly became apparent that nobody knew where my father was.

Jeff and Herbert started calling around, trying to find out what had happened. It turned out that when they reached the hotel, my father had remembered that his stash was still on the plane, and called a cab to take him back to the airport. He didn't want to ask Herbert to take him because Herbert didn't use drugs, and my father always tried not to involve him. The cab took my father out to the tarmac, and he got out alone to retrieve his stash. It wouldn't be difficult; he knew every inch of his plane. He didn't need help finding his stash. He let the back stairway down and went on board to retrieve the drugs. The only light on the field was the head-lights going up to the plane. When the airport police saw a figure getting off the plane at two in the morning, they thought someone was breaking into the plane, so they went to investigate. As soon as they saw that it was my father, they immediately became suspicious. Customs had already been put on alert because of my father's previous arrests. The officers asked my father what he was carrying. There was nothing he could do but admit it was heroin. He had been caught dead to rights. It was Halloween night. While I was falling into a candy-laden sleep after trick-or-treating with my friends, the FBI was arresting my father on federal drug charges.

Though he had been arrested several times by then, this arrest was different from all the others. What made it so serious was that my father had brought the drugs across the Canadian border in his private plane, and by returning to remove the drugs from the plane himself, he had shown that the drugs were brought from Canada with his full knowledge. Bringing drugs across the Canadian border made it a federal offense. If convicted, my father would go to federal prison, probably for decades, and given the evidence a conviction was almost certain.

When my mother received the call at home from Jeff, she didn't immediately realize how serious the situation was. After all, my father had been arrested before. But by the time my father got home a few days later, it was clear that he was in terrible trouble. This case wasn't going away. This time my father's arrest was international news. The *New York Times* ran a lead article on it. Three weeks later the results of the lab tests on the heroin came back, the federal agents testified, and the case was sent to a grand jury. In February 1965 the grand jury indicted my father on four counts of heroin possession and trafficking drugs across the border. In March he flew back to Boston to face the judge and plead not guilty while his lawyers went into a rush of negotiations. When he returned home, he confessed to my mother that he was afraid. There was a good chance he would go to prison for twenty years.

My father canceled his tour starting that spring. Instead he tried to bury himself in his music. Although he had canceled his road schedule, we didn't see him more than usual. We moved to our new house on Southridge Avenue in April, but there was little joy in it for either of my parents. Once again our family was living in suspended animation, waiting for the courts to decide my father's fate. The lawyers argued, and my mother worried, and as the weeks went by, my father began to do some soul-searching. For nearly twenty years he had looked to heroin for escape and pleasure, just as he had in his women. Many years later, my father spoke to me and explained to me how he loved the way heroin made him feel. He never believed heroin was hurting him, since he had been able to build a successful career despite his using. He had always considered his heroin use a personal matter.

Now, though, everything had changed. He knew that if he continued using, he would lose his music, his family, and most likely his life, for he didn't think he would survive in prison. My mother said that for the first time, he faced up to what his addiction was doing to his children. He told my mother that he was going to stop using heroin for me. My dad made a strong and courageous decision to get clean.

That July he flew to Boston to talk with his lawyers, who told prosecutors that Mr. Charles was going to kick heroin to demonstrate how seriously he was taking these charges. The prosecutors were skeptical. After all, how many addicts ever really quit? By the time my father got back to Los Angeles, preparations were already complete. He came home just long enough to pack a few clothes and tell my mother that he was checking in to St. Francis Hospital in Lynwood that night. He decided to quit heroin cold turkey. If he could survive withdrawal, it would be over with and he could get well. His intentions were to get clean as quickly as possible and stay clean.

My mother insisted that he be the one to tell us he was leaving. She wasn't going to do it for him. Dad waited just long enough for us to get home from school. As soon as I got home he asked me to come into his bedroom while he was getting ready to leave. He sat on the side of the bed, packing his socks and underwear in a leather bag while talking to me. He told me he had to go away for a while. When I asked him why, he said, "Daddy has to go get well, baby." I didn't understand what was wrong. I only knew he had to go to the hospital to get better.

An hour later he was gone. On July 26, 1965, he checked himself in to St. Francis. It would be months before he came back to live in our beautiful new home. Meanwhile, I worried. When my mother had gone to the hospital three years earlier, she had nearly died. My next thought was, what if my father never came home? The fate of our family was still in limbo.

If I had seen my father those first two weeks in St. Francis, I would have been even more afraid. His physician, Dr. Frederick Hacker, suggested my father take methadone to make the withdrawal easier. My dad refused. Years later he wrote, "I wasn't weaned. I didn't take pills. I refused to fool with their sedatives and their tranquilizers." He detoxed from heroin without methadone or any other drugs to alleviate the vomiting, diarrhea, tremors, hallucinations, and other effects of the poison coming out of his system. As the Scriptures say, once he put his hand to the plow, he never looked back. He was determined to see it through and come home to us a clean and healthy man. I still can't fathom the strength it took for him to do that.

My parents had agreed that they would keep life as normal as possible for me and my brothers while my father was in the hospital. Before they knew he would be going into St. Francis, my mother had made reservations for us to go to the World's Fair in New York for two weeks, starting the last week of July. My mother's education was limited but she always made sure that we had every opportunity to receive the best education. She even made us read the encyclopedia at home to ensure we were well-rounded. The World's Fair was an ideal opportunity for us to learn about the world. At first she thought about canceling, but the reservations were already in place, and my father wouldn't be allowed visitors for a while anyway. They agreed that she should go ahead with her plans. So my mother and brothers and I boarded the plane and left for New York. My mother's heart must have been heavy, but as always, she turned her attention to taking care of us.

Going to the fair turned out to be a wonderful experience. Nothing could completely take away the knot in my stomach, but the fair was an amazing place, and once we got there, the excitement shoved the anxiety into the back of my mind for a while. We spent days touring the exhibits. The theme was "Peace Through Understanding," symbolized by a twelve-story steel globe surrounded by flags of all nations. The fair was dedicated to man's achievements on the shrinking globe and in the expanding universe, and the exhibits offered a view of the future guaranteed to capture the imagination of a ten-year-old boy. Some of the exhibits were amazing. The Vatican sponsored a pavilion and, incredibly, put Michelangelo's *Pietà* on display. There were also numerous space exhibits that opened up a world far beyond our globe. Like all children in the sixties, I was fascinated by the exploration of space. Men were already orbiting the Earth, and the Apollo missions were right around the corner. I stared enraptured at the Space Age exhibits, watched the new IBM inventions called computers work their magic, and glided through the future in Futurama. Ford introduced the first Mustang at that fair.

My favorite exhibits were those by my hero, the great visionary Walt Disney. Disney had recently perfected audio-animatronics, putting computers to work to animate humanlike creatures. I watched Abraham Lincoln deliver the Gettysburg Address in Great Moments with Mr. Lincoln, an eerily real simulation, and I saw child-size dolls dance in what would later become the Disneyland ride It's a Small World. The Carousel of Progress showed us how far the world had come technologically, its theme song promising "There's a Great Big Beautiful Tomorrow," composed by the Sherman Brothers, who wrote so many of the Disney musicals. We went to the memorial for John Kennedy, who had been assassinated less than two years before. The memorial saddened me. I wasn't ready to remember that dark moment in our history yet. The fair showed me my heritage and the future. I was moved and excited by what I saw.

Even at the time, though, I understood that the fair was a paradox. Walt Disney showed us a utopian society there where all people lived in harmony. The fair also served as an example of President Johnson's vision of the Great Society. Yet outside the confines of the fair, our nation was going through the greatest civil unrest it had ever experienced. Civil rights protesters were marching on Washington and being knocked down with fire hoses in the streets of the South. The Vietnam War had escalated, with thousands of military casualties and protesters being thrown in jail.

The fair was a financial failure, in part perhaps because of the stress of the times. But while we were there, it was a magical place in which to forget about all the pain in our own lives.

Two weeks later we flew home, and before we even landed, reality hit again with a thud. We had heard on television that there was some rioting in Los Angeles, but we had no idea how serious it was until we returned there. As our plane circled to land at the airport, we looked out the window and saw fires burning below, miniature spots of flame in the darkness. As soon as Vernon Troupe, my father's valet, picked us up, my mother turned on the car radio. The first words we heard were "Burn, Baby! Burn!" echoing the Magnificent Montague, a popular KGFJ disc jockey. He used the phrase when he became excited by a good piece of music, but rioters had hijacked the phrase and made it into the war cry of the arsonist. We stared out the car windows in disbelief as we wound through the dark streets toward home. Our city was burning.

Until that week I don't think racial conflict seemed real to me. I had always heard the stories about what was happening in other states, other neighborhoods, and my parents talked to my brothers and me about our heritage and what it meant to be black in America. My perception of the world was that it was a white world and we were just visitors with a pass. Being black in America in the sixties was a struggle. We were surrounded by forces that sought to control and marginalize us. We were looked upon as second-class citizens in our own country. My dad worked hard to survive, to rise out of the humiliation of the South, and to build a future for himself and his family.

Despite the consciousness in our country, most black families I knew were thriving. My father was more successful than most men dreamed of being. Our neighborhood, first on Hepburn and now on Southridge, was populated by highly successful, well-educated African Americans who were thriving in the midst of civil unrest. And not just as musicians or celebrities. Our neighbors, my mentors, were doctors, lawyers, judges, teachers, and entrepreneurs. Major General Titus Hall, who became one of the first black generals in the United States Air Force, lived in Baldwin

Hills. Our friend Mr. Ramirez was an aerospace engineer. Mr. Kaiser was an entrepreneur and Mr. Maurice Hill was a sales executive. These were successful men, formidable African American role models. They were pioneers, African Americans who were given the opportunity to excel in corporate America.

I knew about the civil rights movement, and I was aware that my parents knew Martin Luther King Jr. personally. Like other African Americans, I grieved for those who suffered for our race and celebrated each triumph of the civil rights movement. During our last summer on Hepburn, President Lyndon Johnson signed into law the Civil Rights Act, a landmark moment for African Americans. One year later, shortly after we moved into our home on Southridge, Congress passed the Voting Rights Act, which finally made the rights promised in the Fifteenth Amendment a reality by eliminating discriminatory practices that prevented African Americans from voting. Our family's move from Hepburn to Southridge paralleled a much larger social revolution for African Americans throughout the nation. We were part of a growing number of black families who were "moving on up."

Yes, I knew about racism, but I had never really experienced it personally. For as long as I could remember, I had lived in neighborhoods that, while predominantly African American, included families of all races. Most of the kids I went to school with were white, as was my beloved teacher Mrs. Reynolds, who loved and mothered us all like her own. When my father built our home on Southridge, it was a group of our African American neighbors who had filed a petition to stop construction, claiming the house was too large and would block their views. It was the white family across the street who refused to sign the petition and was the first to welcome us to the neighborhood. There were white families scattered throughout View Park. Most of them still live there. In many respects, I was living in a bubble. Ironically, it was my own people who brought the power of racial anger home to me.

For my children, the Watts riots are something they read about in our history, but for me, the riots were painfully real. When our plane from

New York landed that night, Los Angeles was already burning. The riots were the worst in Los Angeles history to date. They had begun on August 11 with a white policeman stopping a black motorist for drunk driving. A crowd quickly gathered to watch the arrest of the motorist, who failed the sobriety test. The arrest was the catalyst, but the violence that followed had little to do with the original traffic violation. Mob mentality set in, and by morning a full-scale riot was in progress. Watts community leaders urged calm, doing everything in their power to put an end to the violence, but by then the rioting had a life of its own. Thousands of people had taken to the streets, setting buildings on fire, looting the business district, assaulting police and white motorists trapped in the danger zone. Rioters threw Molotov cocktails into local businesses, and when the Los Angeles Fire Department responded to the fires, rioters attacked the firefighters. As Vernon drove us up the hill from the airport that night, we could see the fires burning in the city below. When the sun came up the next morning, we stood on the upper terrace and all we could see—from South Central, to the Coliseum, to downtown LA, up into Hollywood Hills and east toward the San Bernardino Mountains—was thick black smoke. It would be there for days. At night we could see the blaze from our den. I couldn't believe it was happening.

The pictures on television were terrifying, but the news circulating through our neighborhood was even more frightening. Word had reached us that rioters were planning to set fire to View Park and Baldwin Hills, two of the wealthiest black communities in the nation. "We're going to the hills where all the judges, the black judges and doctors and businessmen are. We're gonna' go burn 'em out." I was petrified and confused. We were home alone with my mother. What would we do if they tried to burn our house? What if my dad came home and they threw Molotov cocktails through our windows? My father was blind. How would we protect him? The governor had to call in the National Guard to protect us—a black neighborhood, not a white community—against our own race.

My father was furious about what happened and quite disappointed. Later on, he talked to me about the Watts riots. "Son, it made no sense. I know what racism is. I'm from the South. I had to stand in the middle of a country road after being abandoned by a white police officer. I know how it feels to be disrespected. I've been banned from Georgia—from my own state, where I was born. Martin Luther King has faced tremendous trials. The people around him have been beat down with clubs and sprayed with fire hoses, and they walked for miles just to be able to drink water from somewhere. Now they want to come burn us down for our hard work. I'll be damned. My people. I don't understand it. This is our own people, and everything that we've gained, we just took fifty steps backward. How can anyone honor something like this?" He just sat there with his head down.

We all understood the source of the community's anger, but none of us understood why the rioters wanted to come after us. And what did they think they were gaining by burning down their own people's neighborhoods? It made no sense to me. They started rioting because of the action of someone white and now they want to burn their own people down. I believe the rioters just got angry and took it out on everybody around them. It wasn't about black and white anymore; maybe it was about the haves and the have-nots.

As historians have commented, the Watts riots turned a spotlight on the racial tension between black and white Americans in Los Angeles, but they also revealed a huge division within the African American community. Black community leaders from inside and outside of Watts were appalled by the violence, but the words of local preachers and teachers were widely ignored. Nothing made the problem clearer than the visit of Martin Luther King. He flew to Los Angeles to meet with residents in the riot zone, hoping his message of nonviolent protest would have a calming effect, but if anything, his visit backfired. During the first meeting he had scheduled in Watts, he was surrounded by nearly three hundred people who angrily insisted that they were not sorry for taking part in the violence. Someone shouted, "Burn, baby, burn!" and a crowd gathered around Dr. King, chanting and jeering. He eventually got the crowd under control, but he was so disturbed by what he experienced that he canceled the other visits he had planned in the area. It wasn't safe for him to be there. He left the area that day, citing security reasons. I felt like Martin Luther King had gone through all the pain and struggle in the South for nothing. The Watts riots did not represent the consciousness of Dr. Martin Luther King and the civil rights movement.

The original traffic stop had occurred on a Wednesday night; by Friday morning the National Guard had been deployed into what had become a war zone. The business district had been reduced to rubble, hundreds of buildings were on fire, and troops filled the streets. This wasn't the city I knew. These were pictures out of World War II in my history book. By Saturday night almost 20,000 guardsmen had formed a ring around the city that ran nearly fifty miles. Martial law had been declared, and a curfew was in place. By Monday night the rioting was over. More than 600 buildings had been seriously damaged or destroyed, 857 people had been injured, and 34 people had died. The damage to the city and its residents was staggering. A great effort was made afterward to address the problems that sparked the riot, but the community was never able to rebuild what had been destroyed. The businesses did not come back. Watts remained desolate. Dr. King said it all. "At the center of all nonviolence stands the principal of love." Love builds. Hate destroys.

In the middle of all the chaos, my mother, brothers, and I were locked down in our home in the August heat, worried about my father, frightened of the men with Molotov cocktails who threatened to burn down the homes in our neighborhood. Bobby was only four, too little to understand what was going on, but David and I knew something terrible was happening. At ten, feeling like I was the man of the house in my father's absence and that I had to take care of my mother and brothers, I felt the full weight of that responsibility. By then my father had survived the initial violent illness of withdrawal, and Dr. Hacker told my mother she could see him. Seeing my father meant driving through the riot zone, but with the loyalty and courage that have always characterized her, my mother got dressed the next day and asked Vernon to take her to the hospital.

My mother vividly remembers that drive. As they pulled up to the perimeter the National Guard had established around the city, guardsmen flagged the car to a stop. Vernon rolled down the window and began talking to the guardsman who approached them. From my mother's viewpoint in the backseat, she could see the ammunition belts strapped around his waist. There were rows and rows of the longest bullets she had ever seen. After talking to Vernon for a while, the guardsman waved them through. Vernon drove slowly down the street. On both sides, the street was lined with national guardsmen, stationed a few yards apart, watching. Behind the lines of soldiers were ruined buildings, gutted, burned, looted, and vandalized. Rubble lay everywhere. This was a war zone, not the city she knew.

And she barely recognized the man she found in the small room at St. Francis. My father sat on the side of the bed in his undershirt and slacks, quiet, drawn, somehow smaller. They didn't talk much. He was too exhausted. For the first time the man she had married, always so full of swagger and confidence, was frightened and anxious. Without the refuge of the drug that had poisoned and sustained him for two decades, he was left defenseless to deal with life on its own terms. He also seemed clearly embarrassed to have Mother see him in this condition. They chatted a little, she told him we were all doing fine, and after about half an hour, she kissed him and left. She would be back to see him in two days. For the next couple of weeks she visited him faithfully, every other day, until the doctor said he was well enough for his children to see him. Children were allowed to visit on Sundays.

By that time I was desperate to see him, to make sure he was all right, but I was also frightened because I remembered how my mother had looked when we'd gone to visit her at the hospital after her illness three years earlier. On the way to the hospital, my mother tried to prepare us by telling us that Daddy had been sick. He was getting better, but he didn't feel very well yet. We were to behave, not jump on Daddy or make too much noise. When we arrived at St. Francis, we followed my mother quietly down the hall. She opened the door to his room. It was dark inside. My father never turned on the lights when he was alone. It made no difference to him. My mother turned on the lights.

I didn't recognize the figure in the bed at first. He lay on his side, small and vulnerable, curled up in the fetal position with his back to us. He looked like he was asleep. My mother touched him gently, and he rolled over and scratched his head like he always did when he was first waking up. Then he turned and sat up on the side of the bed. He was wearing his white underclothes. He sat there quietly for a minute, trying to wake up. I looked around the room. Next to his bed was a desk and chair. His glasses and a turquoise-blue domino holder were sitting on the desk. We all stood back from him, suddenly shy. After a moment my father spoke to us softly, calling us over to him. He gave each of us a hug and talked for a minute. He was very soft-spoken, and in a few minutes he got tired and needed to lie down again. My mother told us it was time to go home and let Daddy rest.

Was this my father? I could hardly believe it. My father was bigger than life, and this man seemed very weak. It would be years before I fully understood how strong my father really was in that moment. He had beaten a twenty-year heroin habit with nothing to help him but his own courage, determination, and love for us. He really was the superman I had imagined him to be when I was small. But in that moment, for the first time in my life, he seemed human.

My father remained in St. Francis for four months. My mother continued to visit him every other day, bringing him home-cooked food as his strength and appetite returned. Every Sunday she brought us to visit. Dad never left the facility, even once, for fear he would be accused of using again. For a long time his blood tests showed positive for heroin, despite the fact that he hadn't taken any since he was admitted, and he was watched even more closely. Dr. Hacker reassured him that false positives were not unusual, and eventually the tests were negative. Meanwhile, my father came to trust Dr. Hacker and started talking to him about his childhood, about losing his mother and George, about losing his eyesight. Without heroin as a buffer, the memories that haunted him came flooding back. Facing them must have been harder for him than withdrawing from the heroin. He didn't talk to me about it, and I don't know that he had any closure on what had happened to George or his mother, but he learned to live with their memories without the use of heroin. During his stay he learned to play chess, a game he embraced with a passion.

The months passed, and at the end of November my father was released from St. Francis to return to Boston and the hearing that would decide his fate. Dr. Hacker testified on his behalf at the hearing, and a letter in support of my father written by the original judge on the case who had since died was read aloud. After considering all of the testimony and evidence, the judge placed my father on probation for five years. He could remain free on his own recognizance as long as he made himself available for random drug testing no matter where he was, on demand of the court. Overwhelmed with gratitude and relief at the decision of the court, my father made the agreement and had it written into his contracts that he could leave any engagement without repercussions if the court so ordered. He was as good as his word. Eventually, he completed his probation. He never used heroin again—he had overcome. My father's inner strength was unparalleled. God gave him another chance; he would slay his demons and move forward. It was a humbling experience. Only then, my mother says, did she begin to breathe once more.

CHAPTER 9

All Night, All Day

All night, all day,

Angels watchin' over me,

my Lord.

Bless my home and

family.

Angels watchin' over me.

—TRADITIONAL AFRICAN
AMERICAN SPIRITUAL

SIX MONTHS AFTER WE MOVED TO VIEW PARK, WE WERE finally able to enjoy our new home. The black smoke over the city gradually dissipated, and my fear faded with it. The National Guard packed up and left. Calm returned to the city and our home. The United

States was at war with North Vietnam, racial tension was at an all-time high, and Martin Luther King was marching on Selma, but at home there was peace. The move to Southridge from Hepburn was a new beginning for our family, and a huge relief to me. The walls at Hepburn had begun to talk to me. They whispered of pain and fear, of my father thrashing and hemorrhaging, of my mother carried down the stairs close to death, of my baby brother stretched lifeless on the floor. I could no longer shut the voices out. The house on Southridge was free of them. Its walls were silent, and when the house did speak, it was of peace and hope.

Our house at the top of the hill was a sanctuary and a refuge. From our vantage point we could see the entire Los Angeles basin spread out beneath us. On hot, muggy days, the smog hovered over the city like a toxic cloud, but when the wind rose, we could see the San Bernardino Mountains. In the afternoons the breeze from the ocean would find its way through the hills of View Park and cool us as we played outside.

Our new home at 4863 Southridge was a monument to my father's success. The house was designed by the African American architect Arthur Anderson, and his design approach was brilliant. It was illuminated entirely by natural light from large windows and skylights. Instead of building the house three stories up, he built it on three graded levels to fit the natural contours of the landscape. The highest part was even with our neighbors' houses. We walked in at ground level and then went up or down from there. Altogether there was a drop of about twenty-seven feet from the highest to the lowest level of the house.

The first time my father showed us through our new home, he was more animated than I had ever seen him. Selecting a key from the ring he always carried, he unlocked the door and stood aside to let us enter. As we walked through the entryway, I looked around in wonder. The foyer was marble, flooded with natural light from the surrounding windows. The sheer size of our new home was overwhelming. Our entire house at Hepburn could have fit inside the living room, foyer, and dining room. In the middle of the foyer was a large circular opening cut into the floor, filled with birds-of-paradise, an indoor garden cut into the marble.

A staircase carpeted in red swept upstairs from the foyer. My father's gold records, framed in red velvet with black trim, were displayed on the wall along the staircase. In between the records was a portrait of my parents. Then we entered the living room, which had a ceiling that was nearly twenty feet tall. A beautiful, hand-painted Chinese mural comprised an entire wall, while a second wall was dominated by a huge marble fireplace. We stood there together, marveling at what we saw as my father beamed with pride.

I was standing with the rest of the family, awestruck by what I was seeing, when it suddenly hit me that this was my house. I could go anywhere I wanted. Overwhelmed with excitement, I broke loose from the rest of the family and started running around, looking at everything, wild with curiosity. I raced down the hall and found the den, filled with my father's trophies and plaques like his old office on Hepburn. His Grammys were encased in a glass-front bookcase, and more gold records lined the wall. I turned and ran down the stairs to the bottom level, where my father's office was located. Like the rest of the house, it was huge, and the fireplace shaft from the living room ran all the way down one level and opened into a second fireplace in his office. My father's turntable, speakers, and reel-to-reel tape deck were built into his desk. A large closet housed his tapes and equipment.

The best discovery of all was the entertainment room. The huge marble room—more than 500 square feet—was equipped with everything my brothers or I could want. There was a big color television, a projector, and a movie screen that came out of the ceiling. A built-in jukebox held fifty 45s at a time. It would play all night. There were leather sofas to lounge on, a bar with a soda fountain, and sliding glass doors that opened to a terrace.

Outside the sliding glass doors was our own private playground. There was a tennis court that could double as a basketball court. Next to the court was a fenced-in dog kennel for our German shepherd, King. Best of all, we had our own private swimming pool. It was a large, deep, rectangular pool with a tile mosaic shaped like a piano on the bottom. A hydraulic door made out of marble opened and closed to let the pool cover go forward and retract. In the back was a pool house and storage space for my father's equipment.

When I finished exploring outside, I raced back inside and up the stairs to find my room. There were six bedrooms on the top level, three in front and three in back. My room was in the front, overlooking the street. My brothers' and parents' rooms were in the back. My father had let me walk through the house while it was still being framed, and I chose the bedroom I wanted. Now my bedroom was finished and filled with new furniture.

My father's pride was visible as we toured our new home that day. Southridge was the fulfillment of a promise my father had made to my mother. To build his family a 12,000-square-foot home in 1965 was a remarkable achievement. He could have purchased a house in Beverly Hills like Frank Sinatra, Dean Martin, or Sammy Davis Jr. if he wanted to, but my parents preferred to raise us within our own culture. My mother wanted us to be around prominent, successful African Americans who could serve as role models for me and my brothers, too. Our home was designed as a personal playground for us where we could do almost anything we wanted without ever having to leave. It was built to ensure the privacy and safety that my parents wanted for us. Everything we needed was within the gates around our property. It was a peaceful place for my mother to nurture and keep watch over us. For a poor, blind African American boy from the South, Southridge was a monumental accomplishment.

When we moved to View Park, we began a way of life that most Americans only dreamed of, a life that few African Americans could even imagine for themselves. During the sixties and seventies, View Park boasted one of the highest per capita incomes in the nation for black families. Though primarily African American, View Park was a mixed neighborhood with white, Asian, and Hispanic families as well, the kind of neighborhood where people stayed. Ours was a beautiful, thriving community on a hill far above the oil wells that led to the beach not far away. There were fields with trails to ride our bikes along and beautiful homes that rivaled almost any in the state. Each afternoon the wind rose from the sea and sent cooling breezes up the hill. Our life there was a beautiful season that we never wanted to end.

Even more important than the affluence or physical beauty of our neighborhood, though, was the sense of community that bound us together. Most of the families who lived in View Park had arrived there through courage and hard work, not through birthright or privilege. They were doctors, executives, judges, attorneys, entertainers, educators, and entrepreneurs. Dr. Harris and his family moved there from Hepburn shortly before we did. Dr. Hill, a dentist, lived across the street. So did the principal of the local school and a district judge. Mr. and Mrs. Harrison owned Harrison-Ross Mortuary. My close friend Gary's father owned Thompson Trucking. Another neighbor, Jonathan Leonard, was a well-respected black fireman in Los Angeles. There were several successful entertainers as well. Earl Grant, one of the most talented entertainers of his generation, lived down the block. Nancy Wilson lived nearby. So did Ike and Tina Turner.

There was no neighborhood watch, but everyone on the block looked out for one another. Mothers fed each other's children and called one another if any of the kids were headed for trouble. It was like having several sets of parents. My mother knew that Mrs. Rogers or Mrs. Hill would call if David or I got into trouble, just as they trusted my mother to call if one of their children were in trouble or hurt.

We all lived by the same rules: dinner, homework, home by dark, good sportsmanship, and respect for others. Even our single neighbors took an interest in us. Mr. Grant would stop to talk to us when we were out playing. Mr. Grant was a beautiful man inside and out. He had no children of his own, but he took an interest in us and in his nephews when they came to visit. He was the classiest black man that I've ever known, always impeccably dressed. He wore an ascot and velvet shoes just to walk his dog. Mr. Grant drove an old Rolls-Royce Corniche and always greeted me formally in his soft-spoken voice: "Young man, how are you? Have you been behaving yourself?" He was an old bachelor who never married, and many speculated that he was gay, but it didn't matter to us. He looked out for us like everyone else did. He was our neighbor, part of the fabric of our lives that kept us close and connected. The bonds that were formed on Southridge have stood the test of time, connecting us to this day. Some in our nation still call John Kennedy's White House Camelot. Southridge was my Camelot. We were living the dream.

When it was time to play, View Park was a boys' paradise. Bobby was still too little to come with us, but David and I played together all the time. We remained friends with Anthony and Alfred Anderson, but we didn't see them very often anymore. We would remain in contact with our other friends in Leimert Park as well. The first person I met when we moved to Southridge was Glen Ford, who became my best friend. We played together every day. Two years later, when the Rogerses moved in, David became best friends with Eric Rogers. David, Eric, Glen, Joey, Carlton, and I were inseparable. Sometimes I got tired of David following me, wanting to do everything I did, but most of the time we got along pretty well. We fought like brothers always do, but we were close.

Our manicured street was just blocks away from undeveloped property along Mt. Vernon. We would crawl through the hedges on Mt. Vernon Drive and go into our own little wilderness. There was nothing but brush and ivy and tall grass, with a little canyon down at the bottom filled with Gila monsters and garden snakes. We would hike and catch snakes and play army. Sometimes we'd collect dirt rocks to throw at cars. We got in big trouble if one of the mothers caught us doing that. At home we rode our skateboards down our long, curved driveway in front of our house. If we made the turn at the bottom of the driveway, the momentum would carry us all the way to the end of the block. If we missed the turn, we would end up sprawled in the grass. We played basketball on the tennis court and football in the street. As we got older, we played street football almost every day. If it was daylight savings time, we were allowed to go out again for a while after dinner if we didn't have any homework. If we had homework, that was it. And that was it for everybody on the block. No one else went back outside after dinner on a school night. Our mothers wouldn't let us.

Sometimes David and I were allowed to leave our street to go to the playground at Windsor Hills Elementary School, just a couple of blocks from our house. We didn't go very often during the school year, but in the summer we would meet our friends every day and play softball, football, or dodgeball on the blacktop. When we got tired, we would play caroms on the little wooden boards they had there. Caroms was a kid's version of pool or golf. If we grew tired of the playground, we could walk to the church down the block and play in the sandlot.

The best thing about playing outside in the summer was the ice-cream man. When we heard the music of his truck coming up the street, we'd race to meet it. The ice-cream man was always nice to us, even giving us credit if we didn't have money with us. We would pay him back the next day. In the fall and winter, the Helms Bakery truck came by. I would buy these wonderful golden doughnuts with chocolate icing. The Helms man was good to us, too, always extending credit if we didn't have all of the money. He always greeted us with a smile. Nothing ever tastes as good as the treats we bought as kids from the magical trucks rolling through our neighborhood.

At first we rode our bikes around the neighborhood, but as we got older, we would take our minibikes and dirt bikes into the oil fields, riding up and down the dirt trails between La Brea and La Cienega. These days there's a park there, named in honor of Los Angeles supervisor Kenneth Hahn, but in those days there was nothing but dirt and scrubs. We had to have spark arresters on our minibikes to ride in the area or we'd get a ticket. We were not supposed to ride in there at all because it was private property, but we couldn't get permits to ride our minibikes on the street, so we took our chances. There was a hill in the fields called Devil's Hill, and we used to try to go up it with dirt bikes. I had a few accidents over the years and on one occasion I was injured.

I continued to get into trouble on Southridge the same way I had on Hepburn, usually because I was doing something I wasn't supposed to. One evening I was out in the oil fields with my friend Chris Harris. I was riding my minibike, and Chris was riding his motorcycle. The time crept up on us, and we were racing back, trying to get home before dark. We would both be in big trouble with our mothers if we were out late. I was in the lead with a light on my minibike to guide the way. It was dark by then, and I was saying to myself, "I'm in trouble. We both are in trouble." We came up onto Southridge, and when I started to turn left, Chris hit me broadside. My bike went one way, and I went the other. I slid on the pavement, taking skin off my knee to the bone and breaking my wrist in several places, and landed in oncoming traffic. It's a miracle we were not killed. Chris went headfirst over the handlebars into the pavement, slicing his chin open and knocking out his front teeth. If he hadn't been wearing a helmet, he would have had serious injuries. He was bleeding badly, lying there in the middle of the street. When the ambulance arrived, his brothers, Tolly and Billy, and his father, Dr. Harris, rode with Chris to the emergency room.

He had to have all of his front teeth replaced. Eventually the accident became his favorite story. He would take his false teeth out and say, "Listen, this is how connected Ray and me are. We have been friends since Hepburn, our memories shall bind us forever."

My mother took me to the emergency room, where Dr. Foster met us and they x-rayed me and told me I had a compound fracture of my left wrist. He put a cast on my arm and when my mother was certain I was all right, she told me, "I'm goin' to whip your butt." Never again would someone have to tell me to be inside before dark!

The best thing about Southridge, though, wasn't our house or even our friends. The best thing about Southridge was my father. On Southridge our family found a new home, a new life, and most important, a new bond with my father. The father who came home to us from St. Francis wasn't the man who had come home to us on Hepburn.

After rehab my father found his smile again. It seemed as though his soul had been lightened, relieved. His body was relaxed, the constant twitching and jittering a thing of the past. Until then I had never seen my father in repose, without the continual erratic movement my brothers and I thought of as "just Daddy's way." It was a beautiful sight to see him sitting quietly, relaxed, not moving. With the heroin out of his system, his movements became more natural. He still rocked back and forth like many blind people do, and the occasional twitch remained, but the sweating and spasms were gone. He became more animated, smiled more often. His face would light up, and he seemed more responsive. He even quit smoking for a while. I was used to always seeing him with a cigarette in one hand, but now both his hands were free, and he rested them on his waist when he stood. Now that he was no longer using, he rubbed his arms with a special salve to help his veins heal and over time his arms cleared up. He could roll up his sleeves and go to work again.

It took awhile for my father to get adjusted to our house on Southridge after he came home from the hospital. He had lived there only a few weeks before he went into rehab. The house was extremely difficult for a blind man to navigate because there were so many rooms, so many levels. He had to memorize every room in the house and every piece of furniture in the rooms. I watched him adjust to his new surroundings with the same amazement I had always felt when I watched him move around. Within weeks of returning from rehab, he had familiarized himself with our new house and moved about more freely than he had on Hepburn. On Hepburn he was either in the kitchen or upstairs in his office most of the time. On Southridge he was in every room. He played the piano in the living room and read braille magazines in the den. He moved from level to level at the same pace as a person with sight. Before long he could run up and down the stairs, touching the wall or railing as a guide every now and then to keep himself oriented. Our new neighbors were astonished by the way he navigated our home, and some of my new friends, like my old friends on Hepburn, were convinced that he could see.

I only saw him make a mistake once. Shortly after we moved in, he accidentally stepped in the small garden in the foyer. He made a point to identify its exact position after that, and he never made that mistake again. He would let himself in the front door and walk confidently through the foyer, missing the garden by an inch. It was clear that he knew exactly where it was.

Within no time he had learned the outdoor layout as well and was racing his beloved Vespa around the tennis court at full speed. A few months later, he knew the neighborhood well enough to take the Vespa out on the street. Our neighbor Mrs. Rogers still remembers coming up the hill on Southridge and seeing my father pass by on his Vespa. She nearly had a heart attack the first time it happened. Before long the kids weren't the only ones wondering if my father could see. He eventually ran into a pole on the tennis court and wrecked the Vespa. He was all right, but the Vespa never recovered. It was a miracle he and the motorcycle lasted as long as they did.

Even after watching him all my life, I still couldn't understand how he got around the way he did. I thought back to the first time I saw View Park, flying over the neighborhood in my father's plane. We circled the hills and the oil fields, then the pilot banked right over Southridge and my father pointed down to our new place and said, "There it is!" Then the pilot banked sharply left so the rest of the family could see out their side, and once again my father pointed right at the construction site. I remember thinking, "How the heck does he know where the house is?"

The preoccupation that had characterized my dad on Hepburn dissipated as his drug use became a thing of the past. When he came home from Boston after getting a suspended sentence, he seemed more conscious of us boys than he had ever been. Maybe it was the realization that he had almost gone to prison for two decades. Even if he had survived prison, we would all have been grown men by the time he got out. Or maybe it was just the passage of time that made him want to be around us more. We were growing up, and he was aware of it in a new way. For every parent there are those moments when you wonder, "Where did the years go?" When he bent over to kiss us now after a trip, he would put a hand over our heads to see how tall we were. I think he dreaded the day we would be taller than him.

Sometimes I heard him when he came home from the studio late at night, after we were in bed, and I would quietly walk to the stairs to see him. Often when I got to the top of the stairs, I would look down and see him standing alone in the hall in the middle of the night, perfectly still, absolutely silent, listening to the house. I would sit down and be as still as I could, watching him, wondering what was going through his mind, trying to hear what he was listening to. There's a pulse to silence in the middle of the night. If you really listen, silence has its own rhythm, just as noise does. If I listen closely enough, I can almost hear the house breathing. The walls creak and settle around me. A car passes quietly in the distance. The clock ticking. You feel the pulse of stillness. My father loved that pulse when he could finally hear it. Sometimes I would wake up in the middle of the night and find him standing in the foyer in his robe, listening as the house slept around him, the house he had built. When you're under the influence, nothing stands still, especially your mind. I think that he was getting accustomed to hearing things that he hadn't heard for a long, long time.

Sometimes when he stood there in silence, I wondered if he was praying, thanking God for his deliverance from heroin. He went to church with us in the months following his release from rehab. Before, when he came with us, he would be quiet and withdrawn most of the time, humming softly to himself while the choir sang. Now, though, it was different. Now when the choir sang, the music seemed to penetrate his soul, and sometimes he would sing along. Reverend Durham would say, "I heard, I heard Jesus" like he always had, but now my father would nod and say, "Amen," and he would say, "I heard Jesus," too. Tears would run down his face, and he would reach up and wipe them away.

For most of his life my father had believed that he could not be saved, but sitting in church, feeling the Spirit within him, I think he knew that wasn't true. God had saved him, time and time again, with His grace and mercy. God saved him as a boy when his eyes failed and his parents left him. He saved him as an adult by waking me in the middle of the night and sending me to the room where he was dying. It was God that gave him the strength to beat heroin and go on with his life. I believe that once he had a firm grip on life again without heroin, he never looked back. What an incredible accomplishment. The demons in his life were the painful memories that haunted him. Those memories never went away, but somehow he found the strength to live with them.

Most people believe my father's greatest gift was his music. I don't believe that is true. I think my father's greatest gift from God was his inner strength, and his ability to apply that in his life. That strength enabled him to overcome all obstacles. During that first year of recovery, my father poured his emotions into his music and recorded five songs with the word "crying" in the title, the most famous being "Crying Time." Without the escape that heroin had once provided, music became the refuge for his pain.

I watched the changes in him closely in the months after he came home, taking them all in. I had always watched my father closely. I was captivated by him as a child. Some of it was fascination, but much of it was fear. I never told my parents, but from the day I found him bleeding to death when I was six years old, I feared something would happen to him. When he came home from St. Francis, I worried. Would he fall? Would he hurt himself? I was always roaming around, checking on him. I would go downstairs sometimes and peek in to see if he was in his office. I always had to know where he was. I woke up in the middle of the night if I heard the slightest noise. I would hear someone close a bathroom or bedroom door, and I would get up to investigate. I understood by then what had happened in St. Francis. My father was different now. He was better. But would he stay better? Would he relapse? Would he feel different about us? Would he fall out of love with my mother? It took me five years to stop worrying about him, to realize he really was all right. My little brother Bobby grew up never knowing the man that our father used to be.

It was on Southridge that the Sunday chess games started in the big office downstairs. My father had passed time in rehab learning chess and became fascinated with the game. He was a natural. Chess is a game of concentration and memory as well as strategy, and my father had both of those in unusual amounts. He could keep track of all the chess pieces without seeing them. A few months after he came home, he started holding chess games every Sunday for his friends. I never got to attend one of the Sunday games, but I sure heard about them. The band members would come, along with family friends and a long line of celebrities and musicians, including my dad's old friend Quincy Jones. The games would start in the morning and continue long after my brothers and I went to bed. As she had on Hepburn, my mother cooked and carried food to my dad and his friends all day. Everyone had a story about playing chess with my father. Bill Cosby says that one time he made a move late in the game, and my dad shouted, "Ah hah!" My dad couldn't see the move, but he knew where all the pieces were, and he knew he had him. In fact, my father didn't even need a board. Herbert Miller still laughs when he talks about it. Someone would say, "Pawn B to knight four," and the next thing you knew, there'd be an argument. My father would shout, "Wait! You can't do that, man!" and soon everyone would be yelling at one another, pointing at the chess pieces, and all the time there would be no chess board. Newcomers would look at them moving the pieces around the imaginary board and think they were crazy. But those moments were special for my father, and as long as he was happy, I was okay.

My mother was the center of everything that happened on Southridge, just like she had been on Hepburn. Southridge was her domain, her private sanctuary, and she controlled it. She was a taskmaster where the help was concerned. She made sure the house was kept clean at all times. The sheets had to be ironed. Maids in white uniforms served all our meals. My mother wanted them to share the cooking, too, but that never worked out very well. A great cook herself, she tried to teach them how to cook in the same manner that she did. She would have the maids cook with her, giving them the recipe and showing them how to prepare the foods we liked. Most of the time it didn't work, and she ended up cooking our meals.

One of the maids, Eleanor, was like a member of the family. You can see her in many family pictures. Eleanor's main duties were to help keep an eye on us and to make sure my mother's rules were followed. She did everything from keeping the house immaculate to helping fix our bikes. Eleanor was from British Honduras (Belize), so she spoke with a strong accent. Even her Spanish seemed to have a British accent. She had to learn English while she was working for us, and she had a hard time communicating clearly. When she got upset with us after a frustrating day, parts of her sentences would come out backward, which I found very funny. "Okay, you kids. Come upstairs back!" She was almost as strict as my mother. Eleanor's responsibility was great and she took care of us with love. When my mother's health was failing, Eleanor was always there. I miss her.

Despite my father's fame and affluent surroundings, my mother never thought of herself as a celebrity wife. The phrase I heard about her over and over again was "down to earth." She was a strong and beautiful woman, and when she dressed for an evening out with my father, she looked like his queen. She was very reserved with people she didn't know, and could be intimidating until you got to know her. Right after the Rogerses moved in, their dog bit David, and my mother called Mrs. Rogers. She told Mrs. Rogers that she needed to come over and talk to her about it, and Mrs. Rogers panicked, thinking, "Oh, my Lord, I just moved here and I'm about to get sued by Ray Charles."

When my mother got there, though, she immediately reassured Mrs. Rogers, telling her, "Oh, Ruby, it's nothing, everything's fine. I just wanted to make sure the dog had his shots. David is all right. You never know, the boys were probably doing something to the dog."

Mrs. Rogers was very surprised. She had expected Mrs. Ray Charles to behave like she was someone special. But despite the furs and jewels my father had bought her over the years, my mother remained Della Robinson, the church girl from Texas.

Neither of my parents ever forgot where they came from. People who only knew them as Mr. and Mrs. Ray Charles didn't really know them at all. They forgot that my parents came from humble beginnings, and even when they were reminded, they didn't understand what that meant. My parents understood how blessed they were because they knew what it was like to have nothing. There's an old adage: "Once I had no shoes. Then I met a man who had no feet." They knew what hardship was.

They also knew what racism was. There were no bowling alleys for black people when they were starting out, no golf courses, no swimming pools. If they wanted to swim, they had to go to the lake, the river, or the beach, and even there they could only swim in the designated area. In my father's early years on the road, they had to drive all night because African Americans were not allowed to stay in many hotels, and much of the time, they were not allowed to eat in the restaurants. During a decade of civil rights challenges and victories, my father taught us to have great respect and admiration for Martin Luther King and his tireless pursuit of equality. My father knew all too well about the inequality, unbalanced scales, and injustices suffered by African Americans. Even when I was young, black patrons had to sit in the back rows at my father's concerts when he performed in the South. It made no sense to me. Why would white fans buy my father's records and pay for expensive tickets to see him perform, yet refuse to let my dad's own people sit in the seats next to them? My father used his voice to support civil rights and Dr. King's mission. He would pay a heavy price for doing so and was banned from the state of Georgia, where he was born. My father would use that action against him as motivation to fuel his tireless pursuit of perfection in music and to raise him to another level in society. He knew his music was a universal language, and he created music that bridged the hearts of all races. The only way my father could fight his way through the racial divide in our nation and around the world was through his music. Eventually, the state of Georgia apologized and honored my father in the state legislature, proclaiming his version of "Georgia on My Mind" the state song.

My father had battled poverty and racism his whole life. His closest friends were people who understood what it meant to be poor and black and make their way to a neighborhood like View Park through sheer grit, hard work, and talent. Southridge was a monument to my father's success, something tangible he could feel and experience. When he was just a poor musician playing for Lowell Fulson, Lowell told him that he should be on the corner selling pencils. My father never forgot that insult. It was humiliating, but it made him determined to prove to himself and everyone else that Fulson was wrong. My father went from living on soup to buying his own private jets. His legacy was written into the fabric of American culture. Music allowed him to transcend color in a segregated nation and to achieve the American dream, for himself and for us. He gave us freedom and choices in life. As long as God blessed my father with another day, he worked tirelessly to make the most of his opportunity.

My parents made it clear to us that we were no different from anyone else. They did not want us thinking we were better than other people. It was very important to my parents that we lived a normal life. One of the reasons they sheltered us from the media was to keep us as down to earth as possible.

One of the ways they kept our feet on the ground was to keep the ties to their roots strong. Family friends who had started out with them in Texas remained close. Several of them moved west when my parents did and remained like family members. Herbert Miller, my mother's best friend Bernice, and Jeff Brown had been around as long as I could remember. They had shared their humble beginnings, and now they shared in their prosperity. Nearly all of my mother's family came out and stayed with us at one point. Uncle James and my cousins played with us and went on trips with us as well. My sister, Evelyn, came out nearly every summer. We saw our grandmother regularly. And my granddad Sam, whom my mother says I favor, was often around. We would drive across LA to his little house on Sixtieth Street and spend the day. My father loved Granddad. Granddad had come up poor like my father, and the two of them would sit and talk about the old days. I always felt so connected to my grandparents and family who kept us grounded; they were an important part of my life as well.

But nothing pointed out how far my mother had come more than a trip to Richmond, Texas. The little house where my mother grew up, and where my great-grandmother and uncle still lived, was as far removed from our home on Southridge as you could imagine. The property was on the far side of the tracks in what was once called the colored section of town. Mama Lee's acreage included small clapboard houses with outdoor plumbing. The place had supported crops and livestock when my mother was a child, but as work grew scarce and succeeding generations moved away, the land became overgrown. The grass was half as tall as I was, and to get through it, we had to cut a path with machetes. There were snakes hidden in the grass, and I was terrified of them. My great-grandfather Mike Griffin's parents had bought the land and divided it among their children decades earlier, each child getting ten acres. Mama Lee always called him "my Mike" and spoke fondly of his beautiful red hair. His hair was another part of our heritage. Red hair had been passed down to my mother and to all three of us boys, though Bobby was the only one whose hair remained red.

My father remodeled Mama Lee's house to make things more comfortable for her and Uncle George. But even then, her home was small and humble. Whenever we drove down the dirt road to Mama Lee's for a visit, Uncle George would be waiting outside for us. Uncle George was as country as they come but he always welcomed us with a broad smile and a "Hey, y'all." Mama Lee seemed impossibly old to us. She still knew all the old slave spirituals. She wasn't much more than a generation removed from slavery herself. Her grandparents had been slaves. She would sit us on her knee and sing the old spirituals. She was as sweet a person as you would ever find. My mother calls Mama Lee her hidden jewel, the most precious of souls hidden in the body of a plain old country woman.

There was a small church on the property, Zion Watchtower, where generations of my relatives had worshipped, and so did we when we visited. Most of my ancestors on my mother's side are buried nearby. When Mama Lee died at ninety-eight, we stood together in that tiny country church and sang the spirituals she loved. She was laid to rest with her family and the rest of our ancestors. When the property was finally sold, the family put it in the contract that the church was not to be torn down. The new owners not only kept the church, they repaired it. An active congregation worships there to this day.

THE CHRISTMAS AFTER my father came home from rehab had a special meaning for our family. It was the first clean Christmas he had ever celebrated. My father's valet, Vernon, and I climbed the tall ladder onto the roof and decorated it for the first of many Christmases there. We put up a Santa and sleigh with all eight reindeer and hung lights around the outside of the house. Inside, we put up a big white tree covered with red globes. It was the perfect seventies Christmas tree.

On Christmas morning that year I woke up at about four, too excited to go back to sleep. I decided to sneak downstairs and take a look under the tree. I was too old to believe in Santa Claus, but my brothers still did, and I wasn't quite willing to give up the belief. I wanted there to be a Santa. Even if there wasn't, I knew there would be a pile of amazing presents under the tree.

I crept quietly down the big staircase in my bare feet and peeked around the corner. A light wheel flashed colored lights onto the tree like a mirror ball on a dance floor. The tree was surrounded with big, gift-wrapped boxes, and in the middle of them was a shiny gold bike with a banana seat. It was for me! I knew it. I heard someone move. Was it Santa? I excitedly scanned the room. It wasn't Santa Claus. It was my father, sitting quietly in the chair by the Oriental coffee table.

He was dressed in his nice robe, with his glasses off. His head was lowered and he was singing softly. It was a Christmas song. I don't remember which one. As he sang softly to himself, his body was relaxed, at peace. I sat down to watch him. He didn't know I was there. Everyone else was asleep. It was just me and Dad.

I must have watched him for almost forty-five minutes as he continued to sit there, quietly singing Christmas songs. After a while he got up and walked around the room, touching things, feeling the presents, running his hands over my bike. He sang as he walked, bobbing and weaving to the music in his head. Finally he made his way over to the corner of the room. His grand piano was there, the top raised. On the edge of the piano were the plate of cookies and glass of milk we'd left for Santa. My father picked up the glass and plate, still singing, and made his way back to the chair. He sat down, put the milk on the table beside him, and began to eat the cookies, holding the plate close to his mouth so the crumbs wouldn't spill.

As soon as he took the first bite, I rose to my feet in a flash and shouted, "Daddy! Hey, Daddy! No! That belongs to Santa!"

At the sound of my voice my father almost came out of his skin. He jumped out of the chair, scattering cookies everywhere. He was looking around, his head swinging back and forth, trying to locate the sound, startled and confused.

"Where's Santa, Daddy?"

My dad turned sideways, locating my voice, and blurted out the first thing that came to his mind. "Santa ain't comin', man. You ain't in bed. He ain't comin'. Go to bed!"

I turned and ran up the stairs as fast as my legs would go. I wasn't about to stick around and get in more trouble with my dad.

I had ruined his moment. He had probably just finished putting my bike together when I came downstairs. He loved putting together our bikes; it was one of his favorite things. He sent Vernon home after all the presents were under the tree, and this was his moment to savor. He was in the moment, amid the sounds and scents of Christmas, running his hands over our gifts and imagining our excitement when we woke up in the morning. It's a magical time for a father. Years later I would know that feeling as I put gifts under the tree for my daughters and pictured their faces as they opened them. For my dad, who never had Christmas as a boy, it must have felt like a miracle. My mother said it filled him with joy to be able to provide us with the kind of Christmas he had always dreamed of. The only toys he had as a child were the ones he made.

That Christmas, though, there was an added source of joy. That Christmas, his body and mind were at peace. That night, as he listened to the music of the silence, it sang only of peace on earth and goodwill toward men, and his soul sang back with joy.

CHAPTER 10

Move On Up

Move on up

towards your destination.

—CURTIS MAYFIELD

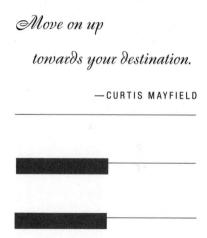

M Y PARENTS MADE ONE EXCEPTION TO THEIR PRIVACY
rule. The summer my father returned to performing after rehab,
my parents allowed the press into our home. Questions were still circulating as he returned to work again: Would the famously addicted musician be able to perform as he had before rehab? Could he stay clean under
the pressure of the public eye? My father invited reporters from *Life* magazine to see for themselves. He started by showing them his two planes, his
new studio on West Washington Boulevard, and his tour bus. He invited
them to Southridge and walked around the house and grounds with them,

chatting with the interviewer while he showed them our home. I trailed along behind him like a little shadow. Afterward, he let them take a family picture. The photograph shows us standing in the curved driveway of our home. My father, dressed in black, is holding my mother's hand. She smiles into the camera, looking contented and relaxed. David and Bobby cling close to my mother, David's hand resting protectively on little Bobby. The scar from the accident is clearly visible on the corner of Bobby's mouth. I stand behind my brothers, grinning into the camera. On July 29, 1966, the *Life* article, entitled "The Comeback of Ray Charles: Music Soaring in a Darkened World," hit the newsstands. It featured photos of my father's personal life, a lengthy interview, and pictures of his triumphal return to Carnegie Hall. Ray Charles was back.

The *Life* photo shoot was the only time my parents allowed the media to have access to our family. This was long before the paparazzi took over Hollywood. There were never any photographers outside our house, even when my dad's problems were spread all over the newspapers. Dad never allowed pictures of the family in his publicity material. He tried to keep our lives private because his was so public. But no matter what they did, my parents could not shelter us completely. Our house on Southridge was on the Tour of Stars' Homes route. Buses filled with tourists would pass by, stopping long enough for everyone to take pictures. If my brothers or I were playing outside when the bus pulled up, people would point and say, "You know whose son that is? Ray Charles's. That's Ray Charles's son." People walking by the house would also stop us and ask, "Are you Ray Charles's son? What's he like?" No one ever said, "How are you?" It was always, "Wow! You're RC's son!" Everyone always asked us personal questions about my father. We were continually bombarded by people wanting to see inside our house. When new friends visited for the first time, they often raved about my father's gold records and went on and on about how amazing our home was. Sometimes we never got around to playing. They were so excited about being in Ray Charles's home that they forgot I was there.

As his oldest son and namesake, I was like a walking billboard. I used my legal name Ray Robinson, but it never seemed to make much difference. Adults would point at me and say, "You know who this is? Ray Charles Jr. Yes, Ray Charles is his father." They would smile at each other and look at me like they knew me. I was shy, and the unwanted attention made me very uncomfortable. David, Robert, and I tried as hard as we could to blend in and not stand out as Ray Charles's children. But everywhere we went, we were reminded.

Just as there were always people who wanted to be near me because I was Ray Charles's son, there were others who hated me for it. Kids would say, "I heard your daddy uses drugs" or "Your daddy cheats on your mother."

I would defend my father and say, "Well, he's taking care of us just as good as your dad." And as on Hepburn, I had to fight. I was always in fights. So was David. If my mother caught us, we would be punished, but we would always start up again. The worst part was that I could never be sure who my friends were.

Somebody was always trying to steal something from me. Once some older kids who were visiting my home with a friend of mine were trying to take clothes from my closet. They weren't even supposed to be in my room, but I wanted to show off my model car collection. When I caught them actually walking toward the front door with some of my things, I stopped them and said, "Are you kidding me? Do you think I'm really going to stand here and let you steal my things right under my nose?"

My mother overheard us talking and came out into the foyer. The next thing they knew, she was in their faces. "We invite you into our home, and this is what you do? You disrespect us? Now you put Ray Jr.'s things down, and if I ever see you around my family again, I swear I'll call the sheriff's department and have you arrested. Get yourselves out of my house, and don't you ever come around here again." They couldn't get out fast enough. As soon as they left, she called the sheriff's department and told them what had happened. I don't think those boys got much of a welcome from "Cotton," the sheriff's officer who patrolled our neighborhood, when he caught up with them. Nobody disrespected my mother.

I was constantly defending myself to other kids about the way we lived. They justified their behavior by saying, "Well, you're rich, I'm not, so . . ." The few times I left the garage open for a minute, someone would steal my minibikes. I had two minibikes and several other things stolen in the middle of the day. I suspected they were taken by some of the same kids who had tried to steal things out of the house. The worst part is that the thieves were other black kids. It really bothered me. I took it more personally because I was being robbed by my own.

When I told my father about it, he said, "Be true to yourself. You know who you are. You need to watch who you bring around. Not everybody around you is your friend. They may want to peer into your life, and they may just want to use you to do that. Not everybody belongs in your private space, son. Be careful. But remember, not everybody you meet is going to have their hand out. Some of them really are your friends."

My mother knew exactly how we felt. She was Mrs. Ray Charles, and people were always trying to dissect her life, especially with all the rumors swirling around her marriage. She never made an effort to explain. She didn't feel she needed to explain herself to anybody. As for our affluent lifestyle, she told me, "Son, your father works hard to maintain a high standard of living for us. I don't care what anybody says about it. People will continue to spread rumors. It is not anyone's business what your dad does and where he is every moment of the day. You have nothing to explain." Those were lessons well learned. My parents had the foresight to know that people were going to try to attach themselves to us for all of the wrong reasons.

Over time I absorbed my parents' lessons and learned who I was and how I would deal with those around me. I've met a lot of people over my lifetime. My parents wanted me to know people from all walks of life. My father would laugh and say, "People are people. You don't talk to people just because they come from a certain background. You talk to them because you want to know more or have a good feeling about that person. That can happen with people from many walks of life. You never know who you're going to meet. That's why you always treat everyone with the utmost respect."

My mother put it more simply. "If that was Jesus, how would you treat him? Treat everyone as if you were meeting Jesus." She told us to treat people with the same respect we wanted from them. We were to be cordial and nice, but we were also to look them in the eye and get a feel for who they were. She taught us to use good judgment.

It was never important to me to spend time with other celebrity kids. I did grow up with Ike and Tina Turner's sons. We were close friends with Craig, Ike Jr., Ronnie, and Michael. I was a little bit older than they were, but my brothers hung out with them a lot. They lived just a few blocks away, and they were all musicians. Tina was extremely nice and cordial to us. She and my mother spoke on occasion by phone. Her four sons were always at our house.

Despite my frustration with being identified primarily as Ray Charles's son, I was fiercely proud of my father and longed to be like him. At the same time I was downplaying my father's name, I would try on his clothes. My father had a lot of clothing that he rarely wore, and sometimes I would raid his closet for something to wear to school. I'd borrow his coats, especially his leather ones. They were too big, so they hung on me. I would take his shoes and put tissue in the toes to keep them on. His velvet shoes were my favorite. I looked like an elf with the toes stuffed full of tissue and pointed up. All dressed up in my dad's clothes, I thought I was the coolest thing since sliced bread. Wearing his clothes made me feel close to him in a different way. I'd walk into the kitchen dressed, all ready for school. My mother would take one look at me and say, "Go right back upstairs and take those clothes off! You look like a little pimp." I never made it out the door.

I was square as a cube from the day we arrived in View Park until the twelfth grade. I went to school, studied hard, and came straight home. I didn't smoke or do drugs, and the parties we had with our friends were good clean fun. We swam, shot baskets, played tennis, and shot pool in the entertainment room. I knew that being Ray Charles Jr. was a huge responsibility. I wanted to make them proud.

Though my father never really gave us the guidance I hoped for, I think he did the best he could. He had never had a father or grandfather to advise him, and he lost his mother very young so he didn't really know how to give us advice. My father did teach me the basics, however. He told me that family always came first and that seemed like a paradox based on his past behavior. He taught me to be myself and never to let anyone tell me who I am. He cautioned me to be independent and to work hard because he wouldn't always be there and one day I would have to make it on my own. He always kept me grounded by reminding me, "No matter how successful you become, you're still a black man in America." Respect was especially important to him, especially for our mother. He would accept nothing less.

When my mother told him that my brothers or I had disobeyed her, he would go ballistic. He would call us into his office downstairs to talk with us. Usually when we were in that office, we were there to get a lecture. If we tried to defend ourselves, he would slam his hand down on the desk and shout, "Shut up! I'm your father. I don't want to hear that you're not listening to her again. Your mother runs things around here. She loves you and she would never guide you in the wrong direction. All I know how to do is play the piano and sing." He didn't believe in spanking us, but he did believe in strict punishment. He was very clear about what was going to transpire if we did not listen to our mother.

He would deal with our behavior when our mother asked him to, but he would not deal with the emotional aspect of our experiences. If we got upset about something that had happened, he would ask us very objectively, "What did you learn?" If we didn't answer to his satisfaction, he would tell us, "This is how I would approach it." He was always calm and analytical but firm. I think it was his way of dealing with our question in the third person, taking himself out of the equation. He always wanted to play the good cop because he was not home enough.

Without question, though, it was my mother who saw to our well-being twelve months a year. Looking back, I don't know how she managed. Our first year in View Park, she had to take care of three very active boys while coordinating the move, adjusting to a new neighborhood, visiting my father in rehab, and coping with the stress of the impending trial.

And that was only the first year. During our first five years on Southridge, she had to have a series of operations to remove the adhesions resulting from the surgery on her appendix, and Dr. Foster had her on frequent bed rest. Though she had survived peritonitis against the odds, she battled the long-term effects for the rest of her life. She was never truly healthy after that. She eventually underwent ten operations and coped with pain and exhaustion almost daily. Pictures of her at Southridge often show her with a scarf or net covering her hair. She lost her hair several times as a result of the surgeries and physical stress. My brothers and I never understood how ill our mother was and how close she had come to death. She would remain ill for a long time.

Our friends were always welcome at our house. I think my mother felt more comfortable having them there where she could keep an eye on us. Our friends ate dinner at our house as often as they did at home. Every night at six o'clock she would serve up a full meal of soul food: corn bread, yams, pork chops, cabbage, greens, smothered steak, or barbecued chicken. Everyone loved her cooking. No wonder they wanted to eat at our house. Once anyone stepped through the door, my mother demanded they show respect, and everyone respected my mother.

And our mother made sure we respected our father as well. That was very important to her. She would tell us about our father's dreams, his struggles, the odds against him. If we complained that he was gone too much, she would say, "Look around you. When you feel like you're doing without something, look around. You've never missed a meal." And if I came to her with rumors I'd heard about him, she always told me, "Ignore the rumors. They're not your problem. Let me handle that. It's your job to respect and love your father."

My mother couldn't help us much with our studies as we grew older because she had little education herself. But she kept on us about our homework, visited teachers, stayed involved, never let us skip school. I only ditched class in high school once in my life, to go to the beach with my friends. I would get caught and Mr. Childress, the vice principal, would call my mother immediately. When I got home, she asked me where I had been, and I told her the truth. She was really upset, saying, "What if something had happened to you? I wouldn't have known where you were." I took my punishment, and I never did it again. More important, my mother did not need to constantly worry about me: she had enough on her plate.

My mother kept us busy and made sure we kept to the straight and narrow. Most important, she led by example. She never took drugs or drank, and she expected the same of her sons. She didn't care what was going on around us. She expected us to follow the standard she kept for herself. My mother brought us up right. She kept us very close, and she dedicated her life to raising us as men the Lord would approve of. Growing up, it was virtually impossible to lie to my mother or go against her wishes. Even when I tried, even when my friends laughed at me, I just couldn't do it. I knew right from wrong. She prayed for us and for our father every day. I believe that God has blessed her with a long life because of her belief in him. If I had adhered to her wisdom as an adult, I would have avoided many traps and much suffering.

Only once as a kid did I go against her teaching about smoking and drinking. My mother liked to give card parties for her friends, and though she didn't drink or smoke herself, many of her friends did. After the parties there would be cigarette butts all over and liquor left in the glasses until the maid cleaned up the next morning. David and I loved to go in after the parties and pretend to smoke and drink. We thought we were so cool. Then one day Mom came through the door and caught us. We knew we were busted in a big way. My mother said, "So you want to smoke and drink? Well, okay."

She got a glass and filled it with Cutty Sark, and then she got my father's unfiltered Kools. She sat there in front of us, holding a belt, and made us smoke and drink it all. First she made us smoke the cigarettes. Then she made us drink the liquor. It tasted terrible. We threw up several times, but she made us finish it. It took us about an hour and a half. By then we were crying and begging to stop. Afterward we were very sick. My father fell down laughing when he heard about it. The story became

My father performing during radio appearances, early 1950s. *(Collection of Ray Charles Robinson Jr.)*

My first Christmas, 1955. *(Collection of Ray Charles Robinson Jr.)*

My mother and father with Tom Bradley, city councilman (and later the mayor) of Los Angeles, 1960s. *(Collection of Ray Charles Robinson Jr.)*

With my brothers Robert and David, early 1960s. *(Collection of Ray Charles Robinson Jr.)*

My uncle George Griffith and great-grandmother Nora Griffith (Mama Lee). *(Collection of Ray Charles Robinson Jr.)*

My first baseball team, the Indians, with coaches Mr. Kaiser and Mr. Ramirez, 1965. *(Collection of Ray Charles Robinson Jr.)*

My father in the privacy of his hotel room during a European tour, 1960s. *(Collection of Ray Charles Robinson Jr.)*

My father performing in concert, 1967, with the Raelettes: Mary Clayton, Alex Brown, Gwen Berry, and Clydie King. *(Collection of Ray Charles Robinson Jr.)*

At a nightclub where my father was performing, 1967. From left: my mother, her friend Viola, Mrs. Durham, Chet and Sadie Shepard, Mrs. Adams, and Reverend David Durham. *(Collection of Ray Charles Robinson Jr.)*

My parents sharing a moment together,
1967. *(Collection of Ray Charles Robinson Jr.)*

My father performing in concert, 1967.
(Collection of Ray Charles Robinson Jr.)

Christmas Day with Dad and the family, 1967. *(Collection of Ray Charles Robinson Jr.)*

With my father on Christmas Day, 1969. Spending time together as a family on Christmas morning was always very important to my father. *(Collection of Ray Charles Robinson Jr.)*

At my graduation from Westchester High School, 1973, with (from left) David, Robert, my father, Mrs. Hall, my mother, Effie Harris (Grams), and Uncle James. *(Collection of Ray Charles Robinson Jr.)*

My graduation present, a Porsche 911T. *(Collection of Ray Charles Robinson Jr.)*

My mother and father at my wedding to Duana Chenier, 1980. *(Collection of Ray Charles Robinson Jr.)*

With my daughters, Erin and Blair, at the LA Zoo.
(Collection of Ray Charles Robinson Jr.)

Erin and Blair on Easter Sunday.
(Collection of Ray Charles Robinson Jr.)

With Stevie Wonder after the taping of *Ray Charles: 50 Years in Music*, 1991. *(Collection of Ray Charles Robinson Jr.)*

My father with Terry Howard in the studio at RPM, Ray Charles Enterprises. *(Collection of Ray Charles Robinson Jr.)*

My father's beautiful and infectious smile. *(Dennis Shirley)*

My father at his Los Angeles studio, March 17, 1998. *(Phil Hewsmith)*

My father surrounded by his children during our family brunch in Los Angeles, 2002. *(Collection of Ray Charles Robinson Jr.)*

With my father. Even though my eyes are closed in this picture, it is very special to me. Many of my personal photos were destroyed in a flood, and this is one of the few images I have of me and my father together. *(Collection of Ray Charles Robinson Jr.)*

Where my father is laid to rest. *(Collection of Ray Charles Robinson Jr.)*

With my mother and
my brothers, Robert and
David, at the premiere
of the movie *Ray*, 2004.
*(Collection of Ray Charles
Robinson Jr.)*

Sharing a happy moment with my girlfriend
Rhonda's parents, Rod and Elaine Bailey,
2004. *(Collection of Ray Charles Robinson Jr.)*

With Erin and Blair at the premiere of *Ray*,
2004. *(Collection of Ray Charles Robinson Jr.)*

Elaine Chenier, 2008. Though Duana and I have divorced, her mother and I remain close and I love her dearly. *(Collection of Ray Charles Robinson Jr.)*

At my granddaughter Kennedy's baptism, with Rhonda and my mother, 2008. My brother Reverend Robert Robinson performed the ceremony. *(Collection of Ray Charles Robinson Jr.)*

Blair and Erin with their mother, Duana, at Erin's bridal shower, 2009. *(Darren Williams)*

Erin and Kennedy before the wedding ceremony, 2009.
(Don Ptashne)

Kennedy at Erin's wedding. *(Don Ptashne)*

Escorting Erin down the aisle.
(Collection of Ray Charles Robinson Jr.)

Erin and Blair with my mother at the reception.
(Collection of Ray Charles Robinson Jr.)

Touched by artist Andrew Lakey's story of overcoming addiction, my father commissioned two paintings of his signature angels. Here, my father is shown running his hand over one of the paintings in 1990. The angels were art he could see. *(Courtesy of Andrew Lakey)*

Seventeen years later, I met Andrew, and he traced my profile for his Silhouettes & Shadows project. *(Doug Brown)*

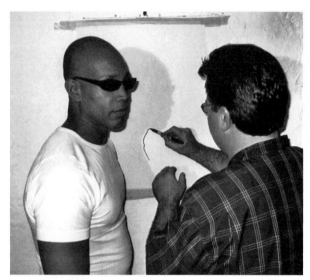

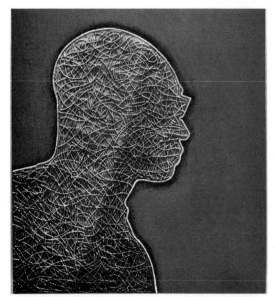

The finished painting, celebrating my journey out of the darkness of addiction with the help of my father, symbolized by light shining down on me. *(Doug Brown)*

legendary in our household. It cured me for years of wanting to smoke or drink. My mother did not have to worry about me coming home drunk or stoned.

In so many ways, my mother was both father and mother to us. She spoke to us about everything she thought we needed to know. About life and people in general. Even about girls. How embarrassing! It was my mother who taught me etiquette and how to dance. And it was my mother who talked to me about the facts of life. She even gave me a pack of condoms. I told her, "But Mom, I'm not doing anything."

She sighed and said, "I know you're not, but you will. You don't think you will, but at some point it will happen. And when it does, I just want you to be responsible." I took it all to heart.

More than anything else, it was playing sports that helped me internalize the lessons my parents were teaching me. By the time we moved to Southridge, sports were becoming increasingly important in my life. My mother had always encouraged us to play sports, if nothing else to keep us busy and help us burn off energy. Surprisingly, my father was a big sports fan. In blind school he had run races holding on to a guide wire and played ball by listening to the ball rolling on the ground. He was fiercely competitive. Luckily, we lived in a city with some of the best sports commentators in the world. I grew up listening to Chick Hearn announcing Lakers games. Vin Scully's voice on the radio during Dodgers games became the backdrop to my childhood. At home in our playroom or driving in the car, we listened to him every spring and summer. My father loved Vin Scully.

If the family attended a Dodgers game while Dad was in town, he would sometimes go with us. My father disliked being in crowds since he couldn't see people coming, and there was too much noise for him to track their movements with any accuracy. People were always coming up to him, shouting, "Mr. Charles!" He tried to be polite about it, but it unnerved him, especially if they grabbed him unexpectedly. At Dodger Stadium he would walk behind Duke or my mother with his arms interlocked with theirs until we found our seats. He always brought his radio along so he could listen to Vin during the game. It was a Super Zenith radio that came in a black leather case. When he folded down the case, the inside had readouts from time zones around the world. It was cool. He carried it with him when he was on the road. Radio was his medium for watching sports. He would sit in the seats with us, feeling the sunshine and the breeze on his face, holding the radio to his ear. He could hear the crack of the bat when someone connected, the cheering and heckling from the crowd, all the while listening as Vin explained what was happening on the field just yards beneath us.

My father even tried to play sports with me. He had taught me to ride my bike when I was little, and he wanted to be able to play ball with me. He decided to give football a try. One afternoon when we were outside, he told me to throw him the football. I didn't want to do it because I was afraid he'd get hurt, but he kept insisting. What I didn't understand was that when he said, "Throw the ball to me," he actually meant I should roll or hand him the ball. That's how they played catch at the St. Augustine school for the blind when he was a kid. So when I finally threw him the football and he bent down to catch it on the ground, it hit him in the head and knocked his glasses off. He didn't say anything.

I said, "Dad?"

Instead of answering, he picked up his glasses and continued to play with me.

When I became interested in baseball, he took an interest in it, too. He asked me to describe the baseball bat, and he ran his hands over it, trying to get the feel of it. Since my father couldn't teach me how to bat or catch like the other fathers could, I had to figure it out on my own. I had to learn everything in fast-forward. Baseball games were like on-the-job training for me. My team was named the Indians. I became good at baseball very quickly, but I really didn't know what I was doing. I was batting cross-handed. Mr. Kaiser and Mr. Ramirez were our coaches. They kept telling me I was going to hurt myself if I kept batting with my wrists crossed, but I wouldn't listen to them. I figured I was doing great the way I had taught myself, so I didn't want to change. But I did correct my grip. One afternoon my father came to one of my games at Baldwin Vista Park. He sat in the bleachers next to my mother while she narrated the game for him. I was hitting the ball like crazy that day, but the coaches kept telling me, "You're going to hurt yourself!" Every time I got a hit, Mr. Kaiser would shake his head and say, "Well, there goes Ray Jr. again."

My father perked right up when he heard that. He beamed his famous smile and said, "That's my son." He would sit on the sidelines and listen attentively to what was happening on the field. He gradually stopped coming to my baseball games once my schedule started conflicting with his.

A few seasons later, I was voted most valuable player. I was thrilled. It was the biggest night of my life. More than anything, I wanted my dad to be there. He promised he would be, but when the night came, he had to leave before I got my trophy. I was heartbroken, and for a long time I was angry and hurt by his absence that night. It was only later that I understood what had really happened. When I had originally asked him to come, he changed his performance schedule so he could be there. The change was complicated because it involved a lot of musicians and a crew, but he did it. And then at the last minute, the promoter changed the time, and there was nothing my father could do but handle his business concerning his performance. Almost eleven years old, I was too young to understand. All I knew was that my dad wasn't there. It hurt him as deeply as it did me because he wanted to keep his promise. Years later he wrote about it in his book. It still bothered him. I understood, and I let go of the disappointing memory. Instead I think of him holding my MVP trophy and showing it to people with great pride.

My father became a serious advocate for the YMCA during the years I was playing. He supported our sports leagues, making sure we had uniforms. Kids who otherwise couldn't afford to participate were able to take part in after-school programs because of my dad. But it was my mother who threw heart and soul into our teams. Because the teams depended on volunteers, all the fathers were required to participate in team activities. My father, of course, couldn't do that. So my mother had to get special permission to perform the duties usually performed by the fathers. She became our stat keeper, raised money, worked in the concession stands, and got other celebrities and entrepreneurs to sponsor our team, including Nancy Wilson.

What she couldn't do herself, she found someone else to do for us. She found mentors for me. One way or another, she made sure I was introduced to men who could help me evolve as a young man. It was through these men that I was able to develop into a good young man and a great athlete. Men like Mr. Kaiser, Paul Ramirez, General Hall, Maurice Hill, Leonard Harris, and Jonathan Leonard took the time to mentor me not only through sports but in life. I found structure in sports, and I learned what it meant to be a team player. We planned things as a group. Before every game, my YMCA Thunderbirds coaches led us in the Lord's Prayer. These men taught me discipline, respect, and sportsmanship. Their sons became my friends. Sports helped teach me what it meant to win and how to lose.

I wonder now how my father felt about being the only dad who couldn't take his son camping or help him swing a bat. It must have been hard for him. Herbert Miller says my father's blindness was a huge issue for him when it came to being a father. He had never done most of the things we were interested in and had no idea how to relate to them. Dad had received only a basic education, designed to help him survive as a blind man in a sighted world. Though extremely intelligent, he had never had a chance to go to college. Outside of his music, he worried that he had nothing to teach us.

I always wondered how my father felt about his blindness, and he used to say, "I'm not blind. I just can't see." He seemed to move through life like a sighted person. In reality, everything he did had to be adjusted to his lack of sight. Whenever he went to a new space, someone had to show him where everything was, lead him around, and point things out until he had a chance to memorize their positions. My mother had been doing that all my life. When he was walking quickly down the hall at home or at his studio during the day, he would say, "Beep! Beep!" to let people know he was coming. If we were walking somewhere in a hurry, he would interlock his arms with ours. In a crowd, he would get behind one of us and put his hand on our shoulder to guide him through. I saw him do this with my mother, Duke, and Vernon, and eventually with me, countless times.

His blindness forced him to trust people. No matter how many precautions he took, he could never be certain what was going on around him. In order to function, he had to believe that the people he relied on were telling him the truth. Some people took advantage of my father's blindness, hiding the truth from him and twisting the truth to their own advantage. That was one reason my mother taught him to print his name when they were first married. She wanted him to be able to sign things himself with his own unique signature, not just use an X or have someone else sign for him.

My father always talked like he could see. If we were looking for something, he would say, "I saw it over there." He didn't carry himself like a blind man. David Braithwaite, who became his sound engineer when I was thirteen, told me he'd hear people say, "Man, this guy thinks he can see." My dad had an uncanny ability to conceptualize spaces in his mind. He would tell Dave, "You gotta concentrate. A man that's sightless has to concentrate, 'cause he has to remember." Nothing frustrated him more than losing his concentration. After a long session at the sound board, he sometimes knocked over his signature cup of coffee. He'd forgotten it was there. He would be upset for the rest of the day. Sometimes after singing for hours, he'd forget his exact location and walk into a wall. There would be a *smack* and the sound of cursing. Everybody in the studio knew better than to try to help him when that happened. You didn't want to be in the room when he got back, either. I used to wonder how anybody could concentrate that hard every minute of the day. It must have been exhausting.

My father looked at things with his hands, like most blind people. That was his way. If he was curious about something, he would ask us questions while he felt it. He often did that when he was given a new toy. He wanted to know what it looked like, how it worked. He would listen carefully as we explained it to him, nodding his head and saying, "You don't say." That was his signature remark: "You don't say."

My father's love was in his touch. There was the way he always stood in front of me and my brothers and placed his hands on our heads, ran his arms down our sides, our shoulders, our faces, under our chins. He would place his hands on the sides of our bodies to see how much weight we had gained around our waists. He would pat us on the chest and the stomach, too. He had done this when each of us was born. And he would say, "You don't say."

I was a teenager when we finally talked about his blindness. He said he was scared when his mother told him he was losing his sight because he didn't know what that would mean, but that she was diligent in preparing him for a world of listening and touch. He could remember vaguely what his mother looked like but described her with loving accuracy. He remembered many of the beautiful things in life—the sun, the moon, flowers, basic colors, butterflies—but he also remembered how poor they were.

Being blind forced my father to develop acutely sensitive hearing, and he never took his hearing for granted. My dad had great respect for Helen Keller. Once he took me by my arms and said, "Can you imagine being in total darkness without light or sound?" He would talk about her genius and the genius of Beethoven, whom he admired greatly, and who could use vibration to compose his music. At one point my dad had an ear infection, and I believe he thought his hearing might be in jeopardy. He said that if he lost his music, he wouldn't know what to do with his life.

During those early years, he was confronted with the question of his blindness head-on. He was in Paris for his European tour and Herbert Miller was with him. They were sitting in my father's dressing room while my dad chatted with the promoter and a writer from the magazine *Paris Match*. They asked, "Mr. Charles, what if you had an opportunity to have an eye to replace the one you lost? What if you had an opportunity to see? Would you seize the opportunity if there was a possibility that surgeons could give your eyesight back to you?"

It was not an idle question. Swiss surgeons were performing a new type of procedure that had restored sight to several blind people. My father went to the College of Surgeons in Zurich to get a diagnosis. They examined my father's remaining eye and told him, "If you had a donor eye, we believe that if the retinas matched, we might be able to restore sight in one eye." So *Paris Match* published an article saying Ray Charles needed an eye. Within days, offers started pouring in. Thousands of people were willing to sell, or even donate, an eye for my father.

My father was shocked and energized by the possibility of seeing. He thought continually of what it could mean to his life. He kept thinking of new things. He would say to Herbert, "You know I don't—I wouldn't even be able to read. It would impact on everything I have learned. Everything that I know, I've learned being blind." It was conflicting. After a lifetime of blindness, the possibility of regaining his sight was overwhelming. He could be blind better than anyone. Ultimately, he decided against the surgery.

When I think about it now, I believe that God took my father's eyesight for a reason. I think perhaps God didn't want him to see the poverty all around him, the hell of the world for a poor black child in the South. My father heard about what was happening, but he never had to watch people being lynched, hosed, or shot as so many African Americans of his generation did. He didn't have to see this horror. Maybe God wanted my father's faith to be complete because he had to depend totally on Him. My father did walk by faith. His path was determined, his road paved by God. Perhaps my father's blindness was his greatest blessing. He was given a special vision to navigate through life with, and it was that vision that gave him his music.

THE YEAR MY CHILDHOOD drew to an end and I prepared to enter high school, two things happened. Robert Kennedy followed his brother in death. I was thirteen years old and in my last year at the Linfield School when he was assassinated. The shooting brought back all the pain of President Kennedy's assassination. The fact that he was killed in my own city made it even worse. Like the riots in Watts, Robert Kennedy's assassination took place too close to home.

Another devastating loss earlier that year was Dr. Martin Luther King Jr.'s assassination. All my life I had heard my parents speak of Dr. King. He was a friend of my father's. My mother had always spoken of him as a symbol of hope. At church and at school we were taught about Dr. King's struggle for human rights and equality for African Americans—for everyone. It was a time of such turmoil in America. It seemed like there was something in the news every day. The riots in Detroit. The Black Panther movement. I saw pictures of Huey Newton wearing a black tam and holding a rifle. Even in California, the Ku Klux Klan was burning crosses on lawns. In the midst of the chaos and hatred stood Dr. King with the promise of a better day. The March on Washington had brought together more than 250,000 Americans of all colors, united in one common cause. It was Dr. King's charisma and compelling plea to America to allow its black citizens genuine freedom that at last turned his followers into a thinking force, not just a working force. God had truly anointed him. But like so many of that generation who stood up for human rights, he was cut down in his prime. The Bible tells us there is no greater love than for one man to lay down his life for another. Dr. King laid down his life for millions of us.

At thirteen years old, I had already seen President Kennedy, Dr. Martin Luther King Jr., and Robert Kennedy shot down in front of our nation. I didn't know what to think. It was difficult to process, and I tried to understand the magnitude of those events. Our country was in great turmoil, with the African American still fighting for equality. The assassinations frightened me and served as a reminder to keep civil rights and being black in America in proper perspective. All three of these great men put their lives on the line to bring Americans together under the law. In the midst of all of his prosperity I worried about my father and the threats he continued to receive. When my dad insisted African Americans be allowed to sit in the front by the orchestra pit along with white concertgoers, he was banned from performing in the South. Some fans embraced his music, but they rejected his race. His music was colorless. If they could see past the color boundaries in the music, why couldn't they see past the color of our skin?

My parents took Dr. King's death very hard. At the forefront of our pursuit of human rights and equality in America stood Dr. King. Dr. King brought the promise of a better day, but he would not live to see it. My father went East for the funeral, and I sought refuge in the music once again—my father, Curtis Mayfield, Sam Cooke, Sly and the Family Stone, the Beatles, the Rolling Stones, Jimi Hendrix, Otis Redding, and the sounds of Motown. The music always lifted my soul. It transcended the boundaries of color and of hatred, creating one world inside the music.

CHAPTER 11

A Song in My Soul

And I'll get along as

long as a song, strong in

my soul.

—VINCENT YOUMANS, BILLY ROSE,
AND EDWARD ELISCU

WHILE THE HOUSE ON SOUTHRIDGE WAS BEING BUILT AS a home for our family, my father was also building a home for his music at 2107 West Washington Boulevard, a state-of-the-art studio with everything he needed to create music and rehearse his band. My first tour of the studio and offices was in 1965, about the same time we moved into our new house. My father and his manager, Joe Adams, showed us the office layout. The building had two floors. The first floor was rented out to the Urban League; the studio was on the second floor. My father's studio was a beautiful space with a minimalist layout and a simple, elegant design. The walls were plain and muted, and there were no windows. There was no art on the walls of the hallway, no furniture or decorative items to get in my father's way as he walked. He moved freely around the building, showing us everything. There were a conference room, small offices for assistants, a kitchen, and bathrooms. Joe Adams's office was on the right.

My father's office, the same size and basic design as Mr. Adams's, was across the hall on the left. It was very large, with a marble table and a piano. The walls were covered with his plaques and awards. There were private bathrooms and a room to store his tuxedos, travel bags, and Ampex tape recorders. My dad always took his Ampex recorders on the road with him when he wanted to work on some music while he was traveling. He had them built into a custom-made canvas case that looked like a suitcase. He could unfold it and use the Ampexes without having to take them out. When we lived on Hepburn, he kept the recorder in the closet, but now it was stored in his office at the studio.

My father was intensely proud of the recording studio. Everything was designed to meet his high standards. Tom Dowd, the sound engineer who recorded and mixed my father's early masters during the Atlantic days, built the original sound board for the studio. My father hadn't seen Tom since leaving Atlantic, but at the end of 1964, while the studio was being finished, Tom was in LA and called Dad to say hello. My father invited him to the new studio and showed him the partly assembled sound board. Tom finished building the three-track control board and taught my dad how to work it. The primary purpose for the third track was for my father's vocals.

Four years later, when David Braithwaite became my father's sound engineer, he rebuilt the board. Like Tom, Dave came from Atlantic and Motown, where they used eight-tracks. Dave totally upgraded the studio, gutting the old board and rebuilding it with eight tracks. In the years that followed, Dave redesigned the board several times, eventually building twenty-four tracks. He set the studio up with new tape machines, microphones, speakers, and headphones. Everything was the best, top of the line, with two echo chambers and four different equalizers. All of the components were built by hand like they were at Motown, even the tape machines. My father's studio had the best, most complex system on the West Coast. David's genius was what made it priceless.

Because my father loved electronics, he was interested in knowing everything about the studio's sound system. He drove the engineers crazy trying to do everything himself. Dave says he would get to the studio and find a pile of chopped-up tape from the night before where my father had stayed late or all night editing alone. There were some things an editor just could not do well if he could not see. It would take Dave half the day to put everything back together. It was like the bike my father put together for me when I was six. Sometimes the seat was adjusted wrong no matter how hard he tried. For the most part, though, the guys who did the technical work in the studio were amazed by my father's ability. He could remember exactly where everything was. He would plug jacks into the complicated board, adjust the controls, and locate components in a closet filled with hundreds of items.

From the time he first walked in the door, to the end of his life, the studio at 2107 was my father's refuge. After he came out of rehab, the studio was recovery. He had his toys, his sweets, and his special brew of coffee, gin, and sugar in his own private sanctuary. Most important, he had his music. He didn't have to hear anything he didn't want to hear while he was alone in the studio. There were no tears, no pain, no voices in his head. There was only the sound of music filling the room. He would sit at the console, puffing on a cigarette, listening to the sounds that only he could hear. Gradually the studio absorbed his scent, just as his office had at home on Hepburn, and Kool cigarettes and Cannon aftershave permeated the walls.

This studio also became his way of having a relationship with me. It was his comfort zone, the place where he was most himself. As I moved into my teens, he began inviting me to come down to the studio to visit him. He would tell me, "I'll be at the office. You can come down and hang out with the old man if you want to." At first Vernon would drop me off.

Later, I drove myself. It was the beginning of a new kind of relationship with my father, his attempt to give me quality time. In the studio with me, he tried to become the father that I needed.

He moved confidently around the room. Sometimes he would find a mike and cord and plug it in himself. If he needed a tape from the closet, he could pull it out unaided. I would sit there for hours and watch him work. The side bar of the studio console was my seat. I would sit to the left, and he would be at the board with his tapes stacked next to him. I watched him work on the tapes, sitting at the board with tape in his mouth, trying to find the levels of the horns, snare, hi-hat, and vocals. I watched him splice the tape the way Dave had taught him. He would listen intently to the tape, stop it, then bring it back. I couldn't figure out how the heck he did it. I watched his whole process as he went about making music and it was fascinating. The studio was his domain.

He showed me how the mixing board worked, and sometimes he had me assist him. When he wanted me to get something out of the closet, he would tell me exactly how to find it—go five boxes up, count three to the left, and pull out the red box. I don't know how he could remember all those numbers and details. Sometimes he had me set up the mike for him so he could sing. He taught me how to punch in for him from the control room to eliminate the sound of breathing. He wanted me to learn the sound board. He would tell me, "Well, this here is the EQ," and show me how it worked. Or he'd say, "Ray Jr., help me splice this tape." A few times we would do those things together, over and over. I think he enjoyed teaching me, bringing me into his world. As a father, he had to be excited at having the opportunity to show me the world he had created. I think he loved for me to be around. He couldn't teach me to throw a football or swing a bat, but in the studio, he was in his element. In his office, sometimes we would just sit and do nothing with the radio tuned to a ball game. He would sit back with his leg over the chair, smoking a cigarette and listening to Vin Scully. Most of the time he would be wearing the jumpsuit my brothers and I had given him for Father's Day. It was brown, with little gold buckles. He liked to change into it between shows. Terry

Howard, a close friend and his music engineer, remembers that jumpsuit well. My father was still wearing it thirty years later. He wore that suit until it fell apart. My father always kept the presents we gave him. Maybe putting on the jumpsuit made him feel close to us, just as wearing my father's clothes made me feel close to him.

Other times we would sit and listen to tapes of his music together. He would listen to the sound of his own voice with the volume low. He would listen to everything in the arrangements. I sat next to him, following the sound, asking him what he was listening for. And he explained to me. He told me what to listen for, describing the sounds in colors. It was in the studio, alone with my father, that I learned to really listen to music, that I fell in love with the process of making music. It was there in the studio that I began to realize how great my father was. There was no one like him.

A lot of the time, we just sat and talked. Alone in the studio, there was no one to interfere with our time together. We would sit virtually in darkness with just enough amber light coming from the ceiling for me to see. I would talk to him about what I was doing, and he would sit quietly and listen. Every now and then he would respond, "You don't say." That was his way of expressing understanding and interest.

Sometimes he would ask me about my brothers, I guess to see if he had missed something important my mother had forgotten to share with him. David and Bobby were taking piano lessons at the same time, and he was interested in their progress. He wanted to know what they were doing, how they were growing. He liked to hear me talk about David and Bobby. It gave him a glimpse into their lives. I knew he talked with my mother about them often, but he also knew that my mother had her own view. She loved us, good, bad, or indifferent. I think he wanted to get a different perspective from me. I believe he began to understand how much he didn't know about us, about our everyday lives and challenges. It bothered me sometimes that he didn't seem to get directly involved, that he always heard about things after the fact. Looking back, I don't think he knew how to be more involved. His own childhood was so different from ours that he couldn't relate. I believe he just wanted to live in his music twenty-four hours a day.

We would also talk about my mother. He was concerned about her health. He would ask me how she was doing physically, how her stamina was. I realized that even when he was recovering, he was extremely concerned about her health. Sometimes I would complain about her, telling my dad she was too demanding, too strict. Afterward he would talk to my mother about our concerns. I don't know what they actually spoke about, but he never repeated their conversations. If I continued to complain, he would tell me, "Hey, that is something you're going to have to discuss with your mother. We've spoken about that already. Speak to her." He always felt that she was doing an amazing job with us, that she was a remarkable woman.

He talked to me about discipline and focus. He was extremely disciplined in his work, and he wanted me to be the same way in mine. I was attracting a lot of attention as a baseball player, and that is when I started to feel that my future was in sports, not in music. I know he wanted me to go into music, but with baseball becoming more and more prominent in my life, he thought it was unlikely I would settle on a musical career.

There were certain topics he did not like to discuss. He was very uncomfortable talking about my interest in girls and avoided any discussion of dating or sex. It was up to my mother to deal with those things. It seemed strange to me that he wouldn't speak with us about it. I knew by then that he had a lot of affairs with other women. My father's affairs were always at my mother's expense, and he had several affairs throughout our time on Southridge. He couldn't very well talk about that with me. I think intimacy was an area he wanted to avoid discussing with me at all costs.

Sex wasn't the only topic that he tried to avoid. Whenever a conversation got intense or emotionally intimate, he wanted to leave or change the subject. When I would try to talk to him about painful issues, about my struggles and temptations, he would steer the conversation in another direction as quickly as he could.

There were only a few times in all those years of studio talks that he ventured into painful territory. I asked him what it was like when he was in rehab. I wanted to know if there was any pain. I told him how I had felt about seeing him so weak and vulnerable. He didn't say very much, just that it was mentally tough and physically painful in the beginning. He told me that later on it was hard in other ways. He mentioned that so many things flashed before his eyes, so many people and memories. That was the hardest part, he said, worse than the physical pain. You just have to make up your mind and do it, he told me.

The most painful subject of all, his childhood, was something he mentioned only once during those years. He told me about George, his mother, Mr. Pit, about the dark. He remembered how dark it was at night in the country with only the moon for light, before the darkness of blindness took even that away. He raised his glasses and wiped away tears as he spoke of these things. He told me that he and George were always together when they were little, always. Talking about his brother was almost impossible. "I just don't know why I couldn't pull him out of the tub." His voice broke, and he couldn't speak. It was clear that he still held himself responsible for George's death. Unable to say anything else, he stood up and walked out the door.

When he came back a few minutes later, we sat in complete silence for a while. He was very solemn, every now and then reaching up to wipe away some tears. After a couple of minutes, he started rewinding the tape and running it again. In my mind the only song I could think of was "Drown in My Own Tears." I could see him immerse himself in the music, listening to his own voice. The tape would end, there would be a moment of silence, and he would start playing it again. Gradually his tears stopped. I realized in that moment that the only way he could deal with the turmoil in his soul was to listen to his own voice singing the things he couldn't say. He went back to his music, for it was there that the pain was lifted. I had never seen him break down like that before. It was so painful to watch, and I didn't know what to say to him. I began to understand how hard it was for him to love somebody when everyone he had loved had left him alone or died.

His mother, George, Mary Jane. Everyone he was close to passed away. There was nothing I could do for him except sit next to him and listen to the music, hearing his voice that day in a whole new way.

During those weekends in the studio, I came to understand that all of my father's relationships were founded in music. The sound of my mother's voice singing had drawn him to her before they ever met. Sometimes I wonder, was it his soul and emotions that he poured into his music that attracted his women to him? He couldn't come to my room for fatherly talks like other fathers, but at the studio, he could speak to me about life, and music. I learned that the only way I could get close to him was to talk about the thing that he loved most, and that was music.

I made a point during those years to go down to the studio and watch the band rehearsals as often as I could. The studio was big enough to hold an entire twenty-piece orchestra. I saw the tryouts for the band and watched my father work tirelessly, driving the musicians into exhaustion as he tried to make the sound perfect. I began to absorb the rhythm of the office, the rhythm of the seasons. Every February and March the band rehearsed as they prepared to go on the road. Every summer they toured from city to city. Every winter there was a holiday concert. And every year, around Christmas, my father would come home for two months before the cycle started again.

Watching my dad work with the band was quite an experience. My father was a notorious perfectionist. He was very hard on his musicians, and some of them resented him for it. Dad knew exactly how he wanted everything to sound, and if a musician didn't understand what he wanted, he would go over that part until the musician got it. It was all about getting it exactly the way my dad wanted it. I remember watching rehearsal one day when my father was auditioning drummers for the road. This young Jewish kid, not much older than I was, came in. He sat down at the drums and started playing with the band, and he was really good, a young Buddy Rich.

I turned to my dad and said, "Dad, this guy's really good."

My father was shaking his head. "Yeah, he's good, but he's not readin' the charts." He was referring to the charts for the musicians to follow.

I said, "What do you mean?"

Dad said, "He's not readin' anything."

The kid was very good, but he had been listening to the other drummers auditioning and improvised instead of following the chart. That would never cut it with my father. No matter how good you were, if you could not read his charts and follow his directions exactly, you wouldn't last.

My father also had a particular way he wanted to record. He always recorded the band first, before the vocals and piano. Until they got used to playing for him, musicians were often shocked by the recording sessions. They were used to showing up, playing, and going home. It was never that simple with my father. He would make everyone work until he got exactly what he wanted, no matter how long it took. Nobody could get anything by him when it came to the music and the chords. He could hear every note and see every color of the spectrum in his music. My dad could listen to all seventeen pieces at one time and pick out every instrument. He'd say, "Drums, what are you doing? Can you read music or not? I don't understand." He could distinctly identify somebody who wasn't following the chart. He would stand over a guitar player and tell him how he wanted it to sound. The guitar player would say, "This? How's this?" And my dad would tell him no and demonstrate again. Hours would go by, and the band sometimes sat in the studio going over a song again and again until he was satisfied.

Part of the reason my father wanted the musicians to play with such precision was that he didn't want the band to get in the way of the Raelettes. He wanted the timing to be perfect. A drummer might not be a brilliant soloist, but if he could keep time exactly the way my father wanted, he was the man my dad would hire. Dave Braithwaite said they had a bass player for a while that wasn't all that good of a musician, but he was very good at following my dad's charts. He never got in the way of the Raelettes, or my father.

It took a long time for the engineers to figure out what my dad was doing with his singing. Dave called my father's approach "the art of singing." Once an engineer figured it out, he became invaluable. My dad would say, "Nope, we didn't get it done," and Dave would stop the tape. Often it would be just a tiny thing like adding an "oh." My father would count with the tape, and Dave would punch in the changes. It was very time-consuming, but the results were usually worth it. When I asked Dave what he learned about singing from my father, he replied, "There's a lot of music within the music." He watched my father eke out everything he could from the music without being repetitive. If you listen to some of the records, you'll hear the same line come through several times, and each time it is different. Dave talks about the way my father sang "Georgia." When it came time to record, he made dozens of small changes, like singing "I say Georgia" instead of just the one word "Georgia." All those hours spent in the studio—replaying, modifying, punching in again—produced the unmistakable sound that was my father's, and are what made him so great.

Everyone including me loved the unique way my father blended R & B, gospel, and country music. In 1962 he'd released two volumes called *Modern Sounds in Country and Western Music*. It caused a sensation at the time among people who thought of him as strictly a soul or R & B artist. But a big part of my father's genius was his determination not to be pigeonholed. He loved music, all genres of music, and he refused to be limited by other people's expectations. What people failed to understand when he first turned to country music was that it was in his heart. He was a huge Hank Williams fan. He had grown up in the Deep South listening to country and western and gospel music. My father had loved singing gospel with my mother and Cecil Shaw in the early days. Gospel was in his bones too. In gospel music, the choir sings and the congregation answers. That's what gave my father the idea of repeating lines in reverse order, backup singers first, him second.

Terry Howard remembers the call-and-response technique my dad took from gospel music. The background singers would sing the lead line, and then my father would sing the back line. He started using the technique when he recorded "I Can't Stop Loving You" as a country song.

The singers led with "I can't stop loving you," and my dad came in with "It's useless to say . . ." Fans thought that Ray Charles singing country music was a ridiculous idea until they heard him perform it. "I Can't Stop Loving You" shot to the top of the pop, R & B, and country charts and stayed at number one for a while. The call-and-response turnaround that came from his country roots became one of my father's musical trademarks.

During the height of my father's music and genius, he was surrounded by the brilliance of the musicians who worked with him—Hank Crawford, Leroy Cooper, Fathead Newman, and most of all, Sid Feller—who made it all work. During their years together, the music seemed to flow naturally from the chemistry they generated. Those years were magical, though I don't know if my father realized how special they were at the time. I always believed that Sid was one of the keys to my father's huge success in the sixties and early seventies. Terry believes it was Sid's orchestration, putting all of the elements together, that made it possible for my father to achieve the sound he did. Sid arranged for my dad, both in the studio and on the road. He knew what my father wanted. He understood that my father's singing had to be perfect and the band had to be perfect, and he knew what "perfect" meant to my dad. Sid worked with him better than anyone else. He understood what my father was trying to accomplish and was not argumentative about it. As Terry puts it, "Sid was able to be in the studio without Ray and still be Ray." Sid would storyboard the ideas or put them into basic note form and then give the arrangement to my dad to tighten up. Sid's arrangements were brilliant. When Sid and my dad got together, it was two geniuses at work. They blended together like the music itself. Sid knew how to orchestrate the arrangements to make the sounds blend perfectly. The records my father made at Atlantic before his collaboration with Sid were powerful, raw, and intense. "What'd I Say" was sheer raw power. "Georgia," "I Can't Stop Loving You," and "You Don't Know Me" were more refined, more melodic. Sid was there all through the ABC-Paramount years, through the high point and new direction of my father's music. It was never quite the same after Sid left.

Their music together became the standard and, like all great music, stood the test of time.

It always surprised me that my father was interested in my thoughts about music. I believe he interacted with me because he could only hear the music that was inside his head. He often asked me what music I liked, whose albums I collected. I believed all great musicians listened to other great musicians around them and those who preceded them. He didn't understand some of the rock-and-roll music I listened to, like the Rolling Stones, Traffic, Led Zeppelin, and Jimi Hendrix. He did like the Beatles. We talked about which Beatles songs we both liked, and ultimately he recorded some of them himself. I loved his versions of "Yesterday" and "Eleanor Rigby." All of my father's arrangements of the Beatles' music were fantastic, and he loved the writing of Paul McCartney and John Lennon.

My father believed in my ability to do whatever I wanted to do in life, but he never pushed me in a particular direction. Neither of my parents tried to mold my interests. They did not believe in pushing their children into a profession. When it came to music, my father would only say, "Maybe you'd like to try the piano" or "Maybe you'd be good with the soundboard." He never came right out and told me what to do. I never had a clear sense of direction about a musical career for myself. I did need his direction.

I didn't want to sing, but I did want to play. My dad got me a Fender Rhodes piano one Christmas, and I played it for a while. He never had the patience or time to sit down at the instrument and teach me, so he introduced me to Marvin Jenkins, who became my piano teacher. Marvin was a little man who looked like an African American Beatle. He dressed like one of the Beatles and his hair was styled like Paul McCartney's. I believed Marvin was the missing Beatle. He was a good teacher, but I could never stay focused. My talent was evident, but I did not devote enough time to practicing because of sports.

I started playing the drums around the age of fifteen and on one occasion my father walked by the den while I was listening to some jazz and fooling around on a drum pad. He asked me when I'd started playing the drums, and I told him I'd been playing with a friend's drum set for a while. The next thing I knew, he bought a Pearl drum set for me. He introduced me to Clarence Johnston, an excellent jazz drummer, and I started learning jazz drumming. I loved playing the drums, and Mr. Johnston was a strict, disciplined teacher. He and I spoke about me playing with my father's orchestra one day if I worked hard. But playing drums for my father was not a high priority for me. He was famous for being brutal on drummers. Being a drummer for my father would have been a nightmare. Also, I wanted to play jazz fusion. By now I was listening to Billy Cobham, Weather Report, Stanley Clarke, Return to Forever, Bob James, Herbie Hancock, Jaco Pastorius, and Miles Davis. Fusion took my mind in a whole new direction, but I was also deeply committed to sports. Nevertheless, I would continue to play the drums. Every now and then I would have my own jam sessions at Southridge. We thought our sound was cool, but the truth of the matter was we sounded like an orchestra warming up.

Learning and playing music when you are Ray Charles's namesake was a daunting task. I knew that even though my father would never push me, he wanted me to be in his business. I believe I had the genes, but I would never strengthen or develop my God-given talent. Becoming a musician required more attention and commitment than I had at the time. When I look back now, it's hard to forgive myself for my lack of focus. I had all the opportunity in the world to nurture the music inside of me, and I still long to play.

I never found a musical career, but I inherited a musical legacy nonetheless. Music was my father's greatest gift to me. It provided my father and me with a common language that enabled us to reach out to each other. Music was his lifeblood, the air he breathed. I do not think he would have survived without it. It got him through the hard times and enabled him to survive the memories that still clung to him. He could escape into a place where he could just be. The music was the thread that bound together his past, his present, his loves, his pain, and his dreams. It was the light through which he could see. When I remember my father in the studio with me, it's like being in a time capsule. I can still see him sitting at the console, framed by the amber light, listening to sounds only he could hear.

Music is my therapy and my refuge, as it was for my father. I came to understand why he loved music so much because I too could find that perfect melody or fragment of a lyric somewhere inside the music that helped me understand and cope with the joys and pains of my own life. I cannot express myself musically in the way my father did, but the music still runs through my body like a current. For years I woke up with music in my head. My mind remains a kaleidoscope of beautiful melodies and the colors of the changing seasons of life. I carry my father's music inside of me. It will never die.

CHAPTER 12

Trouble the Water

Jordan's water is chilly

and cold.

God's gonna trouble the

water.

—TRADITIONAL GOSPEL SONG

OUR HOME ON SOUTHRIDGE WAS LIKE A CASTLE, A fortress built to keep us all safe. It was at Southridge that we left behind the illness and death that had haunted Hepburn. It was at Southridge that my father got well. Southridge was our Camelot. What we couldn't know at the time was that Southridge would also be the place where the foundation of our family would finally crack. It happened slowly, like fissures spreading through a rock. By the time I finished high school, the walls of our home would come crashing down around us.

When I graduated from the eighth grade at the Linfield School after five years with Mrs. Reynolds, I begged my parents to let me leave private school and go to Westchester High School. Westchester was a large public high school with a good sports program and all of the school activities and prom night that go along with a traditional high-school experience. I loved Mrs. Reynolds dearly, and it was hard to leave, but I knew it was time to move on. Mrs. Reynolds remained my friend and mentor, and I continued to visit her through my college years. But I was a teenager by then, and I wanted to experience the variety of people and opportunities that Westchester High could give me.

At first Westchester was a real adjustment. I was accustomed to a self-paced curriculum with a lot of individual attention, so my transfer to Westchester presented new challenges. Suddenly I had to navigate a large campus and go to a different location for each class period. The classes were larger, and I now had to relate to several different teachers at the same time. It took me a while to adjust to the new demands and find a routine for my classes, homework, and sports. After the first few months, though, I settled into the new rhythm of Westchester just fine.

I also found myself dealing with my ethnicity in a new way. Westchester had begun to integrate only a few years before, gradually shifting from an all-white campus to a multiethnic one. All of the African American students at school congregated together. Most of them had a very different view of the world from mine. I was used to going to school primarily with white classmates, and my friends in my neighborhood came from upper-middle-class black families. I moved comfortably into my new environment as I was accustomed to having a lot of expectations placed on me. Some of the African American students at Westchester were bused in from different neighborhoods in South Central Los Angeles. They brought a new atmosphere to Westchester High School, and I wanted to fit in with the other African American students. I wanted to walk the walk and talk the talk. Fortunately, there were some wonderful teachers who were mentors. Then there was the vice principal, Mr. Childress.

Mr. Childress was very strict. When Westchester was first integrated, he would walk the halls between classes, trying to keep an eye on things to avoid what he thought would become a conflict. He was down on any students who didn't follow the rules or do their best. They got an earful from him. I had my days with Mr. Childress as well; other African American students simply hated him. They thought he was a racist. I believed that some days, too. But Mr. Childress was all about order and control. He was strict but fair, and he wanted us all to do our best. Whatever people said, everyone did their best work under Mr. Childress, and there was order on campus. Whenever I did well on something, he would smile at me and say, "Good job, Robinson." It felt fortunate that we had someone who cared about our future.

The teacher who taught me many life lessons was Mr. Spinoza. He was also a friend. We had discussions about my life struggles and my future. Mr. Spinoza helped me stay grounded. He kept an eye on what was going on around campus, and he would warn me about hanging out with the wrong individuals. He would say, "Look, all you're going to do is find trouble with them. You're better than that. Do the right thing." With Mr. Spinoza, it was always about doing the right thing and staying focused. If I got behind in my work, he would pull me aside and ask, "How come you're not in the library studying?" or "How's your project coming along? Are you devoting enough time to your projects at home?" I loved his drafting class. He taught us mechanical drawing, and he even encouraged us to create our own architectural designs. Because of his encouragement, I fell in love with architectural design. I seriously considered becoming an architect.

Westchester High School opened up a new world for me. Mr. McCullough became one of my mentors and made it possible for a group of us to go to Europe one summer for an enrichment program. That summer of 1972, we traveled to England, Sweden, Austria, and East and West Germany. I will never forget our visit to East Berlin, inside the walls of communist Germany. The checkpoint entrance was a grim reminder of Stalin and the communist regime. Our visit to Munich before that year's summer Olympics left me with the same eerie feeling. We were in Munich to visit the famous Rathaus-Glockenspiel and the Olympic Village. Two weeks later at the Olympic Village, Israeli athletes were taken hostage and slain by terrorists. Our trip to Europe was a fascinating and an eye-opening experience.

Our principal, Dr. Herman, and his staff devoted their professional lives to giving us the opportunity to learn and thrive. They took our education seriously, and they were concerned about our development as human beings. For a while I got caught up with my friends and started coming to class late. Sometimes I would get rude and defiant because I was upset about a personal issue. Dr. Herman never let me get away with that. They locked the doors after the last bell, and if you were late, you were called to the principal's office. I was sent to the principal's office once. It was made clear to me that my behavior was unacceptable. I was to be on time to class. I got the message. It was the same message I would get from my mother at home. I pulled myself together and was never called to the principal's office again.

During high school, I was also getting a whole new education about the streets. Neither my parents nor I knew how dangerous the streets of Los Angeles had become until one of my friends, Robert Ballou Jr., was killed by gang members. Robert had gone to the Hollywood Palladium for a concert, and some gang member saw him and wanted his coat. He refused and was beaten to death that evening. Just to think I almost experienced the same fate myself at a festival at Sportsman Park, but I would get to safety. Thoughts of Robert were running through my mind. I will never forget him.

Once I started high school, time would not allow me to continue my visits with my father at the studio as often. Our time together began to erode as I started training more and more for sports. I went from being one of the star players on my little league team to being a star player on my junior league team, the Red Soxs. Scouts were starting to follow our senior league players to identify prospects for their farm systems. I began to receive calls from the Montreal Expos and other major league organizations. I started having conversations with my parents about a career in professional baseball. Our den was filled with my baseball trophies as well as those of my brothers, who were starting to excel in baseball and football, too. Sometimes I would catch my father running his hands over our trophies. Occasionally we still had conversations about me becoming a music engineer. I began to feel him losing hope that I would make music my career. But I had no way of knowing that my career in baseball was not to be. I sustained an injury to my knee that plagued my sports endeavors throughout high school. I ran track and played football for Westchester my junior and senior years, but ultimately my knee injury caused me to retire from competitive sports.

During those days I got to meet one of the greatest sports icons ever. Our doorbell rang one day and I happened to answer. There in front of me stood Muhammad Ali, whom I admired so much. He asked me, "Is your father home?"

I just stood there with my mouth open, unable to say a word. Then he asked me, "Do you know who I am?"

I said, "You're the Champ."

He bent down and started throwing light punches, and I threw some back laughing the whole time. He stopped, shook my hand, and gave me a big smile. Then my mother and I invited him in to visit with my father. I had been around celebrities, great musicians, athletes, but meeting Muhammad Ali was one of the most important moments in my life. He was more than just a boxer to me. He was then and still is the *greatest*.

Like the lives of most teenagers, mine consisted of school, homework, occasional weekends at the studio, and sports. Men like Major General Titus Hall continued to mentor me. Throughout my teens, I was treated like one of the general's family. His encouragement meant the world to me. My coaches continued to watch over my development as an athlete and a young man as well. My dad seemed to have mixed emotions about other mentors during this stage of my life.

Drugs were everywhere during those years. Others around me were smoking marijuana, dropping acid, and taking pills. At parties people would spike the punch with pills and liquor. I did not like marijuana and

I would not touch pills. I didn't even smoke cigarettes or drink. Alcohol and cigarette smoke made me sick. I was very careful. I didn't want these harmful substances in my body. I knew what they could do to my mind and my health. As an athlete it was important to me to maintain a healthy routine. And seeing what my father had gone through, I had experienced the effects of drug use firsthand. I never wanted to make that mistake. Who knew better than I how drugs could ruin your life?

I also had my mother to contend with. When it came to drugs, my mother was not having it. She heard rumors about other entertainers in our neighborhood who had serious drug issues, and their kids were our friends. My mother always kept a vigilant eye on all of us. My own parties were crashed by kids who brought drugs. When she got wind of it, it was all over for our parties. She was famous for crashing parties if she thought something was going on. She didn't care what people thought. If we stayed past our curfew, my mother would show up at the front door of the party. It was embarrassing, and my brothers and I would go to great lengths to avoid it. We would go to great lengths to avoid any kind of conflict with her.

My senior year I tried drugs. A close friend offered me some marijuana and cocaine. I tried them, and it was a bad decision. I didn't know if I was coming or going. It would ultimately alter the course of my life.

My senior year of high school, my mind was dominated by the desire to get my own car. Most of my friends had their own cars by the time they were seventeen. My parents let me drive their cars: a Cadillac and the Mercedes 300 SEL. But it wasn't the same. Like every other teenage boy in America, I wanted a car of my own. During my last year in high school, I asked my mother for one. I knew that if I asked my father, he would just ask her, so I decided to talk to her first.

I said, "Mom, all my friends have a car. I think it's time I had a car of my own. I haven't caused you any problems or been a burden. I will need transportation for college next year. I would really like to have a car of my own."

My mother thought about it and decided that it would motivate me to finish high school with good grades if I had a car to look forward to. So she talked it over with my father, and he agreed that it was reasonable. They decided they were going to pick out a car for me as a graduation gift. My mother wanted me to drive something safe and economical. They discussed getting me a Volkswagen or a Dodge. My father liked the idea.

My dad seemed happy about buying me a car, so he mentioned it to Dave Braithwaite at the studio one day. He rarely spoke to Dave about family issues, but he was excited about the purchase. When Dad told Dave he was going to get me a Dodge for graduation, Dave replied, "Man, don't get Ray Jr. a Dodge. He doesn't want a Dodge. Get him a Porsche." God bless him, my father took Dave's advice.

One day I received a call after I had graduated to come down to the studio, and when I got there, my father told me Mr. Adams was going to take me downtown. "Where am I going?" I asked, perplexed.

My father replied, "Well, you're going to get your car." He was really animated about it. A short while later, Mr. Adams drove me to the showroom of Porsche of Downtown LA. We walked into the dealership and Mr. Adams asked me, "Which one do you like?" He would take care of the paperwork with the dealer. I looked around the room. It was the ultimate teenage boy's fantasy. The dealership was filled with beautiful, shiny Porsches. I chose a gold 1973 911T. I couldn't believe it. That color was one of the most beautiful colors I'd ever seen, and the car was mine.

My dad shared my excitement, but my mother wasn't so thrilled. She was expecting me to drive home in a nice, safe, sensible Volkswagen, not a high-performance sports car. I don't know whether or not she spoke to my dad or Joe Adams did, but one of them suggested I take a high-performance driving course. I had never driven a sports car, and they wanted to make sure I could handle my new Porsche.

They made the arrangements, and I would attend the Bob Bondurant High Performance Driving School. I took my lessons at Ontario Motor Speedway, which was one of the super speedways for NASCAR IMSA as well as Indy car racing. I was a huge racing fan, following the careers of Richard Petty, Mario Andretti, A. J. Foyt, the Unser brothers, Rick Mears, Peter Gregg, and Hurley Haywood. It was thrilling to drive on the same track as those speed merchants. I loved the lessons. I learned defensive driving, how to throw a car into a controlled skid, heel and toe shifting, and how to do apex turns. Then I was ready to hit the streets. I was so excited when I brought the car home that I locked my keys in the car. Racing would become a passion for me. I would race cars and compete in time trials with other Porsche rally clubs.

My father had not ridden in my car or a Porsche, so he asked me to take him to the office. I remember I got him in the car, and by the time I got around to the driver's side to get in, he was flicking the ashes from his cigarette on the floor of the Porsche. I freaked out. "Dad! What are you doing? You're getting ashes all over the floor. Use the ashtray."

He calmly pointed out that he couldn't see where the ashtray was and said, "I'm blind. Remember?" It was very funny, and he made his point.

Whenever I had the time I continued to go to the studio on weekends to visit my father and I continued to seek advice from him even though it was an area he avoided. More accurately, I realized he was not a person who *could* guide me. He gave me no dating advice and avoided talking about women. I guess he worried that his affairs would come up. He relied on reports given to him by my mother and his valet. He did ask me if I was drinking or using drugs. He asked me the same thing about my brothers. He seemed relieved when I said no. It was not an easy subject for him to discuss with us, for he had kept his promise never to use heroin again, although he did have his special coffee and his marijuana to indulge in every day. He taught those around him how to make coffee for him with a layer of sugar, a layer of coffee, and a layer of Bols gin. There was always a mug of the brew on the console of his control board in the studio. There was always a double standard when dealing with my father in so many areas of our lives, but I loved and respected him. My brothers didn't realize this yet, but I did. Now I was developing a full life of my own, and I didn't crave time with my dad as much anymore. I was preoccupied with school, sports, girls, and my friends. For the first time, both of our schedules were full and we only saw each other in passing at home. My father wanted to continue to spend time with me on weekends. He would try to start a conversation saying, "Whatcha doin'? When are you coming down to the studio again?"

I would rush by him saying, "How you doin', Dad? I gotta go. I will call you later, okay?" He never spoke to me about how he felt about me spending less time with him. I guess I grew up too fast and the thoughts of letting go couldn't have been easy. Every parent experiences the pain of letting a child go, and in my dad's case, he had the additional regret of losing the first ten years of my life. Now when he came home from a tour, he would check to see if I was taller than he was yet. He would still put his hands on my shoulders and say, "You've grown." Once I finally grew taller than he was, he put his hand on my head and said, "Oh, you don't say. You don't say."

By the time I turned seventeen and was about to graduate, visits to the studio were rare. I was preparing for another stage in my life. I didn't seem to need my studio visits with my father like I used to, but I still needed his presence in my life.

So much had changed during those years in View Park. Our family was slowly but steadily growing apart. For the first few years on South-ridge, we continued attending Travelers Rest for Sunday worship. But over time, those strong ties began to dissipate. Those were the ties that held our family together. God and church were our foundation. Faith re-mained central to my mother's life.

What a paradox that the studio was a huge factor in the growing sepa-ration of our family. When my father was first starting out, my parents sat down together to discuss business with Jeff Brown in the living room. My father wrote his songs and arrangements at home. When we moved to Hepburn, my father's office became the focal point of his music career. There was a steady stream of musicians in and out of his office, and if I wanted to listen to my father's music, I just had to sit in the hallway next to the door. I sat in that hallway listening to hit after hit my entire child-hood. If they needed a bigger space, the band would rehearse in the living room. All that changed when we moved to Southridge. My father still had a beautiful office at home, but all of the writing, arranging, and recording were done at 2107. If I wanted to listen to my father make music, I had to go to the studio. On Hepburn, he was either on tour or at home. We had him for two or three months of the year. We saw him every day, and at night he came home to sleep in his bedroom with my mother. Now we went for days without seeing him at all. If he was working on some new music, he would hole up at the studio for days on end. He had everything he needed at 2107.

For years my father had been living one life on the road and another at home. His marriage to my mother and the strain of holding it all together took a huge toll on her and our family. We were slowly stretched to the breaking point. In the growing division between my father and those closest to him stood Mr. Adams. The question that still remains is: Was Mr. Adams ultimately the rock that divided the water? My mother and I talked about this many times.

Joe Adams came into my father's life in 1962, three years after the move from Atlantic to ABC-Paramount. During those three years, my father's career had skyrocketed. The homegrown machine run by my father and Jeff Brown had brought him to a level of success none of them anticipated, but it was time for change, for addressing the future and the new challenges my father's career presented. The early sixties had also been a precarious time. Even with all of the success, his public image suffered. There were two highly publicized arrests for heroin possession that threatened his career. Into the middle of my father's complex career instability stepped Joe Adams.

Mr. Adams brought a new sense of organization to my father's enterprise along with a sophistication and sharp business acumen. He was impeccably well spoken, well known, and well dressed, and he carried himself in a professional manner always. He raised the standard for professional behavior in the band, cleaned up my father's public image, and cleaned house. He began to immediately turn my father's negative publicity around and kept my father's private life out of the news. Once my father completed rehab, Mr. Adams screened everyone in the band for drugs. He began to protect the commodity most important to my father—

his image. He took a highly successful business machine (my father) and helped take his career to a new level of success. When my father's personal life was spiraling out of control, and he was on the verge of losing everything, I believe Mr. Adams became the stabilizing force he needed. He kept my father's business affairs intact during a time of great instability. Once the storm passed and my father was back at the top of the charts and in control of his personal life, he prospered beyond his dreams and so did Mr. Adams.

But it came at a huge price. Many of my father's old friends and musicians had to go through Mr. Adams to get to my dad, and they resented it. Jeff Brown, who had been everything to my father for so many years, slowly but surely lost his authority and position. Things reached a crisis and Jeff was accused of stealing money from my dad. Jeff had always moved money around to cover expenses on the road. There was a time in my father's career when his money ran short, and Jeff would pay the band out of his own pocket and reimburse himself when things weren't so tight. Those were the lean years when someone believed in my father. To this day I do not know if Jeff embezzled the money. Everyone tells me a different story. But he did admit to a close family source that he did not have the business acumen to take my father's career to the next level. When Jeff resigned and returned to Texas, I know he loved my father and he was hurt. I also know he was my father's friend. I never saw Jeff again, and I missed him over the years.

From my mother's point of view the biggest problem for our family, as time passed, was that Mr. Adams had his hand in every aspect of my father's life. My mother was no longer allowed to share in any of my father's business decisions, as she had for most of their marriage. Mr. Adams took care of all the household business as well, hiring the gardener, paying the electrical bill, and so forth. In some respects my mother needed his help, since her health was poor for so many years. My mother fought for the right to choose the direction for her personal business with my father, but many of her responsibilities were taken away from her. Making things worse was the fact that Mr. Adams was vocal about his dislike for my mother, according to her. She told me that he made negative comments about her and opposed her influencing my father's decisions. The comments would get back to my mother. It was humiliating and hurt her very much. When my mother expressed her feelings about the negative comments from Mr. Adams and how she felt he was taking over their lives, my father became angry and told her to mind her own business and let him handle their affairs. I felt that my father began to suffer from acute memory loss and he started to detach himself from us. He would turn his back on everyone who loved him, who went to hell and back to keep him alive and protect him from himself.

And of course, there were the affairs. Some of the women referred to themselves as "Mrs. Ray Charles." The gossip columns ran bits identifying other women as Mrs. Charles while he was on the road. There were countless one-night stands on the road, and much of that gossip continued to get back to my mother. Two very public paternity suits were tried over the years, and my mother had the humiliation of sitting in court to show her support while other women testified that Mr. Charles was married in name only and had told them that the child in question was more important to him than his legal children. My dad ultimately fathered twelve children. Articles about his womanizing continued to appear in the gossip columns throughout the years on Southridge. He was always talking to us about the importance of family and of respecting our mother. I guess this was a classic case of do as I say, not as I do.

My father's appetite for women was insatiable. Whatever the reason, his obsession with women caused pain for so many and ultimately pushed my mother to the breaking point. I watched her struggle for years. I would hear her crying often. She became increasingly sad and irritable, harder to get along with. Vernon was caught in the middle. He found himself trying to bridge the divide between my dad and my mother, keeping her informed after she was shut out. Vernon was loyal to my father and didn't want to betray his confidence, but at the same time he loved our family and tried his best to take care of us. He was our confidant, our protector, and our dear friend. During this same time, Mother was struggling with my grandmother's health problems. The years of alcoholism had taken a toll on Grams. As her body began to fail, her mind was affected. She started having delirium tremens, popularly known as the dt's, and they became increasingly frightening. She became paranoid and started to hallucinate. My mother, terrified, called Dr. Foster, our family physician and friend, once again. Dr. Foster told her that my grandmother had to be hospitalized and put on a psych hold immediately or she would die. In great distress, my mother had Grams committed for a week. My grandmother slowly recovered and came out of the hospital seven days later, tired but clearly in a healthier frame of mind. But she never forgave my mother for the humiliation of being put in a psych ward. My mother now had to live not only with the fear that it would happen again but with the pain of her mother's blame.

After nearly two decades of being the good and faithful wife, my mother started to find herself again. She had always followed the Bible's injunction to submit to your husband, and she firmly believed that my father was rightfully the decision maker and head of the household, so she had always tried to accept my father's indiscretions and commit herself completely to him and to her children. As the years passed, though, it became more and more difficult for her to do so. My father had the continual adulation from his fans, and in his studio he was the king, maybe even the dictator. The money controlled everyone and everything in his world. When he got home, he expected my mother to be at his beck and call as well. Now, however, she wanted more independence. After years of being housebound, she wanted a life of her own. My parents started arguing more and more. She was starting to say no to him, and he didn't like it.

As my mother's health improved, she wanted a chance to get some exercise and go out with her friends, so she became part of a women's bowling team. One night my father came home and found her on her way to a bowling tournament. He insisted that she skip the tournament and stay home with him. She refused. They began to argue, and the argument escalated into a screaming match. Then he got physical with her.

I had heard the shouting, and I knew something was wrong. My father came to my bedroom to explain. He was furious that my mother was threatening him with divorce. All I could do was vent my own anger. "Dad, all these years she's put up with all the other women, the newspapers, the drugs, the other children, everything. What did you expect? That she'd put up with it forever?" When my father replied that I was taking my mother's side, I told him that I was sorry he felt that way.

That was the end of the marriage as far as my mother was concerned. She had tolerated all of his behavior, but she would not tolerate his hurting her physically. She hired an attorney and began the process of legal separation. He had always said she was the love of his life, and he thought they would be together forever. Somehow he had convinced himself that his affairs shouldn't matter to her as long as she was his wife and he took care of her. I wondered how he would have felt if my mother had had an affair with another man. Yet he couldn't understand her feelings. I loved him, but he just didn't get it.

All of our lives, our family had been number three. His first priority was his music, and that took most of his time and energy. His second priority was his women he spent so much time with. His third priority, our family, was waiting to greet him with open arms at home, as we always had. My mother loved and protected him at a great cost to herself. She always had his back. If she felt he needed to be confronted, she would do so, but she never let anyone else criticize him. Not even us. To this day, if anyone says anything critical of my father, she will stand up for him, and she still reminds us that he loved us in his own way and gave us a life second to none. But eventually her life with my father wore her down. I don't know how she dealt with the threats, the drugs, and the humiliation for so many years. He took their marriage for granted. He thought she would always be there, no matter what, and for many years she thought the same thing. He loved her until he died, but I don't know if he ever truly understood what he had in her. He could not have had a better woman at his side.

The long process of my parents' separation and divorce began that year. It would ultimately drag on for four years, shaking the foundation

of our family to the core. There's a parable in the Bible about the foundation a house is built on. The foolish build their house on the sand of their
own sin and confusion. The wise build their house on the rock of God's
word, and when the storms come, the house is shaken but not destroyed.
Our lives and our beautiful home on Southridge had been built on sand.
As each storm hit, the foundation was gradually washed away. Our home
collapsed, and as the Scriptures say, great was the sound of its fall. I felt
like the walls of my life were coming down around me again.

CHAPTER 13

Dancing with the Devil

A fever-minded young

man with infinite

potential...

Dancing with the devil,

smoked until his eyes

would bleed.

—IMMORTAL TECHNIQUE

IN THE SUMMER OF 1973, THE LIFE I HAD KNOWN WAS ENDING. The foundation of my family had been damaged and our lives would never be the same. I was anxious to escape the turmoil at Southridge, eager to break free from the anger and confusion at home and strike out on my own. I had just graduated from Westchester High School and was preparing to begin college in the fall. I remember waking up one morning that summer with the voice of Marvin Gaye on the radio singing "What's Goin' On." The song echoed the sign of the times around me. Our nation was in the middle of a bloody war in Vietnam. I had just registered for the draft on my eighteenth birthday a few weeks before. Some of my class-mates were leaving for Vietnam; some of them never came back. Nixon was in the White House, and the nation was about to endure the national disgrace of Watergate. African Americans continued to struggle for civil rights. The Nixon tapes would soon reveal the contempt that our own president had for the people of my race. It seemed like there was turmoil everywhere I turned. I sought change in my life, to go far away from all the tension and misery.

I had decided to attend Pasadena City College, a two-year college, with the intention of transferring to the University of Southern California. I was happy with my decision to attend PCC because I had done enough research on the school to discover that it was one of the best junior colleges in the nation. Its graduates went on to transfer to the top universities. Also running through the track of my mind: maybe Pasadena City attracted some of the prettiest girls in the state, all hoping to ride the queen's float on New Year's Day. I thought that was pretty interesting. And my parents told me they were getting me an apartment in Pasadena. I hadn't expected that. An apartment of my own would give me some space and indepen-dence. I was really excited.

During the summer of 1973 I went to work for my father at RPM International for the summer. It wasn't exciting work, just a little book-keeping. I wanted to take on some responsibility for myself and make some extra money. The summer did give me a glimpse into the work-ings of Tangerine Records, my father's record label. I would also get a chance to see firsthand that his publishing company was flourishing. He was recording artists such as Ike and Tina Turner, the Ohio Players, Louis Jordan, and Percy Mayfield. It was a good experience for me to see the process from the inside.

I didn't see very much of my father, just a fleeting glimpse and a conversation or two. I didn't really want to have too many conversations with my father about the separation. It was a difficult time for him. It had been four years since Sid Feller departed, and without his old team of collaborators, his music was changing. He continued to make good music, but he hadn't had a big hit for several years. He was working as hard as ever, but the money wasn't coming in the way it had. He was still angry about his separation from my mother. Everything out of his mouth was "Your mother this, your mother that. She asked for the separation, I didn't." I was struggling not to get in between my parents because I loved them both, but my father wanted me to take his side.

My mother, however, wanted me to remain close to my father. She told me, "What is happening between your father and me is not your fault. Your father needs you, too." I didn't believe that at the time. I was upset with my father, and I blamed him for the collapse of the marriage. My mother was hard to live with, taking her anxiety and frustration out on me and my brothers. But I knew she was very unhappy, filled with a sense of failure about her marriage and frightened about the future. I worried about her health and what might happen to her. I was spending more time alone in my bedroom listening to music. I asked God to help me make sense of it all.

That fall I moved into my apartment in Pasadena. I loved the city immediately. Just to the north was Altadena, a treasure trove of beautiful African American girls. Pasadena moved at a slower pace than Los Angeles, and I liked that. There was still enough night life to enjoy myself on the weekends. The atmosphere was more laid-back, tranquil. My spirits rose as I began to shed the burdens of home and start focusing on my own life and my studies.

My cousin, Greg Shaw, would share my two-bedroom apartment. He had been living in Pasadena for a year, so he helped get me acclimated socially. Paul Hall, my friend and classmate from Westchester, would attend PCC that fall as well. During my first semester I was rehabbing my knee. My plans to play football came to an abrupt end when I reinjured my knee on the first day of spring practice. I did not know how severe my injury was yet, though. After hearing the opinions of several orthopedic surgeons, I decided to have surgery.

Southridge was a very private and sheltered environment for me, so it took some time to settle into my new life in Pasadena. I began to frequent parties, meet girls, and develop new relationships. My weekends became busier and busier. But I was focused on my classes and having fun. I was heady with the thrill of independence.

When I wasn't partying on the weekends, I was "Porschen' it." That was my term for racing my Porsche in time trials around California. It was a great release. The thrill of going more than a hundred miles an hour on a professional racetrack was a rush. Some of my friends owned Porsches and other high-performance cars as well. We would rally up to Hearst Castle and the Monterey Peninsula. In the early hours of the morning, at two or three o'clock, when the roads were deserted, we would race through the canyons that led from Pacific Coast Highway to the 101 freeway. Those canyon roads twisted and turned, with two-hundred-foot drops, and we would take the curves at high speeds. It was dangerous, but we loved the freedom and the feeling of speed. I loved to drive my Porsche alone up Pacific Coast Highway at night, to Port Hueneme and back. The white foam of the waves would be glimmering in the dim light, and the roar of my Porsche engine was like a lullaby. Those drives gave me peace of mind.

It took a while to get adjusted and learn to manage my time. By the second semester I learned to play hard and study hard. Once I settled in, it became a must to focus on my studies. Believe it or not, I was attempting to double-major. I really loved architecture, but ultimately I chose business as my major, with economics as a minor. I thought in the future I would work for my father's company, Ray Charles Enterprises. Once I made the decision, I was able to find a balance between school and sports-car rallying and parties.

That first year my mother watched me from afar. When I came home to visit, I would tell her stories of my new adventures. She saw me becoming caught up in my new sense of freedom. I was beginning to feel like a legend in my own mind. She told me, "Okay, Mr. Man, you're the king of your own kingdom right now, the kingdom of Knuckle Dom. Watch the decisions you make and the people you choose to hang around. Be very careful, son." She knew about my racing, and she felt that what I was doing was dangerous. "Slow down, or you're going to have a rough road ahead."

College had become the distraction I needed from the problems at home. That first year of college, I came home only for the holidays, although every now and then I would drop in during the week to check on my mother and make sure she was all right. She didn't say much about what she was going through but it was clear to me that she was heartbroken and filled with regrets. There was nothing I could do to help her through it. I did not see my brothers very often, either. For two years I simply lost touch with David and Bobby at a time when they needed a big brother. All of our lives had changed and we were moving in a new direction. I knew they were still in sports. David became an all-American linebacker for Montclair Prep. But the tension at home separated us instead of uniting us. We all suffered individually in our own way. My life in the fast lane only covered up the confusion and pain that still lay underneath the façade. I was trying to survive emotionally. Though my life appeared to be an endless party that year, underneath I was headed for a collision with myself.

My second year at PCC I had detached myself emotionally. Nothing at home was going to change, and I wanted to get on with my life. I simply tried to stay focused on the future because the time was approaching when I would have to submit my applications to USC or Whittier College for the next year. I had great support from Roland Sink, my teacher for business math analysis and calculus. He became a mentor to me and some of my classmates. He constantly motivated us to excel, and excel we did. He was an alumnus of USC, and he wrote a letter of recommendation for me to attend USC for the fall semester.

After I chose my major, school became very intense. I was accepted to USC and to Whittier College as well. I spent my last semester at PCC preparing to transfer to either Whittier or USC. I was also preparing for surgery on my left knee. The scan revealed a torn main ligament and two torn cartilages. My surgery was to be performed by Dr. Clarence Shields of the Kerlan-Jobe Orthopedic Clinic. My father sought out one of the best orthopedic surgeons in sports medicine. It was major surgery. There was no arthroscopic surgery at that time, so it was extremely painful. It took six months to fully recover: two months in a cast and four months of rehab. My knee injury would end my quest to play professional baseball or football, but some of my friends and fellow athletes would go on to have successful careers in sports, including Rod Martin, Wendell Tyler, Wyatt Henderson, Ricky Odems, Jack Steptoe, Fred McNeill, and Sidney and Tryon Justin.

It was during that second year at PCC that I met the woman who was to become my wife. Chu and I invited a few friends over for a Halloween get-together, and my friend Dwayne arrived with an attractive woman dressed in a white racing outfit. We were introduced and I was immediately attracted to her. Her name was Duana Chenier and there seemed to be some chemistry between us, though it would take some time for our relationship to develop. That was also the year that I met Rhonda Bailey, a Creole beauty in her own right, whom I was extremely attracted to as well. She would return to my life twenty years later and become the love interest of my life today. But at the time, I continued to stay focused, study hard, and have some fun, too.

I celebrated that summer with a big blowout party with some friends on Southridge. We invited all of our friends. It was a wonderful hallmark for me as I prepared to enter Whittier College. That July my family went to Montreal for the 1976 Summer Olympics. My friends Paul and Tommy Hall joined us there with their mother. We celebrated the victories of the Spinks brothers, Sugar Ray Leonard, and Bruce Jenner, who all won gold medals. Montreal and the Olympic Stadium were magnificent. It was a wonderful time for our families to be together and reconnect. It was great to be with my brothers, almost like the old days on Southridge. I loved my brothers very much, and Bobby had grown two or three inches. While we were together, I was filled with hope and optimism.

In August I returned to enter Whittier College. Both the city of Whittier and the college had originally been founded by the Quakers. It was small and peaceful, with only about 1,400 students. It was also the alma mater of President Richard Nixon and where George Allen had coached football. The college, which had long been fiercely proud of its most distinguished alumnus, was in the first throes of the humiliation that was Watergate. Whittier's motto was "Light, Poetry, Truth, Peace, and Love of Knowledge," all the things I was seeking in my life. But living on campus would not give me the privacy I was accustomed to. So I moved back home and used the lower level of Southridge as my private space as my father had.

I pledged the Lancer Society the first semester. The Lancers, an indelible part of campus history, was a private school society formed on February 13, 1934, with thirteen original members and modeled after the example set by King Arthur and the Knights of the Round Table. The mission of the Lancer Society was to maintain loyalty and the true spirit of Whittier College, to instill the motive of service without reward, to continue a social agenda, and to maintain the activities for the betterment of the students as well as the college. By pledging the Lancer Society, I would belong to the history and tradition of the college. I would have a bond for life with those who preceded me and those who would follow. I was invited to the Lancer rush with my friend Phillip King. We attended a few other rushes but decided to pledge the Lancer Society because of the caliber of its members and its history at Whittier College.

Pledging the Lancers was a challenge and a real adjustment. As time passed, Phillip and I learned about the importance of our brotherhood and our responsibility to one another. The Lancers became a moving force for me to socialize, to learn how to communicate, to understand others. I needed the camaraderie and the bonding. The Lancers reminded me of Camelot, a perfect world built on peace and love where all the people were one. The Lancer Society gave me a place to belong.

Meanwhile, my relationship with my father had become strained. After four years of separation, my mother had finally filed for divorce.

My father became very bitter for a while, but ultimately he would accept that his marriage was over. I chose to remain as neutral as I could with my parents. But my dad and I still had our differences. Despite them, he made sure my tuition and my living expenses were taken care of while I was in college. Time always seemed to ease the tension between us, allowing us the opportunity to share some time together again.

I continued my studies at Whittier in business and economics and a minor in philosophy. My relationship with Duana was serious by this time and we started discussions about getting married. Outwardly, my life appeared to be fine and I was moving forward, but inside, I was filled with turmoil. Trouble was echoing inside, and I simply wanted to escape. I was about to start down the same path as my father. The path of self-medication and destruction.

My first steps were innocent enough. During my first year away from home, I had begun to drink and dabble in cocaine socially. I occasionally smoked a little marijuana with my buddies, but I didn't really like it. It made me paranoid, and I hated the way it smelled. I didn't like going around reeking of marijuana, and I couldn't go home smelling like that. It was like being a walking billboard: I'm high. So pot smoking didn't last long. But I had already crossed the line.

By the time I got to Whittier, social drug use seemed ordinary to me. It was at Whittier that I started snorting cocaine more frequently. It was everywhere in the circle I ran with off campus. I didn't think twice about doing coke. As long as I limited my use to weekends, I felt it was not interfering with my life and school. If I had stopped there, I might have been all right. But I didn't stop there.

One evening in 1978, I was invited to a party at a house in the Hollywood Hills. It was an exclusive party, and you only got in by special invitation. The host was called Angelo. That night I drove to Laurel Canyon in my Porsche, the engine humming as I made the turns. Laurel Canyon winds through the Hollywood Hills from the San Fernando Valley to Beverly Hills. Ascending that road is like leaving the city far behind. The area is thick with trees and foliage, and houses perch on hilltops or hide in small glens below. Narrow two-lane roads branch precariously off the main road at irregular intervals. Residents love the area because it is beautiful, private, and secluded. It is a haven for the wealthy and for those with secrets to keep.

That evening I pulled into a parking space where the small road I was following reached a dead end. It was quiet and serene. There were trees all around, and I could hear the trickle of a creek in the background. Nestled under the trees was a sprawling, rustic house. I felt like I had walked into a fairy-tale scene deep in the woods. As I stepped over the threshold, two of the most beautiful women I had ever seen, dressed seductively, greeted me. I looked around the room and saw that it was filled with more beautiful women. I stopped dead in my tracks. The most striking of all of them was a tall woman with long, gorgeous legs. She beckoned me in. In the den where everyone gathered was a large glass aquarium filled with sand. A boa constrictor lay coiled on top of the sand. I walked through the house and out the back as though I were in a dream. But inside, I could see Angelo, brewing a gaseous liquid that rose from the plate like a Christmas tree. I wasn't sure if he looked like a wizard or a mad scientist. I was mesmerized but curious. There were people walking around wired for sound, and some of them from Hollywood's A-list.

I thought I had found Paradise. What I didn't know is that I was standing on the edge of a precipice. I stepped over the edge that night when I took the pipe that Angelo offered me. It was pure cocaine, etherbased. When I breathed it in through the glass pipe, it took me to a place I had never imagined. I was gone in sixty seconds. It was the most intense and profound sensation I had ever experienced. It lasted for ten minutes, and within those ten minutes I went to a place I never wanted to return from. I left every problem, every fear, every anxiety behind. I knew in that moment that a thousand journeys there would never be enough.

What I didn't yet understand was that one journey there was already one too many. In that moment, I entered a battle for self-control. It would challenge every fiber of my moral being. It made everything I had learned until then, from my father's addiction to my mother's warnings, irrelevant. None of that mattered anymore and the worst part was that I knew better. And I continued down that path anyway.

That night was the first of many. For months I became obsessed with that euphoric feeling. Three or four times a week I would make that drive into Laurel Canyon, alone or with friends, and leave the world behind. It was expensive, consuming, and slowly taking me away from my friends and family. I gradually began to see through the façade, and one night Angelo whispered in my ear that the tall woman, the most beautiful and seductive of them all, had been born a man! Nothing in that house was real. As the pale light of the morning shined through, I noticed the boa hanging lifeless over the side of the aquarium. I realized everyone in the house was lifeless, too. It was all an illusion.

It took this jolt to bring me back to reality. One evening a few months later, driving to a club, I got into an argument with Duana. She was angry with me about my obsession with Laurel Canyon, with my endless quest for the perfect high. Distracted by the argument, I angrily turned my head to say something to her. My Porsche hit the car in front of us and went all the way up under it. The hood of my Porsche became an accordion with substantial damage to the frame. Even more remarkable, by the grace of God neither Duana nor I was seriously hurt. I wound up selling my Porsche because of the damage.

The accident was a wake-up call. Something had to change in my life. I canceled all of my classes for the fall semester to regroup, and recommit myself to my studies and my relationships. I was able to do all those things, and I returned to Whittier the following semester. But even though I made a successful return the next semester, I knew I had ventured into uncharted territory. I had opened a door that I couldn't completely close. I had violated all of my principles and experienced something I never should have experienced. I had tasted the fruit of the forbidden tree. Once you taste it, eventually you want more.

In June 1980 I would finish my major in business and economics at Whittier College. Once again, I prepared to move forward. My future was filled with promise and my life was back on track. I was to be married to Duana that August, and wedding plans were in the works. Our wedding party was very large and the ceremony took place at St. Bernadette Catholic Church in Baldwin Hills. Elaine Chenier prepared the New Orleans–style wedding and Southridge was the perfect backdrop for our reception. Maybe it was fate I met and married Duana Marie Chenier. Our families had old ties. Her grandfather Rip Robert and her grandmother Miss Mary were old friends of my father from New Orleans. In the early days, when my father was on the chitlin' circuit, Miss Mary would invite him over and cook gumbo for him. Rip was my father's friend and promoted his concerts in New Orleans. Over twenty years later I would marry Rip's granddaughter.

The morning of the wedding, I waited nervously for Dwayne Bonner, my friend and one of my groomsmen, at Southridge. He pulled up in a black Rolls-Royce Corniche convertible. He got out of the car wearing his wedding attire, gave me a big smile with his arms open wide, and said, "Junior, are you ready? The Corniche is my present to you and D. Congratulations. I love you."

When we arrived in front of St. Bernadette, all of my groomsmen, our guests, and our friends were waiting out front. I greeted everyone with a smile, and then my best men, Dwayne Booner and Shedrick Nance, decided it was time to go to the front of the church and wait. We came in down the right side of the church, and when we reached the front I turned around to see how many people were in attendance—the church was almost full. I never expected so many people. I was immediately overcome by anxiety and I retreated to the restroom and locked the door. I peered into the mirror and asked myself, Are you ready?

I could hear Billy Preston's "With You I'm Born Again" playing in the background. Then someone knocked on the door, and I heard my father asking, "Son, are you coming out?" I was very surprised to hear his voice. I knew he and Bobby were aware of the wedding date, but I had not spoken to either of them since my father's tour began in Europe.

I replied, "Not yet."

Dad said, "Why not?"

I replied, "I'm a little nervous."

My father said, "Well now, son, just open the door."

As soon as I opened the door he reached out and hugged me tight. It meant the world to me to see him. He'd rearranged his schedule to fly home just long enough to see me get married. This day the music did not come first. My brother Bobby was on tour with him, but he missed his connecting flight and didn't make it to the wedding. I wanted him to share that moment with me along with David. When I approached the altar to wait for my bride, I saw my mother and father sitting together. My mother looked beautiful in a purple dress and a lovely hat. My father sat close to her, beaming. I couldn't remember when I'd last seen them together like that, looking happy. I knew they had put their feelings aside to share this day with me. It was one of the first signs that some of the bitterness was beginning to fade. My mother told me later that she kept reminding my father that even if they couldn't live together, we could still be a family.

After I arrived at the altar with a smile, I turned toward Duana as she walked down the aisle toward me, and we exchanged our vows. Our introduction as Mr. and Mrs. Ray Charles Robinson Jr. represented a new beginning for us. We exited St. Bernadette to the applause of over four hundred guests. *Jet* magazine attended the wedding to write a story and to take some pictures of us and our family. As we met our guests and our wedding party at the front of the church, Dale escorted Duana and me to the Rolls. We stood in the backseat with the top down, smiling and waving to everyone for several minutes until we finally sat down for the ride to Southridge.

Everyone was there to greet us when we arrived. We partied for hours, New Orleans–style. Elaine and my mother had done an amazing job preparing Southridge. There were guests all around the pool area, the tennis court, and the upper-garden terrace, and inside our home was filled with music, and we second-lined the day away. It was a day filled with joy that we shared with our family and friends. As we finally drove off that evening, I looked back and saw the walls of Southridge lit up behind us. Our house looked like a castle. In that moment, I thought maybe Camelot would be possible after all.

CHAPTER 14

From the Heart

I will protect you

and respect you.

—JEROME POMUS AND
KENNETH HIRSCH

DUANA AND I SETTLED IN TO BEGIN OUR OWN HAPPILY EVER after. We moved south to Irvine in Orange County, and I went to work as a loan officer for Centron Financial, a mortgage banking firm in Newport Beach. The Rancho San Joaquin condominium complex where we lived was a beautiful setting to start our lives together. Next door was a golf course and a tennis complex. During our first year of marriage we found out Duana was pregnant and we decided to move back to Los Angeles, closer to our families. Nineteen eighty was not an ideal time to be in real-estate finance. That January my grandfather died. I loved him dearly. It was yet another loss in a family that was already diminished. With all of my grandparents gone, Duana's pregnancy couldn't have come at a better time. We needed new life in the family, and my mother needed the comfort of our presence at Southridge, which had become a lonely place. We moved into the lower level of Southridge, which we had all to ourselves, and eagerly awaited the birth of our first child.

On October 23, 1981, at Daniel Freeman Memorial Hospital in Inglewood, my daughter Erin Brianne came into the world. After hours of anxiety while my wife was in labor, I watched as my daughter was born. I held my breath until I heard her cry. The doctor handed her to me, and I held her for the first time. I started to check her limbs, counting her fingers and toes. I put my finger in front of her eyes to see if she would respond. My father's anxiety was passed down to me; he felt his blindness may have been hereditary. It was the first question my father had asked my mother when I was born. Once I knew Erin was all right, I was flooded with relief and joy. I just stood there and gazed at her. Her birth was the most incredible experience I had ever had, a miracle from God. She had light brown skin, a full head of hair, and almond-shaped eyes. I know all parents think this, but I truly thought she was the most beautiful baby I had ever seen. I nicknamed her "Tinkerbell." It was something about her smile. The nickname stuck, and my friends and I called her Tink as a child.

After her birth the gnawing worry I had felt as a child at Hepburn returned. What if something happened to Erin? My fear was worsened when I heard that a prominent athlete had two children die of SIDS—sudden infant death syndrome. No one knew what caused SIDS, and there were no warning signs. I was petrified about losing Erin to SIDS. I would wake up in the middle of the night and watch her sleep. I would put my finger by her nose to make sure she was breathing. Sometimes I would pick her up in the middle of the night and hold her. Duana would get angry with me for waking her. Other times I would pick her up when she was crying, lie back down, and let her sleep on my chest so she could hear my heartbeat.

I would lie still like that for two or three hours until she was asleep again. Her bassinet was on my side of the bed. I just needed to be close to her. I wanted her to know that I was there and would protect her.

Duana was also overprotective and wanted to do everything for Erin. But I was determined to care for my daughter myself. One day when I took her into the bathroom to change her diaper, I locked the door, prepared the water, and bathed her by myself. When I carried her out, she was all clean and diapered. My wife was mad at me, but Erin was my child, too, and I wanted those special moments with her. Erin remained the center of our lives for the next three years, until our second child was born. We held Erin so much during the first year that she rarely got a chance to walk on her own. Then on her first birthday, Erin was sitting on the carpet in the entertainment room full of children who had come for her first birthday party. After watching the other kids walk around for a while, she pushed herself to her feet and started walking, following the other children. We all watched Erin take her first steps anxiously. It was a wonderful day. Southridge was filled with children and laughter and full of life once again. Life was good.

When we learned about Duana's pregnancy, we decided to move back to Southridge. Part of the plan was for me to go to work for my father. I had chosen my majors in business and economics with my sights on joining the publishing end of my father's company. I felt that with my educational background I could make a contribution. But when I asked my father for a job, he failed to offer me one. The best he could offer me was a minimum-wage position helping out around the studio. I was shaken. But I could not support a wife and child on minimum wage.

At that time he was leaving for a tour in Japan, so I asked if I could go on tour with him as his assistant. He considered my request for a few days. Eventually he agreed, and that December I left to join him. I've never regretted that decision. It became a fond memory and a way to reconnect with my dad.

I arrived in Tokyo, and was met by some tour representatives. My father and the band were already in Nagoya. His representatives were very thorough and efficient. They put me on a high-speed train, and there was someone there to check in with me at every major city en route to Nagoya. It was my first time in Japan and I was very excited. I peered out the windows as the Japanese landscape rushed by. When I arrived in Nagoya, I was escorted to the Hilton Hotel, where I met my father.

I fell quickly into the routine that my father followed on the road. During the day, while he was sleeping, I was free to sightsee, and I took in as much of Japan as I could. When he was awake, I was on call to assist him. The hard part was the actual traveling. My father never left the hotel until the last minute, so we were always in a rush to make a plane or train. It made me a nervous wreck. We usually got to the plane just as they were shutting the door. We would be walking at what felt like ten thousand miles an hour, my father following behind me with one hand on my shoulder. Meanwhile, I carried all of his personal bags. He always had a pile of bags with him. I would rush through the airport with my father attached to my shoulder and my hands filled with my bag, his garment bag, his radio, the case with his tape recorder, his coat, and his personal bag. It weighed a ton, and it was hard to walk and carry it all. I learned a new respect for his valets.

We had arrived back in Tokyo, and the first night in his hotel, he got up in the middle of the night and headed for the bathroom. Still half asleep, he accidentally went out the door into the hall instead. The next thing he knew, he was standing in the hall in his underwear, locked out. Somehow he found his way down the hall to my room and knocked on the door, calling, "Let me in!"

Awakened from a sound sleep, I yelled, "Dad? What are you doing?"

He said, "It doesn't matter what I'm doing, just open the door! If you don't open the door, I'm going to go down to the lobby like this."

I staggered out of bed and opened the door. There stood my father in his underwear. He told me what had happened, and I got him back to his room. My father was irritated, but I thought it was hilarious.

We didn't talk about father-son stuff for two weeks. We just laughed and had a good time together. We talked about music as we always had. We went out to dinner, which is something he rarely did. He was extremely self-conscious about eating. We went out together with the promoter. We had never done that before. During this fleeting moment on the road with my father, the past was lifted.

My favorite part of the tour by far was helping to prepare him for a concert. He had a preparation ritual that he always followed precisely. We would go through his clothes together, and he would ask me to identify every piece by color and style. I would put everything together, from the tie to the socks and shoes, and lay them out in the dressing room. The band leader, Clifford Solomon, would come into his dressing room and get the numbers of the music for the night. All the songs were numbered, and my father would call them off to Clifford. A few minutes after Clifford left, the band would go onstage. My dad would have a white towel in front of his chair, and he'd sit there with his shoes off and his feet on the towel, sometimes smoking a cigarette, and listen to the band through the speakers. When the band hit a certain point in the music, he would say, "Okay, let's go."

He would start his ritual. Then he would tell me what to bring first, asking me to hand him each piece one at a time until he was completely dressed. I would straighten his tie. I always had to tell him to brush his hair. The entire time he was dressing, he was listening to the band. As he sat there, I could see him begin to transform. He would start patting his leg and bobbing his head, then throw his head back and say, "Listen to Clifford!" It was like watching the music being injected into the core of his soul. By the time we left the dressing room, he was bobbing and patting his leg in time to the music. He would jerk me back and forth as he danced and I'd say, "Man, this is wild, Dad!" "Listen, that's my band!" he'd say. While I guided my father to the stage, he would be infused with energy. I, too, would feel the music. The connection and the experience was simply electric as the current of his music ran through my body.

We would stand in the wings waiting for the announcer's voice to come booming out: "Ladies and gentlemen, the genius of Ray Charles!"

I would lead him onstage, still bobbing and jumping, and feel a shot of sunshine as we walked into the stage lights. He could feel the warmth of the lights and hear the crowd roaring and I could feel the electricity of the crowd, too. I would guide him to the piano, making sure that the mike was set, and that the seat was in its proper position. Once everything was in place, I would leave the stage. As I was walking off, he would stand there with his hand up in the air for a moment, and then he would jump up and start patting his leg, and it was on. He would sit down and plunge into his musical journey once more. I would stand in the wings and watch. It was magic watching him perform. The air was filled with applause as the audience embraced him. And he would embrace them back with his music, giving them what they had come to see. For the duration of the concert, my father and the audience and the music were one—a love affair.

After being on the road with him that December, I understood why my father said he would never retire. He always told me that he wouldn't know what to do in retirement. Watching him for those weeks, I understood why retirement was out of the question. The music was a part of him from the beginning, and it would be part of him until his last curtain call. Everything about it—the dressing room, the lights, the energy, the crowd, and most of all, the music—was the heart and soul of my father's existence. It was his lifeblood, and he would never leave it until he heard God's call.

As much as I loved touring with my father, I couldn't stay out on the road. I didn't want to repeat my father's pattern by being away from my family most of the year. I would miss them too much. But I wanted to prove to my father that I could be an asset to his business, so I decided on a venture of my own. My friend Eugene Rhea and I decided to use his production company, Underdog Productions, and invested our money in putting together a concert featuring my father at the Santa Monica Civic Auditorium. We were going to promote a Ray Charles concert. We used Eugene's production company name in dealing with Ray Charles Enterprises because I didn't want my father to know I was involved. The only one who knew was Warren Stevens, the booking agent at the time, and he kept our secret. I believe Mr. Adams also knew, but my father did not know that I was promoting his concert. My involvement was confidential.

On the night of the concert, I was very excited. I knew that it was part of my father's contract that he must be paid before he went onstage. The promoter would have to give a cashier's check to either my father or Mr. Adams before his performance. I walked into his dressing room and said, "Hello, Dad." He was surprised to hear my voice. He said, "Hmm. I didn't expect you to be here tonight. What are you doing here?"

And I replied, "Well, I have your check."

A strange frown came on his face, and he started moving his head from side to side. He said, "What are you doing with my check?"

I said, "Well, you're working for me tonight, Dad."

He said, "What do you mean? I don't understand what you're talking about."

I told him, "You are working for me tonight. Eugene and I are promoting this concert. I told them not to tell you."

He slapped himself on the knee and said, "Well, I'll be damned." And he looked down and said, "Well, you have a lot of nerve, 'cause I wouldn't have put my money up like that."

I asked him, "What are you saying? That you're a risk?"

"I'm not a risk. I always play. Concerts are risky."

So I said, "Well, then go out and do a good job, so we can sell out the next show."

For a minute he just sat there, taking it in, and then he said, "Damn. Yeah. I like that."

I didn't make a fortune that night. We sold enough tickets to make some profit. But it was a learning experience. I had never promoted a concert before, and I didn't really know what I was doing, but it went well anyway. I had achieved my main objective, which was to prove something to my father. I wanted to demonstrate my business acumen. In less than four months, I had put together a successful concert for him. It felt great handing him that check.

I felt that I had proven my point, but I knew I would need more work experience and a successful track record before I tried to join my father again. So I took a job as a financial adviser for New York Life, and we moved out of Southridge to Culver City.

When Duana announced that she was pregnant with our second child, I was thrilled. This time we chose a birthing room at Kaiser Permanente Hospital in Los Angeles, and this time our mothers were able to join us and share the experience. My mother would coach and encourage Duana during delivery. I brought a video camera to record the birth. On January 8, 1985, Blair Alayne was born. For the second time, I was having the most remarkable experience of my life. Afterward I brought the videotape home and shared the experience with Erin, showing and explaining her sister's birth to her. I wanted her to be a part of her sister's birth, even though she wasn't old enough to be in the delivery room. Later I took Erin to the hospital, and she was able to visit and hold Blair. She looked at her tiny sister with tenderness and wonder. That was the beginning of a long, close relationship between them. My daughters are still very close. I taught them that no one and nothing should ever come between them, not even Duana and me.

I called Blair "Binky." That was her nickname. My girls were Tink and Binky to me. My anxiety about SIDS surfaced again with Blair's birth. I wasn't comfortable putting her in another room, even with a baby monitor. So I would turn on my side and sleep with her in the curve of my body. I slept with her for months that way until my wife finally said, "Okay, that's enough. She can sleep on her own." Blair was four months old, and having her in our bed continually had begun to create problems in our marriage. Duana put Blair in her crib, and from that night on, Blair slept in her own bed. I understood Duana's frustration with me, but my fear was real. I was serious about watching over my children. Having Erin and Blair close to me during their infancy relieved my anxiety and fears.

I had a wonderful family that I loved. I should have been counting my blessings, but I wasn't. I became self-absorbed, struggling with my career direction and trying to figure out which direction my life was headed, trying to establish a more sound foundation. In the midst of all this I decided to do the worst thing I could have done: I had an affair with a mutual friend's sister. Inevitably, my wife found out, and it destroyed all the trust in our relationship. The tension in our relationship continued to build until it became unbearable. I apologized, but I could not take back what I'd done. It was wrong and irresponsible. All my life I had been angry with my father about his infidelities while married to my mother. Now here I was, less than five years into my marriage, and I had already begun to follow the same pattern. I wasn't unhappy and I had no logical reason for doing it. Ultimately, Duana and I separated and I bear the responsibility for the sadness my actions brought into my children's lives. Our separation and divorce was an extremely negative experience.

All of our lives became more complicated after that. The girls were back and forth between us, but eventually I would get custody and move back into Southridge with the girls. Southridge was a safe and sound environment to raise the girls in, just as it had been for me. The grounds of Southridge became a great shelter of love and security for my children, where they could grow up with their grandmother to nurture them when I was working, as she had nurtured and protected me. Their grandmother's cooking became the standard by which they judge all good cooks. To this day they both swear that my mother could make Malt-O-Meal taste like cake and ice cream. She cooked for them, mothered them, and when necessary, reminded them that she still had the switches on reserve.

My mother was a huge help, but for several years the girls spent most of their time with me. It took me a while to figure out how to manage my personal life and my business life. I had to divide my days like most parents. It was a challenge being in sales and balancing my workday going back and forth in the middle of the day to pick Erin up from preschool, take her to day care, and then come back and pick both girls up by six o'clock. Eventually, I got the hang of it.

I cherished my time with my daughters. I wanted to be the kind of father to them that I had always needed for myself. I wanted to be there for them physically and emotionally, to be the kind of hands-on parent that my mother was. I learned to braid their hair. I made it a point to know their teachers and monitor what the girls were learning in school. When Erin started kindergarten, I worked diligently with her at home. I wanted her a step ahead of her class. I always made her do more than what was required. She hated it at the time, of course, but in the long run she appreciated it. Her grades were proof of her hard work.

I belonged to the PTA for Windsor Hills Magnet School in View Park. The school was starting to look a little run-down. Some of us parents volunteered to take time off from work and paint some of the school's worst classrooms over the summer so the teachers and students would come back to fresh-looking classrooms. We bought the paint ourselves. We raised money for the school whether it was raining or the sun was shining. My mother had done the same thing for me.

I was always particular about the girls' appearance. I chose their outfits to make sure everything went together perfectly. Eventually Blair got so tired of it that she threw a tantrum and refused to get dressed unless I began to allow her to pick out her own clothes. She promptly put on half the things in her closet. Her color coordination was something to be desired. But she was very pleased with herself.

The girls' favorite thing to do at Southridge when they were small was to get into my Grandmother's bathroom and closet. She had every product imaginable, and Erin and Blair would sample her powder, lotion, and perfume. Her closet was like Disneyland to two small girls. It was big enough to run through, and the girls would dive into her clothes and try on her hats. My mother had an amazing collection of beautiful hats and shoes. A Southern girl at heart, she never lost her love of a striking hat.

It was the little things that created the happiness in our lives during those years. Our house was always filled with music. We didn't watch a lot of television, but I played jazz, R & B, and, of course, some of their grandfather's music. It was the closeness that defined us during the girls' early years. I loved waking up with them climbing in the bed and playing with me. I remember spending most of one summer inside with both girls because they had chicken pox. And I was proud of my skills as the tooth fairy. I kept a big bag of change handy, and when one of them lost a tooth, I would dump the change by her pillow. It wasn't until years later that I found out they heard me. I tried to tiptoe, but the clanking of the coin bag was a dead giveaway. They pretended to be asleep so I wouldn't feel bad, but they knew early on that the tooth fairy was Daddy.

I even enjoyed their mischief. It reminded me of my own at the same age. I would go into their room and find sandwiches and other food wrapped in napkins under their beds. There would be ants everywhere. I would find out that they had collected a considerable amount of food that I thought they had eaten. I had to laugh since I did it myself as a kid, stuffing Spam and vegetables under the red seat of my chair in our kitchen on Hepburn. Erin played violin in the school band, and one day I went into Erin's bedroom when I heard her practicing the violin—at least I thought she was practicing the violin. She was actually sitting cross-legged on the bed reading a book. It turned out she had taped her violin lesson and was playing it while she read. When I walked in on her, she had that deer-in-the-headlights look. I had to turn around and walk right out again because I couldn't stop myself from laughing. I had to admit, it was pretty good. It's amazing what children can come up with.

I enjoyed answering their questions. I explained to them how birds fly, and all of the endless whys and why nots. When we went to the beach, I explained the motion of the waves and told them why sand crabs dig their way into the sand after the wave retreats. Eventually there were a few questions that caught me off guard. On one occasion, after the girls would take a bath, they asked me why hair grows on certain parts of the body. I couldn't think of a thing to say. Every now and then I would have to tell them, "Okay, I have to call your grandmother and let her answer that question for you." And I would.

Being with the girls was the joy of my life, my favorite thing. When they would crawl over me and run their hands across my face, it reminded me of the way my father would run his hands across my face. I would touch their faces in return. Our lives were a cycle of home, school, homework, and recreation, creating balance in their lives like so many parents do. Their smiles were my world.

My photos of my children during those years remind me of how beautiful life was and how blessed I was. A picture of little Erin, with her fat cheeks and beautiful almond eyes, smiling. A goofy shot with both girls holding their pigtails up in the air. Me sitting at a baseball game with Erin on one knee and Blair on the other, all of us watching the game. Blair dressed as a bumblebee and Erin in a pink princess dress for Halloween. Me bent down with their arms around my neck at the Los Angeles Zoo. Sitting on my lap at Easter in their fluffy new dresses. Erin sound asleep in my arms on the couch. These are the images that still live in my memory and my heart. In every photo they were happy and the love we shared shines through.

When my father was in town, I would take the girls to visit with him. He still came back to the house now and then, and when he did, they would see him at Southridge. When we visited with my father at the studio, I often took them with me. Once we were inside the studio, my father would greet them with the ritual I knew so well from my childhood. He would stand Blair and Erin in front of him one at a time and feel their faces, their arms, their waists, to see how much they had grown. Then he would have them sit down next to him at the console while he worked. I wanted them to sit still while Grandpa was working, but it was too intriguing. They were as fascinated as I was by his ability to work the soundboard. His hands would move confidently over the complicated dials and jacks, making adjustments, marking the tape for editing. Like most people, they had no idea how he could perform so many tasks while being blind.

When my father stopped working we would go to his office to talk for a while, and the girls would explore his office. His office was large, filled with gifts from fans—flowers, toys, candy, and stuffed animals. His office had a big closet filled with his personal and performance clothes. The girls would go in there to play like they did in their grandmother's closet, except they didn't try his things on. Blair was fascinated by the sequins, bright colors, and loud prints he wore onstage. One day my father had some of his stage tuxedos hanging on the door, and she asked her grandpa if he knew how loud and flashy his clothes were. He didn't seem surprised. He told her his clothes were supposed to stand out so he would be the center of attention onstage, and he guessed that they did that all right.

They were also convinced that Grandpa had played a lifetime joke on everybody. Like me when I was little, they thought for sure my father was only pretending to be blind. One afternoon Erin and Blair were playing quietly in the corner of the office farthest from my dad while he was talking to me. They had been looking at all the gifts, and they decided to get into one of the candy boxes. Sliding over the carpet to the table, they opened one of the boxes very carefully so that it didn't make a sound. They almost jumped out of their skins when my father's gravelly voice rang out, "Baby, I wouldn't eat that if I were you. I'm not sure how old those sweets are." He not only heard them open the box; he knew which box they were opening. They looked at each other in shock. Grandpa can see! Grandpa can see!

My father was their "funny grandpa," full of jokes, making them giggle, and he was gentle. When they think of him now, they always remember his energy. He rarely sat still. He moved and fidgeted in his chair constantly, bouncing around like a kid. If they wanted to have a treat or play with a toy, he would let them, but they always had to ask first. He was very strict about that. They were not to take things without asking. Whenever he saw them, he would say, "Come to me if you need something, baby. Ask me. Call me." They knew their grandpa would help them if they needed him.

As children, my daughters didn't really understand what it meant to be Ray Charles's granddaughters. They knew he was a singer, of course. They listened to him in the studio and on records at home, and I took them to several of his concerts. Sometimes they watched from the wings; other times they sat in the audience. They loved his music, but to them, he was just Grandpa. They couldn't figure out why other kids would ask to see their rooms when they lived at Southridge or seemed fascinated by the tile mosaic of a piano on the bottom of the swimming pool. Erin and Blair didn't see our family name as anything special.

They thought they were living a normal life and that everyone lived like they did. Erin didn't realize that she lived a privileged life until she was almost twelve. Then, people stared and pointed, just as people had once stared and pointed at me and my brothers. Eventually Erin and Blair began to realize that their grandfather was special to the world as well as to them and that the unwanted attention was an unavoidable part of being his granddaughters.

Their own special moment came when they were included in a *People* magazine photo shoot with their grandfather and their images were seen all over the world. Only then did they begin to realize how famous their grandfather really was. Erin and Blair would grow into their lives as the granddaughters of Ray Charles just fine.

I was extraordinarily blessed. I believe if I had remained true to my mother's advice, I could have lived peacefully and happily with my children and spent more time watching them grow up to be the beautiful young women they are today. I fully intended to do that. But the road to hell is paved with good intentions, and I had started down that road the night I entered that house in Laurel Canyon and took the pipe the devil offered me. I had embarked on a path that would lead me not only to relive my father's mistakes but to make my own.

CHAPTER 15

Sinner's Prayer

Well if I've done somebody wrong, Lord, have mercy if You please.

—LLOYD C. GLENN SR.
AND LOWELL FULSON

THE EIGHTIES HAD BEGUN AS A TIME OF GREAT HOPE FOR me. I finished college, married, and embarked on a life of my own as a husband, father, and businessman. The initial trauma of my parents' divorce was behind us by then, and at my mother's urging, we were beginning to function more like a family again. Underneath the bitterness of their divorce, my parents claim they still loved each other deeply. If my father had had his way, they would still have been married. And though my mother could no longer live with the pain of a deeply troubled marriage, she was determined to hold on to the good things that survived. We were still a family, and though my father and mother were no longer husband and wife, they were still our parents. As the pain of the divorce began to subside, my father found it easier to be a part of our family again. But despite the best of intentions, the sins of the father are all too often an affliction passed on to the next generation. Now fathers ourselves, my brother and I would soon have to face our own failures.

In 1982, shortly before Erin's first birthday, my brother David brought a tragedy into the family that none of us could have foreseen. After leaving college, David had begun touring with my father. At twenty-four, David was already using a variety of hallucinogens. My dad knew that David was using drugs, and he told him that if he caught him using on tour, he would fire him. David thought our father's attitude was hypocritical given Dad's history, but he accepted the terms for the length of the tour. Once the tour ended and the band went on hiatus, however, David felt justified in returning to his old habits. When my father found out David was using again, he reminded David of the "no drugs" rule and promptly fired him. David was furious. He thought his behavior while they were on hiatus was his own business. He lost his temper and called Dad a hypocrite. A nasty argument followed, and David stormed out.

Still angry, David turned his anger into rage by using an abnormal amount of PCP. He wanted to hurt somebody, and he did. He doesn't remember anything specific about the assault, but he retains enough of the memory to know that he committed the crime. He was arrested and put in jail to await trial. My parents were devastated. My father went to visit him and cried, asking David if it was his fault, if he had been harsh and unfair. He felt sick with guilt over his own drug habit. David explained to our father that it wasn't his fault. David pled guilty to the charges and was sent to a maximum security prison, first to Chino and later to the state prison in Vacaville. His son, Little David, remained with my mother at Southridge.

That year my family began a ritual of monthly prison visits that went on for nine years. None of us could believe what had happened, and all of us blamed ourselves to some extent. I felt I had not spent enough time with him and become so wrapped up in college and new independence that I hadn't been there when he needed me. I couldn't comprehend what had happened. What had happened to my good-natured brother who spent his life trailing along behind me?

Our father had been jailed briefly for possession, but those had been one-night stays in the local jail. This was nothing compared to what David was experiencing. He was surrounded by brutality, witnessing other inmates maimed and killed in front of him. My parents found themselves sitting in the same room with Charles Manson on visiting days. It was like a bad dream. If David survived and was released someday, what kind of man would he be? How could anyone survive that hell intact?

While all this was happening, I was building another kind of prison for myself. Duana had said there would be no using cocaine when we got married, but I hadn't completely given up snorting it. I used cocaine occasionally and I didn't pay attention to the writing on the wall. But as my marriage disintegrated and I began to lose direction, I started using more often. By the time I separated from Duana, my drug use had begun to escalate.

Things were going well professionally. I had left New York Life and was working successfully for Mony Financial. As long as cocaine didn't affect my work, I thought I had things under control. I always waited until the girls were asleep or visiting with their mother before I used, so I didn't think it was affecting them. But my mother had noticed a change in me, and she wasn't pleased, to say the least. She knew I was using drugs again, and we had words about it more than once. She did not want drugs in her house. When the arguments continued, I decided to move out of Southridge and get a place of my own with my children. I found a split-level apartment in Culver City, and in the summer of 1988, we moved out of Southridge.

The girls loved our new place, and so did I. But without my mother's presence, there was no one to notice or comment on my behavior. I quickly escalated from snorting to smoking, because it was more intense. As the weeks passed, I remained blind to my growing addiction. Like cancer, addiction goes into remission, but it never goes away. It grows unseen, and when it surfaces again, it seems ten times worse than it was before. The moment you allow yourself to entertain the thought of using again, you are in danger. The moment you act on the thought, you are in its grip more powerfully than ever. After years of occasional use, my body reacted badly to the drug. I often felt sick and disoriented.

One night while the girls were asleep, I was downstairs, high, when Duana happened to call. When I answered the phone, she said, "You sound funny. What's going on? What are you doing?" I said things were fine, that the girls were asleep, but she didn't believe me. She recognized the symptoms. A short while later I heard her banging on my door, yelling at me to let her in. When I opened the door, she could see that I was high. A huge fight ensued. She woke the girls, packed a few of their things, and took them home with her.

I was angry at first, convinced that the people around me were over-reacting to a little recreational drug use. But gradually even I began to realize I was losing my grip. I had escalated from freebasing to smoking crack. When I was smoking ether-based cocaine in West Hollywood, I knew it was pure. But with crack, I could never be sure. It might have been mixed with heroin; it might be mixed with anything. One night after getting high at home, I thought I was having a heart attack. The left side of my body went numb, my heart raced, and my legs collapsed under me. I had no idea what I might have ingested. For a few terrible minutes, I thought I might die.

The drug itself wasn't the only danger. I was also interacting with a whole new set of people. Crack wasn't a rich man's drug. To get it, I had to go to the streets and buy from dealers who didn't care if I lived or died. I was no longer doing drugs in a wealthy enclave with the rich and famous. Some of the people I dealt with were extremely dangerous. I began to look for people I could use with "safely."

It was becoming apparent to me that I was in trouble. I searched the phone directory for an AA hotline to get information about meeting locations. I finally called AA and spoke to someone about getting help, but I never followed through. I told myself that I could beat the problem myself. I believed it was a simple matter of willpower. I refused to acknowledge the feelings that had been dormant deep within me, forcing their way into my consciousness. The failure of my marriage, the stresses of the separation, and my fear that I was incapable of being a good father had brought up my most deep-seated fears. I had suppressed a lifetime of pain, so when the pain became unbearable, cocaine felt like my best friend. I felt I had no one to talk to about my feelings because some of my close friends were using, too. I was no longer doing drugs for the high; I was self-medicating. I had crossed all of my personal boundaries into a dark place, and I was alone there. In the past, getting high was something to do with friends. Now I was isolating, seeking solace and relief. It had become a compulsion to continue until I was totally out of funds or completely exhausted. One night I looked in the mirror, and for a moment, I thought I was looking at my father.

I knew I had to do something or I wouldn't survive. I decided the answer was to go away for a while, to get clean and reflect on my life. The girls were still with their mother, so this seemed like the ideal time. I took thirty days off from work and flew to Hawaii. When I reached Honolulu, I checked in to the Sheraton Waikiki and took a room on the twentieth floor facing the ocean. The island became my refuge, and surrounded by all the natural beauty, I found peace again. Every evening I could watch the sun set over the water from my balcony. At night I walked the beaches, listening to the rhythm of the waves hitting the shore. Afterward I would lie in bed, praying and listening to the ebb and flow of the water. I would leave the lanai door open so I could hear the ocean. As the drugs worked their way out of my system, my head began to clear. I felt my body and spirit begin to reenergize. The striking natural beauty and the solitude surrounding me enabled me to face the seriousness of my situation.

I knew that if I did not get a grip on myself, my family would suffer and I could die. They were already suffering. We had been through this with my father, then with David, and now with me. If I didn't change, another generation of Robinson children would grow up suffering from the effects of drug addiction that almost destroyed my childhood. I did not want to do that to my children. I promised myself that I would make the changes that were necessary to put my life in order. Thirty days after landing in Hawaii, I returned to Los Angeles healthy, energized, and determined to stay clean. Shortly after I returned, Duana brought the girls back. My life seemed whole again.

With my life back on track, I decided the time had come to renew my relationship with my father. I resigned from Mony Financial and talked with my father about my future with Ray Charles Enterprises. By this time I'd had some professional success and experience of my own, and I felt I was ready to work for my father. I awaited his decision with great anticipation. No one was more surprised than I was when he said yes, I could come to work at Ray Charles Enterprises and we would see how things went.

As I entered into this new professional relationship with my father, I also began a serious relationship of another kind. Walking down Venice Beach shortly after my return from Honolulu, I ran into a woman I had met briefly a while back. Her name was Kim. She seemed to be a kind person in every way, and when we began spending time together, I found myself falling rapidly in love with her. Kim and I seemed so right for each other, I couldn't believe how fortunate I was. In only a few months, I had gone from loneliness and despair to a new relationship with a wonderful woman, to working with my father and my reunion with my daughters. Life couldn't get much better. I was still cautious, aware that the new situation was fragile, but for the first time in a long while, I had hope. The summer of 1989 was a time of hope, of new responsibilities and expectations. The Berlin Wall was coming down. I flashed back to my trip to East Berlin years before, when the dismantling of the wall had seemed a distant dream. Everything around me was changing. My daughters were growing up. Erin was in third grade, and Blair was starting kindergarten. Maybe I could change as well and leave my old demons behind.

I threw myself into preparing for my new role at my father's company. My first order of business was to acquire the rights to my father's life story. The rights had been optioned by producer Larry Schiller and were about to revert back to my father. I formed a production company, Red Cap Productions, with Larry Fitzgerald, Mark Hartley, and Doug Brown, and we optioned the rights to the life story. Doug still has the original treatment in braille for "The Ray Charles Story." Our production company negotiated a production deal with New Visions Pictures. Taylor Hackford and Stuart Benjamin would executive produce the film. With the production deal in place, I was ready to go to work. I brought something to the table as well.

My personal life was stabilizing, too. Most women were put off by the idea of dating a single father who was raising his children, but Kim seemed to accept my situation. She made a real effort to be part of my daughters' lives and the only request I made of her was to be a friend to my children. We moved in together and she started assuming some of the responsibility for taking the children to school, helping them with their homework, and taking care of the house. I began to think of her as a partner in raising my children. It was more than I had hoped for. Once again it seemed I had found the perfect family life that I had always dreamed of.

I should have been happy, and on one level, I was. But as my life began to flourish, the more uncomfortable I became. Maybe I didn't know how to be part of a happy family. I didn't feel deserving of one, yet when I came home each night, they still greeted me with smiles and hugs. I didn't feel worthy of such unconditional love. I carried a deep sense of shame for my behavior in the past. The more they loved me, the more unworthy I felt. I began to ruin joyous moments with self-doubt and fear. I was in control for the moment, but I didn't know how long that would last.

Ray Charles Enterprises was thriving. My father's Diet Pepsi commercials were a huge success. I continued to develop my own projects. I was still working diligently to bring my father's life story to the screen, and I had begun developing a project that became *Ray Charles: 50 Years in Music,* a special that I was co–executive producer on along with Greg Willenborg for the Fox Television Network. The guest stars included Stevie Wonder, Willie Nelson, Gladys Knight, Quincy Jones, and a host of other celebrities. The concept of the show was that my father would sing duets and medleys with the stars. The show did extremely well for Fox television. My father loved performing with his friends and it was a good start for my production efforts. I started RCR (Ray Charles Robinson) Productions, a marketing company that promoted and sold merchandise related to my father's name and likeness. I designed a biographical booklet, "My Early Years," along with other memorabilia for RCR. The merchandise was sold at concerts, on television, and through a variety of other marketing venues. The business relationship was working. My father had a tremendous amount of faith in my creative ability, and he backed his faith with action.

As time passed, though, my anxieties related to my relationship with my father began to creep into the business. My personal feelings gradually became intertwined with our professional relationship. I always arrived at the office before he did, so I would be at my desk every day when he walked in. I would sit there and hear him walk through the hall, hear his keys jingling as he greeted everyone. But he never stopped to put his head in and say hello to me. In fact, for the most part, he very seldom came around to my side of the building unless he needed something out of the wardrobe room. It started bothering me, and over time, it festered. What I didn't know was that every day when my father walked into the building, he would ask, "Is Ray Jr. here yet?" He always wanted to know that I was there. Once he knew I was safely there and working, he would go on about his business. I didn't find out until later that he checked on me every day. All that time I was in my office brooding, creating a problem in my own mind.

My feelings began to eat away at me. I just wanted a closer relationship with my father. I wanted to build a new father-son relationship. All of a sudden the congenial relationship I now had with my dad wasn't good enough. For him, just knowing I was there was a good feeling. But it wasn't enough for me. I tried to press him into a relationship he wasn't ready for, and in doing so, I began to ruin the relationship that we had. I slowly started to detach from him.

I had begun withdrawing from Kim as well, feeling more and more unworthy of her love, too. We began to drift apart. I was steadily destroying every relationship that mattered to me. It made no sense, and I started my self-destructive cycle again. The more unhappy I became, the more I turned to drugs for relief. I started bingeing, all night. At times, I would disappear for days without anyone knowing where I was. Afterward I would regroup and stay sober and functional for a while, but inevitably I would lose my grip and begin bingeing again.

The addiction that consumed me had become a battle for my mind and soul. I was spiritually lost. I wasn't chasing a high anymore. Drugs were no longer a relief; they were a source of paranoia, anxiety, and hopelessness. Late one night after bingeing all day, I called the paramedics because of a sharp pain in my head. I thought I was having an aneurysm. The paramedics came and examined me and confirmed that my blood pressure was extremely high. They asked me if I had taken any drugs, and I told them I had. They explained that I was having a severe anxiety attack and that I needed to calm down and get some rest. One of the paramedics patted me on the shoulder and told me, "You don't need to do this to yourself. Mr. Robinson, asking for help doesn't make you less of a man." He was thoughtful and very kind.

I knew he was right, but I didn't stop. I knew how much I was hurting everyone, but the more I thought about it, the more I would spiral out of control. I had never felt more alone. Deep in a drug-induced state, sometimes I thought I heard my mother's voice, my children's voices, my father's voice calling me. Today, I believe in my heart I heard all the prayers and voices of those I loved calling me back from the darkness.

The ones I was hurting the most deeply, of course, were my children. They would get up in the middle of the night sometimes and watch me as I once watched my father, but I was oblivious to their presence too. I would be walking around the house pacing back and forth. The cocaine triggered spells of obsessive-compulsive disorder. It was frightening for them to see me that way. They didn't know what was wrong with me any more than I had known what was wrong with my father when I was their age. The worst thing, though, was my disappearances.

My daughters knew something was seriously wrong. Everyone was making up excuses for me, telling them that "Daddy was sick"—the same thing my mother had said to me about my dad. They accepted the excuses. My children loved me with all of their hearts, just as I had loved my father. But like my father, I had brought the dark world of drugs into their lives. I was spiraling out of control. They were living with the same constant fear I had lived with as a child. The situation couldn't continue indefinitely. The girls' mother successfully sued for custody. The court determined that my children were no longer safe with me. I had failed my children on the most basic level, and I was overwhelmed with despair. Everything I cherished was going up in smoke.

The pernicious cycle put a tremendous strain on my relationship with Kim and my children. Kim and I were to be married, but that would not come to fruition. Eventually my relationship with her and my children became unbearable for all of us.

When she left, I continued my downward spiral. Everyone was concerned about me. My mother was sick with worry about what I was doing to myself, reliving her worst nightmares with my father. I knew I was breaking her heart, but I couldn't stop. My father was worried, too. When my dad learned that Kim had gone home to Connecticut and my children were back with their mother, he knew something was seriously wrong.

He sat me down and said, "This is just not like you. What are you doing? What's going on?" When I finally confessed that I had a drug problem, he was upset that I hadn't come to him for help. He did not understand what I was going through. And he didn't understand that he was the last person I could tell. I was too ashamed. My father told me that if I didn't stop the cycle I was caught in, I would lose my family. I knew he was right. He told me, "You've got to get hold of yourself, or I'll have to send you away to rehab. It's for your own benefit." When my father asked me if I wanted to go to rehab, I said yes. He told me he would make arrangements for me to be admitted to the Betty Ford Center. But deep inside I just wasn't ready, and when the time came to leave, I refused to go.

My father wasn't going to let me off the hook. He had no intention of sitting by and watching his son self-destruct. Once again, he took me aside. And once again, I found a way to pull myself up by my bootstraps. I stopped cold, and I regrouped. On the surface, my ability to stop without help seemed like a good thing, but in reality it was pushing me further and further away from admitting that I was an addict and was powerless over my addiction. But as long as I continued to believe I could stop on my own, I would never get the help I needed. And as long as I ignored my emotional pain that drove me, I would never be able to stay clean for long.

I was on the brink. I did not know if my life would ever be the same again, and I admitted myself to the Betty Ford Center. I was there for thirty days. I sought recovery with other high-profile celebrities and business people during my stay there, and I heard other shocking stories during the group sessions. I found out there were other people who were suffering just as much as I was. On the surface these people looked perfectly fine, but they too had serious issues. I realized that I was not alone in my suffering.

Unfortunately, in my case the Betty Ford experience was not enough. Being there brought up so many issues I had never dealt with that I came out thirty days later in worse shape than when I went in. I needed to go into a sober-living community. It never occurred to me to go to my father for help. If I had, I feel certain he would have helped me. But I didn't, and within days of leaving Betty Ford, I relapsed.

My mother confronted me and said, "You've got to go back. You have no choice." I knew she was right. Within thirty days of leaving Betty Ford, I moved into a sober-living program in Long Beach called Get Off Drugs (G.O.D.). It was not a twelve-step program; it was a program built around spirituality and abstinence. The sober-living house was in an area infested by drugs and prostitution. In the midst of all this confusion and corruption, G.O.D.'s house stood as a beacon of hope. Under the direction of Pastor Irene Robinson, who introduced us to the power of God and prayer, I would embrace Jesus Christ as my savior. In the chapel there, I would lie on the floor in front of the altar and pray that God would heal me of my addiction. And he did. I lived there for a year and a half, and during this time, I received counseling and began to get to the root of some of my most deep-seated issues. It was the first time I had any real clarity about my behavior and the trauma I carried inside.

For my first nine months there, I did not hear from my father. He was still angry and wanted me to get well without any interference from him. Eventually, though, he did call and ask me how I was doing. I knew he was concerned about me, but he never came to visit. The counselors at G.O.D. told me to be cautious about going back to work. They advised me that it would be a mistake for me to return to Ray Charles Enterprises. They felt it was a toxic environment for me. Being around my dad every day would trigger so many deep-seated memories and anxieties. Despite their advice, though, I wanted to return to Ray Charles Enterprises if my father would take me. I needed to reconnect and prove to him that I could still be a success.

In 1996 I returned to Ray Charles Enterprises. I continued to live in the sober-living home until I left on tour. My father welcomed me back with open arms, though on different terms. I would have the opportunity to build RCR Productions from the ground up. I would have to roll up my sleeves, pick myself up, and prepare to go on tour to sell our merchandise. I needed to complete the designs I had already started and pick up the production of my merchandise. I learned that while I was in rehab, my father and Mr. Adams had continued the work I had already begun. It was a great confidence builder to know he still had faith in my abilities. I agreed to his terms, and that summer I went back on the road with the band. The merchandise was received very well. We were gone most of the summer, finishing in Atlanta for the 1996 Olympics. It was great to be working again and earning the trust of those around me.

Before I left on tour I began developing the Web site raycharles.com. I envisioned a site where his fans could keep in touch with him, stay updated on his concert schedules, and buy his merchandise. My father loved the idea.

Things were going well, I was in a new relationship, and my misplaced self-confidence led to two serious mistakes. The first mistake was to not have a support system when I moved out of the sober-living facility. I had been sober for two years by then, and I thought I was ready. The second mistake was getting involved in another relationship too soon. I flew back to D.C. that fall to see Lisa. I thought I was ready for a new relationship, but as soon as I got engaged, the same anxiety from the past began to resurface. I became increasingly short-tempered, and I recognized the symptoms. I told myself, "You need to check yourself." It was then that I knew I had not dealt with all of the things I needed to deal with. I had never consulted a doctor about my anxiety attacks, so I sought release from the pain in the same place I had always gone. Abstinence from using was simply not enough.

As soon as I got off the plane when I returned from Washington, D.C., I crossed the line for the first time in two years. I knew the perils of using cocaine and I did it anyway. Once again, I was in that self-destructive state of mind. Worse, I brought my fiancée into my world of chaos. Against my better judgment, we were married in Las Vegas. Our marriage didn't stand a chance, and within a year I was separated for the second time. Once again, I had hurt someone I cared about. I deeply regret it. I had become the King of Pain and was still searching for answers.

Eventually my relapse was obvious and I would show up to work under the influence. My father confronted me and said he loved me, but he could not watch me go through this again. I would have to work from another location. I would move RCR Productions to my loft downtown. I continued to work with my father, but from a distance.

I believe that I broke my father's heart that day. He couldn't understand how I could come so far and then let it all go. He told me that he knew I had worked extremely hard, that I had accepted his challenge and made a success of RCR Productions. He seemed proud of my accomplishments, but he couldn't understand what was going on in my mind. He was struggling, questioning if my behavior was his fault, if he could somehow have prevented my relapse. Just as with David, he thought he had failed me. He was disappointed. My father couldn't understand why I didn't just stop cold turkey and stay clean like he had. I was disappointed in myself. That disappointment fed on itself, and for the next year I continued to run RCR Productions until my sister Raenee was brought in to run the day-to-day operations. It was only by God's grace that I survived.

CHAPTER 16

If I Could

If I could, I would

teach you

All the things I've never

learned.

—MARTHA VANESSA SHARRON,

KENNY HIRSCH, AND

RONALD NORMAN MILLER

AS THE NEW MILLENNIUM BEGAN, MY HOPES ROSE ONCE more. I had been clean for two years, and I felt it was time to make amends with my father. I arranged to meet him at the studio on the weekend. Once again we reconnected over some new projects. We were still seeking a production deal for my father's life story.

When I entered the office, he was sitting at his desk in his usual position, with one leg hanging over the side. He looked tense. I walked over to where he sat, said, "Hi, Dad, it's been a long time," and bent over to kiss him on the forehead. He looked up at me and rose to his feet. After a brief pause, he began to look over me as he had when I was a child. He ran his hands over my shoulders and down to my waist, then put his hands on my wrists and squeezed to see how thin I was. He nodded and said, "I see you've been taking good care of yourself." He sat back down, and I sat in front of his desk.

I could see that his hair was grayer, and this day he looked tired. His voice was soft as he spoke to me. "I've been getting reports about you from your mother. Seems like you've been through some more personal discovery about where you've been and where you need to go. Well, I just want you to know I love you." My father seldom expressed affection in words. Every now and then he would say, "I love you, dirty drawers," as a term of endearment, but that was rare. I was touched by his words.

"I love you, too, Dad," I told him, and then I began to talk to him. I told him that the bad choices I had made in life were not his fault. It was true that his behavior while I was growing up had an effect on me, but it had also shown me the dangers of addiction firsthand. No one knew better than I did how serious drug addiction could be or how much it affected a family. I had ventured down that road with my eyes open. And then I told him, "I know you were disappointed in me. I hope you can forgive me."

He sat silently, looking at the floor. I knew without his saying so that he forgave me, but he couldn't find the words at that moment. I had been through the same fire that had tried him so many years ago. We shared about our failures and also our triumphs.

We talked for hours after that, catching up on all we'd missed in each other's lives. We talked about the past, about my children, about my plans for the future. I told him about the projects I still hoped to develop for him. He listened carefully, nodding. I knew he had to be holding his breath, hoping I would be able to follow through this time. He was willing to give me another chance, and I was determined to make the most of it.

I returned to my father energized and determined. I was ready to handle business. I plunged into a whirlwind of activity, moving forward on several projects at the same time. One of the first concepts I pitched was a project that eventually became the album *Genius Loves Company*. It came at a time when my father was feeling the loss of so many great musicians who were his friends. Dizzy Gillespie had died, and my father had begun to realize that he would never be able to play with many of his friends again. Don Mizell and I originally came to my father with another duet concept for a CD, and we sat down to discuss the possibilities. We talked about him doing duets with Paul McCartney, Steve Winwood, Natalie Cole, Willie Nelson, and other great artists. Ultimately, some of the artists we proposed to perform on the CD did. Once again, my father would perform with the artists he loved and respected. That was all he wanted to do. I took pride in watching the success of the CD. It sold more than three million copies and would become my father's grand finale.

Another project close to my heart that year was the gospel Christmas concert DVD *Ray Charles Celebrates Christmas with the Voices of Jubilation*. Stuart Benjamin, of Benjamin Productions, brought the idea to me. It immediately sparked my memory of a conversation I'd had with my father a few years earlier. He was talking about gospel music, and he said, "Hey, this is how me and your mother met, you know." I knew he loved gospel and that it had been in his heart to make a gospel CD with a gospel choir one day. He had wanted to make a gospel CD with his friend James Cleveland, but he lost his inspiration after Reverend Cleveland passed. I knew gospel would bring him back to his roots. Stuart asked me if my father had performed gospel before and if he would consider the idea. I could serve as a catalyst to inspire my dad to consider the project. After listening to a recording of the Voices of Jubilation Choir, he asked to speak to Stephanie Minatee, their choir director. Stephanie and my father would meet, and their personal and musical chemistry was instantaneous. "Christmas Jubilee" was born.

The Christmas concert was a wonderful experience to share with my father. To his surprise, I came at Stuart's request. I wanted Dad to know I was directly involved in helping Stuart promote the event for Benjamin Productions. I appeared on a morning show and conducted radio interviews promoting the concert. I spent a wonderful two days with my father while they rehearsed and prepared for the performance. He was so excited about performing with the Voices of Jubilation Choir. Stephanie, Vernon, Stuart, and I shared my father's joy together, and the success of the gospel performance that evening. My father, the Voices of Jubilation, and the audience were moved by the spirit of the performance that night, which came from the depth of their souls.

I was proud of the work I was doing, but the greatest joy came from spending time with him. We attended a Green Bay Packers game one evening, something we hadn't done together in a long time. It was incredibly cold that night, but we were given a luxury skybox for the game, where it was warm. My father listened with Vernon as I sat with my eyes glued to the field. I was a huge Brett Favre fan. I was with my father, and I had a wonderful time.

My return to the entertainment business also gave me the opportunity to produce an independent film. A mutual friend introduced me to Anatoli Ivanov, an accomplished Russian writer, director, and cinematographer. We discussed his plans to shoot a film in Moscow and St. Petersburg about Aleksandr Pushkin, the great Russian writer. Pushkin's great-grandfather, Abram Petrovich Gannibal, had been born in Ethiopia. Abram served as a page to Peter the Great, who educated Abram in France as a military engineer. He went on to become governor of Reval and was responsible for building many of the sea fortresses and canals in Russia. I was intrigued by the notion that Pushkin was of African descent, even more so when I learned that he was passionate about his African lineage. The idea of exploring Pushkin's African roots through Russian culture fascinated me. The independent film project named *Black Prince* was critically acclaimed and won the Grand Jury Prize at the New York International Independent Film and Video Festival. It starred Russian prima ballerina Anas-

tasia Volochkova, of the Bolshoi Ballet, as Pushkin's wife; Georgian actor
Levan Uchaneishvili as Pushkin; and me as Roy Charles (Gannibal).

The making of the film was one of the most fascinating experiences of
my life. I flew to Moscow in 2002 to begin production. The ancient beauty
of the city was powerfully moving. From my hotel window I could see
the Kremlin outlined against the evening sky. I remembered the images
of Russia from during the cold war and how terrifying they were. As a
boy, I had been afraid that Russia and the United States would engage
in an apocalyptic war, but now I was walking the streets of Moscow, experiencing Russian culture and history. In St. Petersburg I stood on the
landing in the harbor and watched the great ships sail in as part of the city's
three-hundredth anniversary celebration. I was taken on private tours of
the Hermitage Museum and Peter the Great's summer palace. I visited
the classroom where Pushkin was taught, and I filmed scenes inside his
apartment along the canals of St. Petersburg. I watched the Bolshoi Ballet
in their home theater, toured cities along the Black Sea, and stayed at the
Grand Hotel in Nevsky Prospekt, where I visited the Church of the Res-
urrection of St. Petersburg.

As much as I loved Russia, though, the project closest to my heart was
my father's life story. It was burned into my soul. Stuart Benjamin, Taylor
Hackford, and I had been on a quest to bring it to the screen for fourteen
years. We had pitched the project to major studios and production compa-
nies over the years with no success. Given the ultimate success of the film,
it is incredible how difficult it was to get backing. One of our meetings
with potential backers is funny in retrospect. Reggie Jackson, an associate
of mine, and I were meeting with a production company and one of the
vice presidents of William Morris. We sat around the conference table as I
pitched my father's story. I told them about George drowning in the tub,
my father going blind and being sent away to blind school at eight years
old. I described his mother's death when he was fifteen and his struggle
to survive as a blind black orphan in the South. I told them about his trip
to Seattle alone, about his breakthrough success in the music business,
about his heroin use and how he had beat his drug habit. I told them about

my parents' love story, and I also told them about the other women and children. Most of all, I told them about my father's triumph over the many obstacles that made his journey seem impossible.

When I finished, there was a short break while they conferred. When we sat back down at the table, one of the producers said, "Gentlemen, we're sorry. There's just no story here." I was dumbfounded. No story? Then I was questioned about my authority to represent my father. One of the VPs of William Morris asked, "Are you even empowered to bring us this story? We would need a letter from your father saying you have the right to represent him."

I picked up the conference-room phone and called my father. "Is this Ray Charles?" I asked.

Dad said, "Yeah, son, what do you need?"

"I'm here with one of the VPs of William Morris and another production company speaking to them about your life story. I am being told there's no story. But they want a letter from you stating that I have the right to represent you."

My father replied, "Just walk out of the meeting." And that's what I did.

These kinds of meetings were a familiar part of our journey. No one was willing to invest the funds necessary to make a film about the life of a poor, blind African American musician from the South who just happened to be Ray Charles, a music icon.

In the long run, the rejections we received for more than a decade turned out to be a blessing. They ultimately led us to Philip Anschutz, a highly successful businessman who had the vision to see the story's potential and the commitment necessary to make *Ray* the high-caliber film we all needed it to be. After hearing us out, he said, "This is not just an African American story. It is a triumph of the human spirit. It is an American rags-to-riches success story." Mr. Anschutz's production team included Crusader Entertainment and Bristol Bay Productions. He was committed to keeping the film focused on its central message: the rise of a man who came to greatness against all odds. Mr. Anschutz refused to include scenes showing sex or graphic drug use. He wanted the film to be appropriate for everyone. James L. White had come on board to write the screenplay. He bonded immediately with my parents as well as with me, and that bond breathed life into his screenplay. Taylor Hackford was destined to direct this film. Taylor understood all of the elements that made my father's story great and how the music could be used to drive it. "Unchain My Heart," as the film was originally called, finally went into preproduction in 2003.

I was thrilled to have the project under way, but I also felt a tremendous sense of responsibility for the way the film would represent the events of my father's life. There was a lot of controversial material in the film, and I wanted it portrayed properly. Both of my parents were still alive. I did not want anyone to sensationalize his story; his life and all that he accomplished spoke for itself. My father was a star and provider for his family, but my mother was the foundation of our family. I wanted that to be made clear. If I felt the film was not representative of my family, I was going to have to bring it to my father's attention. That may have resulted in a complicated and expensive legal battle. But Taylor and the rest of the production team soon put those fears to rest.

The ensemble cast that Taylor assembled was simply amazing. They were dedicated to the film and treated my father with great respect whenever he was on the set. Taylor chose Kerry Washington to play my mother, and I thought she was a fantastic choice for the role. Taylor chose Jamie Foxx for the lead. Jamie is not only a fine actor; he is also an accomplished singer and classically trained pianist. Apparently, the first time he met my father, he sat down at a piano and played until my father slapped his leg and laughed in approval. My first day on the set, I met Jamie and told him, "I know that you can do it. And if you win, we all win." I spoke with him about a few of my father's mannerisms; other than that, he came prepared indeed. That preparation showed in his performance. In New Orleans, I walked onto the Hepburn set, and Jamie was outside on the porch playing a keyboard, weaving back and forth. As he continued to play, I watched him closely, and began to get an eerie feeling. It was almost as though I were looking at my father when he was young. It was as though my father's spirit was using Jamie's body as a host. Jamie's performance was electrifying. It was the perfect story, the perfect actor, and the perfect time.

We shot the film in New Orleans, and I quickly fell in love with the city. So much of my family's history is there. My grandfather was from Baton Rouge, Louisiana, and my children's family on their mother's side were from New Orleans. My father had played there as a struggling musician, back in the days when a home-cooked meal from Miss Mary was a blessing and a treat. The city itself embraced us with open arms. Most of the crew was from New Orleans, and the people were extremely hospitable to me. During my visit, I dined at some of the best restaurants in New Orleans but I became a regular at Delmonico's, one of Emeril's restaurants. I ate there almost every night, and they always had a table for me and my favorite sorbet prepared for dessert. They treated me like royalty.

I expected the filming of *Ray* to be one of the high points of my life, the culmination of a fourteen-year quest. The film was everything I hoped for. What I hadn't realized, however, was that the film would force me to relive all the trauma, fear, and anxiety of my childhood. I hadn't dealt with memories and anxieties as my father had. The day I first walked onto the Hepburn set, I began to get uncomfortable. The set looked exactly like the house I grew up in. For a moment, I felt like I was actually there again. There was my father's grand piano in the living room, and on the office wall were the plaques, gold records, album covers, and *Billboard* covers. Standing there, looking at all the familiar objects, my childhood came rushing back, with all the pain I had tried to forget. I had to get out of that room on set immediately. From then on I sat in another room and watched the filming through the monitor. I would go back and forth inside the room, never staying too long. I hoped the feelings would go away, but as the days went by, they would get stronger. One night, after I returned from the set of Hepburn, I went back to my room and used some cocaine for the first time in three years. After being clean for so long, it made me sick and a little disoriented.

It was about this time that my youngest daughter, Blair, came to New Orleans to visit me and watch production. I was excited to see her and eager to show her around the city. I took her to Café du Monde in the French Quarter and showed her around. I introduced her to Jamie Foxx and some of the other people on the set. Once she got comfortable, she started venturing out on her own. She visited her cousins and made friends with some of the people she met. New Orleans is an exciting city, and Blair seemed to be having a wonderful time. We made plans to go to an NCAA championship game that weekend.

After my experience on the set of Hepburn, I had already started to self-medicate. On the day of the NCAA championship game, I decided to finish the cocaine I had left. Instead of getting high, I got sick and began having an anxiety attack. I thought I might need a doctor. I told Blair I was feeling sick and couldn't go to the game that night, but she knew all too well what was really wrong with me. She and her cousin Claudia took a taxi to the game and they spent the evening sitting in the corporate box with Jamie. Claudia tried to comfort her, and Blair made the best of the situation. By the next morning I felt better, and I did not use the rest of the time she was there and while I was in New Orleans during production. We continued to enjoy New Orleans. We spoke about that event. I tried to relieve her anxiety, but I knew I had hurt her and revived the old memories about me in the past. I was painfully aware of the irony that my attempts to deal with my own childhood trauma had revived my daughter's as well. Blair returned to Los Angeles a few days later. I saw a doctor, who helped me flush the drugs out of my system.

Four weeks after we started filming *Ray*, I had to leave New Orleans and return to Russia to work on *Black Prince*. Rumors circulated about my departure, and I had left so abruptly that even my father didn't know why I was gone. By the time I came back to the States, the film had wrapped in New Orleans and moved to Los Angeles to complete shooting. I was in LA briefly, but then I had to go right back to Russia. I made several trips back and forth to Moscow. Out of the country, I missed the wrap party, the group picture, and all the other celebratory rituals that occur when a production finishes filming. I missed the satisfaction and joy of completing *Ray* on set with the cast, crew, and production team. And I missed the opportunity to express my gratitude to the amazing ensemble of individuals that brought my father's story to life in a way that exceeded my greatest hopes and expectations.

IN DECEMBER 2002, on one of my brief trips home from Russia, I received a call from my father. He said he wanted me to come to a brunch he was having with all of his children. I realized that he wasn't just referring to me and my brothers; he was referring to all of his offspring, including my half brothers and half sisters I'd never met. I knew something important was in the air because he had never called us all together before. I was also struck by the fact that he made the call himself. Usually he would have someone else call if he was arranging a meeting. If he was calling everyone himself, it had to be important. I had been talking to my father by phone periodically, but I hadn't seen him for about six months. I wondered what the meeting was about. There was an uncomfortable feeling in the pit of my stomach that something was wrong.

Walking into the brunch that day was unsettling. I was curious about my siblings I was about to meet, but I was anxious, too. We all introduced ourselves and hugged. I found myself watching them intently, trying to see family traits I recognized. My feelings were mixed. On one level, though I knew some of my siblings, it was exciting to meet my other siblings up close and personal. On a deeper level, it was difficult thinking of what my mother had had to endure in knowing about most of my siblings. Almost all of them were there except for Margie Hendricks's son, Charles, and Sandra Jean Betts's daughter, Sheila. In attendance were Louise Mitchell's daughter, Evelyn; Mae Mosely Lyles's daughter, Raenee; Arlette Kotchounian's son, Vincent; Gloria Moffett's daughter, Robyn; Mary Anne den Bok's son, Corey; and Chantelle Bertrand's daughter, Alexandria. I knew the meeting must be an emotional roller coaster for my other siblings as well. In spite of the awkwardness, though, it was ultimately a comfort to finally meet the brothers and sisters I had known about most of my life. I hoped that we would be able to start new relationships that were based on more than just shared genes.

My father looked uncomfortable at first as we all milled around, making introductions and getting to know one another. Once everything settled down and we had a chance to eat, he got up to make an announcement. He said that he had set up an individual trust for each of us. We looked at one another, and a murmur ran around the room. No one had expected this announcement from my dad. My father seemed relieved, as though a burden had been lifted off him. He said that Mr. Adams would take care of the details and give us instructions on the disbursement of the money he had put in trust for each of us. Then he sat down, and Mr. Adams got up to speak.

Mr. Adams began to talk about the estate and the money our father had set aside for us. My father had referred to a single disbursement, so we were all surprised when Mr. Adams suggested to my father that it might be more prudent to disburse our funds over a four-year period rather than a lump sum. Mr. Adams would serve as trustee for all of our trust funds. As I listened to him, it was clear Mr. Adams would be in control of my father's estate and our individual trusts. After this uncomfortable announcement, we all gathered around my father to take family photos. These would become the first and only pictures of almost all of my father's offspring together with him.

Everyone said their good-byes, but as I prepared to leave, I began to get a sense of urgency about my father. It wasn't anything I could put my finger on, just a general uneasiness about him and his health. He was next to me as we walked toward the door, and we stopped to talk briefly. As I was about to leave, my dad suddenly grabbed me by the arm and asked me to wait. He was standing behind me when he said it. He started squeezing my arms and then ran his hands over my shoulders. I was startled. He hadn't done this in a long time. He put his hands on my waist and patted me. I asked him what he was doing. He replied, "Just stand still a minute. I want to see you. I'm just trying to see you, son. I love you. You know that."

I didn't know what to think. This wasn't like him. I pulled Vernon aside and asked him if something was wrong. Was there something I needed to know about my father's health?

Vernon said quietly, "You need to come to the office and speak with your father. In private."

I felt a knot of worry in my stomach. I asked my father, "Is there something about your health I need to know?" He wouldn't give me a straight answer. I asked him again, but each time, he evaded my question. The feeling of uneasiness stayed with me.

IN 2003 I RETURNED to Moscow to finish *Black Prince*. Shortly after I arrived, Anastasia and I made a trip with Anatoli to shoot some pick-up scenes at a monastery in a secluded area some distance from Moscow. The monastery was nestled in the countryside, and it was a beautiful hidden gem of antiquity. The church inside the walls of the monastery was more than three hundred years old, older than our nation. On the afternoon of our arrival, I ventured into the church to pray and found repairmen restoring the image of Christ. The moment I entered this ancient place of worship a stillness came over me, and I got the chills. I sat in one of the pews and let the silence embrace me. For more than an hour, I sat in that stillness, feeling it penetrate to my soul. I had never experienced anything quite like it.

Later that day Anastasia, Boris, Anatoli, and I were taken to holy ground. A priest from the monastery led us there through the woods, about fifty minutes from the monastery. He was a small man, no more than five feet tall, with a beard that came down to his waist. Among the ancient trees, he looked more like a character of myth. There was a baptismal pool and a well where the priests brought flowers and prayed over the water. It was freezing that day, less than thirty degrees, and I found myself transfixed as I gazed at the water. The place felt holy, and people came from miles around to bless themselves with the holy water. If the house in Laurel Canyon had been the house of lost souls, then surely this was the pool of salvation.

Without stopping to think, I said, "I'm going to get a blessing today," and jumped into the ice-cold water. I began splashing my face with water and continued to pour water over my face with my hands cupped for more than five minutes. As the water cleansed me, I felt deep chills running through my body, as if I had been touched in a way that had nothing to do with the cold. Something was happening to me, a deep sense of an awakening, a blessing I had never experienced before. I couldn't put a name to what I was feeling, but it was beautiful. After watching me for a few minutes, Anastasia got into the water, too. Afterward, we exited the pool, she filled a bottle with water from the well to take back to the monastery, and I continued to splash my face with the water from the well. Eventually we returned to the monastery, where we spent the night. The feeling that had filled me in the pool stayed with me. When we returned to the monastery, I had no desire for anything, only to be alone with God in solitude.

The next morning we returned to the city. Anatoli wrapped our film a few weeks later, and we would travel to Sochi, a coastal city on the Black Sea that is referred to as the Russian Riviera. We attended a film festival there where our film was well received. Instead of going home after the festival as I'd originally planned, I decided to stay in Russia for a while. I had a girlfriend there, and there were other projects I wanted to develop in Moscow. I began looking for an apartment in St. Petersburg. Once again I would return home briefly during the summer of 2003.

During the months I was in Russia, I'd gotten in the habit of reading the news on the Internet every morning to keep track of what was happening at home. One morning in Moscow at the end of September 2003, I saw a news article announcing that my father had canceled the remaining dates on his tour. That was highly unusual. I knew he had postponed his tour when he admitted himself to St. Francis, but this information caught me by surprise. My mind flashed back to the last time I had seen him, at the brunch with all of my brothers and sisters. The uneasiness returned. Something was wrong.

I rushed back to my room at the hotel and called Ray Charles Enterprises, where I spoke with Valerie Ervin, Mr. Adams's assistant. I asked

her, "Is my father okay? I read in the news that he's canceled all his concert dates."

Valerie said, "Your dad hurt his hip, but he's okay. I'll have him give
you a call, though."

I felt somewhat reassured, but I still needed to speak with my father.
Despite Valerie's promise, I did not expect my dad to return my call so
soon, and he would have to catch up to me while I traveled back and forth
to Moscow.

I had traveled to St. Petersburg to see my friend Alla and I was in my
hotel room when the call came through. I heard a soft voice say, "Hello.
Hello." I could barely hear the voice, and I didn't realize at first that it was
my father. His voice was so soft, and my father always started phone conversations with me by saying, "So it's you. It's your father."

I said, "Who is this speaking?"

He replied, "It's your father."

I immediately replied, "How are you? Are you all right? What's going
on with your health?"

He just replied, "Well, how are you?"

I told him, "I'm great. I'm in Russia finishing a film. I started making
this film before we started the production of *Ray* and I had to return to
finish shooting. How are you and what is happening with your health?"

He said, "Well, you know, I have some pain in my hip. I had to have
some surgery. I'm a little tired. Son, that chemotherapy kicked my butt."
He paused a moment, and my mind raced. Chemotherapy? That meant
cancer, but he did not go into any details about his condition. Then he
continued, "Son, it's just nice to hear your voice. It's just good to see another day."

My heart almost stopped. I knew at that moment that he was dying. He
didn't say so. He never used the word "cancer." But I knew. I didn't know
what to say to him. The shock was overwhelming. A thousand thoughts
raced through my mind. Until that moment, I had truly thought that my
father was immortal. In many ways, so did he. He had always been larger
than life to me. I had never imagined him becoming terminally ill.

His world had been turned upside down. Strangely, my life began to flash in front of my eyes even though I was not the one dying. All the pictures of my father in my mind started flitting by. My mind kept going, beyond the pictures of the past to pictures of the future I had expected us to have together. All the conversations we would have. The walks we would take. The tours I would go on with him. Helping him when he grew old. Having him there to experience his granddaughter Blair's singing career. It had never once crossed my mind that we wouldn't have more time together.

After a moment my father broke the silence. He sounded tired. He said he had just finished chemotherapy and was pretty worn out, but he needed to hear my voice. I told him I would be back as soon as I could, and I rang off. I finished up some business and then took a plane back to Los Angeles. It was October 2003. I checked into a hotel room close to the airport. I didn't plan to stay long. I just needed to see my father.

It was several days before I was able to visit him. When I did, I took my daughters with me. He was still spending a lot of time at the studio. I was tense and anxious as we went upstairs, wondering how he would look. When we walked into his office, to my great relief, he didn't look as bad as I feared. He'd lost some weight, and his skin was very dark, somewhat like my mother's when she had peritonitis. But he was up and around as usual, still pretty vibrant and able to have a sound conversation. There were no serious signs of deterioration. He'd had time to recover from the stress of chemotherapy and was feeling stronger.

The first thing he wanted to talk to me about was my film obligations. I was shooting two films simultaneously. He expressed his disappointment that I was not in the production photo shoot for *Ray* at the studio. I reassured him that Mr. Anschutz was adamant that the film be made with dignity and discretion. I also told him that I'd had complete confidence in Taylor Hackford. Taylor cared deeply about this film and about presenting my father's journey as the triumph it was. Our conversation seemed to reassure him and clear the air.

Then my daughters joined in. Blair continued talking to her grandfather about her plans to sing. She and my father talked about the music business for a while, and my father told her that he wanted to help her get started. He had all the studio equipment she needed to work on her first CD, and he said she could use his recording studio. He was excited about the possibilities and Blair was, too. Then I gave my dad the big news about my older daughter, Erin. She was pregnant with her first child. He was surprised by the news, but he got a kick out of the fact that I was going to be a grandfather. It meant another generation of Robinsons. I was elated for my daughter, my dad's third generation unfolding before him and my becoming a grandfather. For Erin's part, she was excited about the baby and looking forward to putting her grandfather's great-grandchild into his arms. He told us he was working on a new CD. Finally we said our good-byes and I told him we would see him soon. As we were leaving, my dad said, "By the way, Ray Jr., I want you to hear some of the new tracks."

It was the last time I would see my father face-to-face and alive.

CHAPTER 17

Unchain My Heart

Unchain my heart.

Won't you set me free?

—TEDDY POWELL AND

ROBERT SHARP JR.

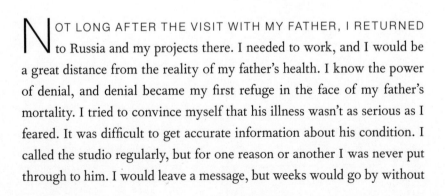

N OT LONG AFTER THE VISIT WITH MY FATHER, I RETURNED
to Russia and my projects there. I needed to work, and I would be
a great distance from the reality of my father's health. I know the power
of denial, and denial became my first refuge in the face of my father's
mortality. I tried to convince myself that his illness wasn't as serious as I
feared. It was difficult to get accurate information about his condition. I
called the studio regularly, but for one reason or another I was never put
through to him. I would leave a message, but weeks would go by without

hearing anything back. I did talk with him a few times. Usually, I would be told that he was napping or with the nurse. I knew that my half sister Evelyn, who is a nurse, was helping with his care. My father was seeing almost no one. But Mable John, who was a former Raelette and remained one of my father's close friends, was one of the few people allowed to visit him. A minister for many years by then, she became a spiritual adviser for my father as his health worsened.

After a while, I didn't hear from him at all. When the reality that my father was dying made dents in my shield of denial, I took refuge and dwelled in the memories of my life as his son.

In April my father's studio and office at 2107 were declared historic landmarks in an outdoor ceremony. I was not notified of the ceremony. I watched the dedication on CNN. The mayor was there with other civic dignitaries and a line of celebrities to dedicate my father's building. The ceremony began without my father. As the dignitaries took turns making speeches, people watched the door, wondering if he would make an appearance. Finally, near the end of the ceremony, the door opened and my father was brought outside in a wheelchair. He was pushed close to the podium, where he was lifted from the chair and supported on either side by Clint Eastwood and Cicely Tyson. My father was gaunt and drawn. I was stunned by his appearance, fighting back tears as he whispered a thank-you to the city for the honor. After struggling for a moment, he finally managed to whisper, "I'm weak. But I'm getting stronger." He was carefully lowered into the chair and wheeled back inside. The newspaper photos of that day told the story of my father's fate.

I returned to Los Angeles to await the birth of my granddaughter. I tried to concentrate on the blessing that was coming, but I was also worried about my father's health. As the stress mounted, I turned to self-medicating once again. Cocaine was the only way I knew to find emotional relief. But instead of providing relief, the drug magnified my fears. I moved into another hotel, isolated and overwhelmed. Looking back at that time, I was filled with self-recrimination for my behavior. It should never have been about anything other than the present, my family, and their needs. But instead I was caught in a vicious, selfish cycle that made a difficult situation intolerable.

I struggled to pull myself together as my grandchild's birth drew near. I managed to regroup, and I promised Erin that I would be there for the baby's birth. She was very excited. On the way to the shower, I called her to say I was on the way. Though I had stopped using, I looked awful and I felt ashamed. I simply did not want to embarrass her. I did not show up to the shower. She got through the shower as best as she could, and the week before the birth, she went to visit her grandfather and tell him the baby was due any day. I missed that visit, an opportunity to see my father again, because yet again I had stopped communicating and continued to isolate myself.

On March 11, 2004, Kennedy Michelle Williams was born. I would see Erin and Kennedy for the first time weeks after her birth. I was finally able to hold her, and she was a beautiful, healthy baby. My hand gently traced her face and I touched all of her limbs. At the beginning of May I admitted myself to a sober-living home. My family put me in touch with a family friend, Danny Laws of Laws Support Center, and he agreed to admit me into one of his homes. For the next four months, this was where I lived. I still hadn't been able to see my father.

Erin had called her grandfather almost as soon as Kennedy was born, but like me, she could never get through. My mother, meanwhile, had been delivering my father's favorite foods to the studio, to encourage him to eat. By the first week of June, Kennedy was almost three months old, and Erin was anxious to show off her baby to her grandpa. My mother had arranged to bring some of his favorite pies to my father that week, so she suggested Erin come along and bring the baby. Erin was very excited, and they agreed it would be the perfect chance to see him. That way my mother could share the joy of introducing their first great-granddaughter to my father.

On the afternoon of June 10, 2004, I was at Aron's Records on La Brea with Blair. I had just finished a month in sober living and was spending as much time as possible with my daughters and grandchild. Erin was at home with Kennedy while Blair and I shopped that day. The phone rang at her house, and when Erin picked up, it was her aunt Inga, a close friend of her mother's. Without any preliminaries, Inga asked, "Are you all right?" Erin had no idea what she was talking about. Inga told her, "You need to turn on the news. Your grandfather's passed."

Erin was stunned, but her first thoughts were of me. She realized I hadn't heard the news, for I would have called her. She knew I was out with Blair and that the news would soon reach me. She didn't want me to find out over the radio. Erin immediately called Blair's cell phone and gave her the news. Blair was standing in the record store looking at CDs when the call came. She said, "Oh, no!" and then looked at me, standing a few feet away. Walking away from me to hide the conversation, she told Erin, "I don't want to tell Dad. He's going to lose it." Blair called her grandmother Elaine Chenier and asked her to call me. A few moments later my cell phone rang, and Elaine told me with great kindness that my father had passed away. I almost fainted from the shock. Wouldn't somebody have called us if he was that close to death? I immediately dialed Ray Charles Enterprises, but the line was busy. I was desperate to find out what was happening and why we were not notified before the information was released about his death. Blair and I got in the car and raced over to 2107 W. Washington. When I turned on the car radio, I heard the announcement. Mr. Adams had issued a press release before informing the family. We would receive the news from one another or from a radio or television broadcast.

When we reached Ray Charles Enterprises, I pulled into the driveway. Blair and I climbed out, but we couldn't go any farther. The gate had been closed and locked, preventing entry through the driveway. We tried entering the building through the front door, but that was locked, too. Frantic, I called the office again. I identified myself and said Blair and I could not get into the parking lot. The person replied, "Mr. Adams has locked the building."

Incredulous, I said, "You mean we can't come inside?"

The voice calmly replied, "No, Mr. Adams doesn't want anyone in the building."

A thousand things were swirling through my mind. I couldn't take in what was happening. "I don't understand . . . then can I speak to Mr. Adams?"

The reply came, "Mr. Adams is not available." There was nothing to do but leave. I never received a call from Mr. Adams about any aspect of my father's death. Not one word.

The radio and television bombarded us relentlessly with news surrounding my father's death. It was painful to listen to, yet it was our primary source of information. The local news showed Johnny Grant, honorary mayor of Hollywood, next to my father's star on the Walk of Fame on Hollywood Boulevard. The star was already surrounded by flowers and flocks of mourners. The news of my father's death traveled extremely fast. The papers reported that "Mr. Charles died surrounded by family and friends." Family and friends? Whose family? I found that a very interesting statement. My father's complete medical diagnosis was never fully disclosed to me. We later learned, through the media, that he had died of acute liver disease.

I needed a friend to talk to, someone who would be there in the midst of my grief and confusion. A few days later I received a call from Rhonda Bailey, a friend from my college days. She said that she had heard the news about my father and was calling to tell me I was in her prayers, that she was there to support me in any way I needed. I was surprised and deeply touched by her offer of friendship. That phone call ultimately would be the beginning of our new relationship. I am deeply grateful that she offered her heart to me at a time of tremendous emotional turmoil. I don't know where I would be today if she had not stayed in my life.

Stunned and grief-stricken, the family gathered to comfort one another and decide what to do next. We were able to find out that my father's body was at Angelus Funeral Home on Crenshaw at Thirty-ninth. We decided to have a private memorial service in the chapel there before the public memorials began. We contacted our close friends and our families, and we contacted Angelus to inform them of our plans to have a private memorial. Our plans were set in motion by my brother Robert. We were informed that we would be met with opposition by Mr. Adams. But we moved forward anyway.

As everyone arrived, we gathered outside the funeral home. My mother and daughters were there, with Erin holding little Kennedy, and we stood at the entrance, greeting our family and friends. Once everyone was assembled, we entered the building, but Mr. Adams and private security quickly moved to prevent us from going farther. Mr. Adams told us that we did not have permission to let "these people" view our father's body. The people Mr. Adams was referring to were family members and our close family friends who knew my father but who would not be attending the funeral at the First African Methodist Episcopal Church, better known as FAME. "If your friends want to see Ray Charles," he told us, "they can go to the Los Angeles Convention Center and look at him there like everyone else."

I cannot begin to explain how disgusted and angry everyone felt. A heated discussion started as security blocked our way. Erin took Kennedy outside, away from the crowd, to calm the baby down. There was confusion and pandemonium. My brother Robert took the funeral director aside and spoke to him privately, then the funeral director spoke to Mr. Adams. Eventually Mr. Adams agreed that the family could enter the viewing room to see our father's body, but our friends would have to wait in the chapel.

Our friends were directed into the chapel. Then Mr. Adams and his security took us down the hall to the room containing my father's body, unlocked the door, and we filed inside. Mr. Adams closed the door, leaving his security outside the entrance. We gathered around my father's coffin. He looked so thin and frail, as he had years ago lying in the bed at St. Francis. We were all struggling for control of our emotions as we looked at him, especially my mother. Meanwhile Mr. Adams stood there, watching us. We were intensely aware of his eyes on us. Even in death, we were not allowed to be alone with my father. We struggled with a mixture of grief and anger.

We could have our private memorial in the chapel on the condition that my father's coffin remain in another room under lock and key. Robert led us through the brief memorial service. Our friend Ollie Woodson, who also loved my father dearly, sang "Walk Around Heaven All Day."

I spoke about Ray Charles Robinson: his humble beginnings, his loves, his pain, his dreams, his rise to fame, and our relationship. "Ray Charles became the man he was meant to be, with music flowing through his veins. He lived for the enduring love and embrace of his audience," I said with love and respect. I promised my father that I would be a better person. I said, "Dad, you can rest now." Saying that tore me apart inside, and I continued to mourn in private. Our family would have our memorial.

ON THURSDAY, Ray Charles Enterprises put my father's body on display at the Los Angeles Convention Center. Eric Raymond, a spokesman for Ray Charles Ent., my father's publicist, announced that "the star's family requested that he be put on display as a final tribute to his fans." That was news to me. His open coffin stood on a raised blue platform surrounded by candles and floral displays. To the right of his coffin was a grand piano, the lid raised, with one of my father's sequined jackets lying on the piano bench. Large pictures of my father in one of his last performances were displayed on an overhead screen. Thousands of mourners filed by to pay their respects. Many of them signed a condolence book or one of the large posters of my father displayed in the lobby. My family did not go. Erin was puzzled by the public display. Why would they put her grandfather's open coffin in such a huge public venue? It had not yet dawned on her that he was an American icon, loved by his fans. To her, he was just Grandpa.

Another service was held in Los Angeles on Friday, June 18, at FAME, one of the highest-profile African American churches in the country. The huge sanctuary, which accommodates 1,500 people, is beautiful. A wall-size mural in primary colors and gilt forms a backdrop to the choir loft. On the way to the church, I rode in the limousine with my mother, my daughters, their mother, my brother David and his wife, and my granddaughter, Kennedy. The streets around the church were blocked off. As we neared the church, we could hear police and news helicopters circling overhead. When the chauffeur opened the door, we were swarmed by an onslaught of paparazzi. Hundreds of floral arrangements, including a huge wreath of chrysanthemums spelling out the letters "RC," surrounded the church. The entrance was packed with mourners still trying to get inside. Some of the 1,500 Hollywood A-list guests had been in line for more than two hours, inching their way through a tight security check. Security guided our family safely to the main entrance. We were silent, grim. Erin clutched Kennedy tightly, overwhelmed by the pressing crowd. The family entered the church by the main aisle. The sanctuary was packed. We could feel the stares of the crowd as we were led to the front pews and seated. It was at that moment, surrounded by thousands of people inside and outside the church, that my daughters finally understood the magnitude of their grandfather's celebrity.

A few feet in front of us was my father's closed casket, covered with red and white roses. A note on the roses said they were from Joe Adams and his wife, Emma. Mae, Mary Anne, and Arlette, all of whom had borne a child by my father, sat in the family area, one row behind my family and my mother. It was uncomfortable for everyone. Even in death, my father's indiscretions followed him. I had developed a relationship with my siblings' mothers, but their presence was a painful reminder for my mother.

Robert, the only family member to participate in the memorial, opened the service. He told the congregation, "If you would do something for my family today, why don't you stand on your feet and give God some praise—because we're here to celebrate God today and thank God for this man. He's blessed us, He's blessed us. Say hallelujah! Say hallelujah!" And the congregation responded "Hallelujah!" It echoed in the vast sanctuary. It was difficult for us to feel joyful that day. Reverend Jesse Jackson praised my father as a maestro. Clint Eastwood spoke of my dad as an educator who had taught the country the meaning of many genres of music, particularly the blues. Glen Campbell paid his respects. Stevie Wonder and B. B. King sang musical tributes. Everyone fought tears as my father's good friend Willie Nelson sang "Georgia," my father's signature song, and we all laughed when Willie said that after losing a chess game to my father, Willie asked him, "Next time can we play with the lights on?" Quincy Jones and Bill Cosby, who were unable to attend the service, recorded tributes that were played. My family appreciated the heartfelt tributes. The most poignant moment came from my father himself. His deep, gravelly voice filled the sanctuary with one of his final recordings, "Over the Rainbow." I was in the audience looking on rather than being a participant at my father's funeral.

When the service concluded, our family was shown out to the limousine again while my father's coffin was placed in the hearse. We formed part of a funeral cortege that went first to 2107 Washington, where we paused for a minute in tribute to my father's musical legacy, before continuing on to Inglewood Park Cemetery for a private service. Everyone crowded in front of my father's crypt at the mausoleum, where Mr. Adams conducted a brief ceremony, which was followed by a repast at FAME. By then we were so exhausted and emotionally drained that it was all a blur. When we finally got home, the evening news was showing clips from the funeral. Erin and Blair had phone messages waiting, all of them with some variation of "We saw you on television!" My children hadn't realized they would be on the evening news. It was another loss of privacy that only the families of public figures can understand.

Tributes poured in from around the world, but I couldn't take them all in. My friends called and e-mailed from all over the world—Russia, England, Italy, France, Switzerland, Jamaica, and Germany. Their messages were heartwarming, as were the calls from my friends in the States. I want to thank Kim Davis for expressing her sympathy by offering her home as a place for all of our friends to meet in our time of grief, and Lorraine Dillard for her support in bringing together all of our friends from Hepburn and 6th Avenue. Those gatherings really touched my heart. I would also like to thank Jeru and Natalie Morgan for their considerable and deeply appreciated efforts as well.

I would reunite with Rhonda Bailey for the first time in several years at Lorraine's. Rhonda was a blessing. She not only offered her friendship but her love as well. She went out of her way to help me through and out of the turmoil I was experiencing. She took a real chance inviting me into her life during the height of my emotional instability and grief. Her love and support became a stabilizing force in my life and I love her for that.

Ray was about to be released, and I still had not screened the film. I had promised my father that this film would represent our family well, so I tried to screen it the month he died. I couldn't do it. I tried, but before I was an hour into the film, the pain was too acute. I had to abandon the effort. It was too soon. By the end of that summer, Universal was screening and was promoting the film heavily, and I knew I couldn't wait any longer. I had to screen the film, and I needed to get my mother to see the film as well. With my father's passing, her approval was crucial to me. I scheduled a screening for my mother, Rhonda, her parents, and me. Stuart Benjamin and I were on pins and needles, waiting to see how my mother would react. The film was a tribute to her as well as to my father, and her reaction was important. Her support was vital. Her work with Kerry Washington and James White were crucial to the story. When the film ended and the lights came up, my mother told me, "Ray Jr., I like the way our family was portrayed." I was flooded with relief. It was all the approval I needed.

The day *Ray* premiered was extremely difficult for me. My thoughts were on my father. I had dreamed of us watching the film together. I struggled to keep my emotions at bay. I sat in the theater that night with my family and friends and a gifted production team that had finally made my dream a reality. The moment the lights went out and the film started to roll, I celebrated a quiet victory over those who said this film would never be made. My mind went back fifteen years to Red Cab Productions, to the day I walked into my father's office to ask him if I could have the opportunity to bring his story to the world. Even with my father's blessing, it took Taylor, Stuart, and me over a decade for *Ray* to become a reality. I was filled with respect and gratitude to Philip Anschutz, Crusader Entertainment, Bristol Bay Productions, Taylor Hackford, Stuart Benjamin, and James White for not sacrificing the integrity of my father's life. Once again, when the film was over and the lights came up, I smiled and wiped the tears from my eyes. My father will never be forgotten.

After the premiere, I found myself falling into a deep depression. I carried a heavy burden of grief and guilt, and of what could have been. Regrets assailed me. I had assumed that someday everything would be made right. Now it would never be made right. It was too late. I had been so busy wishing for a different kind of father that I had missed the opportunity to relish the one I had. At this point I was living in a five-star hotel in Beverly Hills, and I decided to visit someone I knew. When I got to the room, there were drugs, which was the worst possible scenario in my frame of mind. This time I plunged deeper than I ever had before.

Even though I was isolating, I was communicating with Rhonda and my children. Rhonda was adamant about seeing me, but I refused. I did not want to take her any farther down this path with me. My children came to visit one evening, and when they saw my condition, they began to worry. As the weeks passed and my condition didn't improve, the girls begged their mother to help. They were frantic with worry. Duana spoke to everyone she could think of, and finally she called Ray Charles Enterprises. She talked to Valerie Ervin, and told her I was in desperate shape. She pleaded with Valerie to speak to Mr. Adams and ask him to use some of his authority to release funds to get me into a good treatment program. When Valerie called back, she said that she had spoken with Mr. Adams, and he had decided not to take any action to help me. Family spirits were low, broken by their fear for me. Duana worked for some attorneys at the time, so she asked them what options were available for me. They contacted the drug court to find out what the legal process was. They were told that the only way I could be forced to get help was to be arrested. The courts would either jail me or put me into mandatory rehabilitation. But it might be the only way to force me to take a hard look at myself. I had never been arrested for drug possession or for being under the influence.

On February 3, 2005, two police officers showed up at the door of my room at the Dunes Inn–Wilshire. They told me they were there on a tip that I was in possession of illegal drugs. I spoke with the officers for twenty minutes. I told the LAPD officer that I had used cocaine the night before and I was not under the influence at that time. They searched my room, found a small amount of drugs, and arrested me. I voluntarily took a urine test, which came up positive for drugs, as I knew it would. I could have denied using cocaine and called an attorney, but I didn't. Instead I told the officer that I needed help. I was angry that I had put myself in this position in the first place, but I was no longer in denial. I had followed my father a step farther down that dark path. Like him, I had now been arrested for possession. The next day articles were in the paper and on the Internet with headlines reading, "Ray Charles' Son Arrested on Drug Charges." It was humiliating. But my arrest and the court would ultimately get me into a more sound treatment program. And it probably saved my life.

Eleven days later, on Valentine's Day, my father was awarded eight posthumous Grammy Awards, including Record of the Year for "Here We Go Again" with Norah Jones and Album of the Year for *Genius Loves Company*. Jamie Foxx and Alicia Keys performed a musical tribute in his honor. Once again I was not notified about either the Grammy Awards presentation or the NAACP Image Awards tribute. *Ray* was also nominated for six Academy Awards: best picture, best director, best actor, best editing, best sound mixing, and best costume design. At the ceremony on February 27, Jamie Foxx would win an Oscar for best actor, Paul Hirsch for editing, and Scott Millan, Greg Orloff, Bob Beemer, and Steve Cantamessa for best sound mixing.

ALTHOUGH THE ARREST had served as a form of intervention, I was the one who ultimately made the decision to go into treatment. I had grown up worried about whether my parents would be there to see me reach adulthood. I lived with the constant fear that one or both of them would die. As a father myself, I had come full circle. Now it was my mother who wondered if she would outlive me, and my children who feared I wouldn't be there to see my grandchildren grow up.

With the agreement of the court, I voluntarily checked in to sober living. I agreed to supervision by Impact Drug and Alcohol Treatment

Center, which works in conjunction with the court and other service agencies. They are a key part of the alternative-sentencing program that refers offenders to addiction treatment rather than to jail. They monitor program participants carefully, conducting random drug tests and requiring weekly counseling and strict accountability. Impact also makes regular reports to authorities on probationers' progress and conduct. If the staff believes someone is not attempting to follow the program, they have the ability to send that person to or back to jail. They offer services on both an inpatient and outpatient basis.

I elected to enter the program on an outpatient basis, remaining under Impact supervision while returning to sober living at the Laws Support Center. That didn't last very long. The sober-living facility was too close to the neighborhood where I used to get high, and the temptation was too great. Impact requested they move me to a different sober-living arrangement, where I remained for six months before moving to Marina del Rey. By June 2006 I had been sober for one year. One year of following the program and remaining clean enables participants to graduate from the program. I was proud of my success.

And how did I celebrate that success? I got high. Incredible, but true. For forty-five days, I binged. Ridiculous as it sounds, I even called my Impact counselor, Colin, to tell him that I was bingeing. Then one day, seven weeks into the binge, something strange happened. I looked in the mirror, and once again found myself staring back in despair at a blurry-eyed image. I don't know why, but that morning, my father's words from five years earlier came back to me. He had told me that one day, without rehab, without help from anyone, I would just decide to stop treating myself in that manner, and when that happened, I would stop. And I did. It was September 8, 2006, my sobriety birthday. I have celebrated three of them so far.

Once I was clean, I went back to Impact and talked to the alumni and the newcomers about my experiences. Most of the staff members are graduates of the program, so they understood what I had been through. Together we developed a follow-up program for Impact alumni called Still

Here. Every other month we meet with recovered and recovering addicts to renew our commitment and offer support. We talk about the challenges of remaining clean, take part in group discussions, and have fun together. The ongoing support and sense of connection have proved invaluable for many of us. I continue to attend meetings and remain in contact with my sponsor, and I do not take sobriety, my life, and, most important, my family for granted today. I know I will have to live the rest of my life one day at a time. But that is okay.

Now that I have finally gotten my life together, everything is so much better. I keep it simple and I thank God for his blessings. My life is not a happily-ever-after story; my family and I are still tied up in legal challenges. Yet, I feel fortunate to be able to rebuild my life spiritually and financially.

In so many ways, life is better than I once dreamed it could be. I needed to talk openly about my failures and my addiction, for the best use I can make of them is to help others learn from my mistakes. Today I live and feel my emotions instead of hiding from them. I have learned to forgive, as I have been forgiven. I have learned humility. After a lifetime of judging and blaming my father for the ways he hurt us, I repeated some of the same mistakes. It is deeply humbling to recognize that and move forward. Our relationship was bittersweet, but I loved him and I know he loved me. I am profoundly grateful for the love and forgiveness of my daughters. They are amazing women and I love them. And I draw strength from the knowledge that I am helping to break the chain of addiction that has crippled my family for two generations. Everything in my father's life and mine happened for a reason. It has led me to the place where I am today. God has spared me the fate that has claimed so many. I am still Ray Charles Robinson Jr., but these days I know who that is.

I am still here, moving forward with hope and optimism. As my father once said, it's good just to see another day.

Epilogue

*But still I hold my head
up high and sing,
Please free my heart and
make me strong to carry
on each day.*

—ARLETTE KOTCHOUNIAN

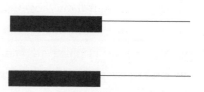

AS I MOVE FORWARD WITH MY LIFE, I CAN'T HELP BUT RE-member that I tried so hard to understand my father, who never called just to say hello or stop for a visit at my home. But, it's a new day. I forgive him as I have been forgiven. I'm learning to forgive myself for my shortcomings and I gain strength from the knowledge that God has given me another chance to do it right. My relationship with my dad was bittersweet, but there is no doubt he was a great man. I respected him as my father and I loved him. I know he loved my mother and his children. He loved all of us in his own special way. I am Ray Charles Robinson Jr., and I am proud to be his son. When I listen to my father's music, it reminds me of the man he was and the man he wanted to be. His music still communicates to me in God's common language, which fills my heart and soul. My father is resting now and our beautiful season will have to happen in another space and time.

Thanks to God's grace and His mercy, I have stopped the pain. I realize I have another chance at a beautiful season with Rhonda. We are looking forward to our future with promise, love, and respect for each other. I realize by arresting my addiction my children, my mother, and my brothers can move past our pain collectively. It is not too late to build a stronger family foundation through forgiveness, communication, and love. I hope my bond with my other siblings becomes stronger. They are part of my life, too. I have come in from the rain, I have found my reality, and I have been humbled by the road it took to get here. Today, I walk with my head held high so I can continue on the path God paved for me.

MY FAMILY IS DOING WELL. My mother is our foundation and she continues to keep our family together. Her voice still echoes faith and truth. She lives with her family memories and her beloved dogs on ten acres in Riverside County. Her health remains stable. There have been more surgeries, resulting from the one so long ago. But her spirit and love for her family remain strong and the warmth and dignity that have always characterized her still shine through. She remains beautiful inside and out, possessing that stunning smile, and the power to turn heads in her Sunday suit and hat still. Her days on Southridge are long gone and the memories linger, but wealth and fame were never a priority for her to be happy. At heart she is a faithful worshipper of Christ and goes to services every Sunday. She loves to visit her grandchildren and great-grandchildren as much as possible, and cooks for us every now and again. The same beautiful black-and-white photos of her and my father sit on the baby grand piano in the living room. And somewhere in the piles of boxes in her garage, I'm fairly certain there is a very large collection of hats, shoes, trophies, and memories of our childhood.

My little brother Bobby is Pastor Robert Robinson now. I am extremely proud of Robert and what he has accomplished. In 1985, God gave him a vision of himself as a pastor. When he realized it was not a hallucination caused by drugs, he walked into our mother's bedroom, sat down, and said, "Tell me about Jesus." So she did. He enrolled in divinity school, and three years later, he graduated and became a minister. With some of my father's stage presence and a strong speaking voice, he is an imposing figure in the pulpit. If you look very closely, you can still make out the scar from the accident with the electrical cord that almost took his life. He has our great-grandfather Mike's red hair. Robert now has a ministry in a small church in South Central Los Angeles. His church is a light on a hill, offering refuge and respite to those who are in need of food for the soul. My mother is his most devoted parishioner.

David has shared some of the same struggles I have. He has been sober for seven years now, living, like me, one day at a time. He refers to his years in prison as his "college." It was there that he learned some of life's most soul-searing lessons. He will tell you that it was the love and prayers of his wife, our mother, and family that kept him strong. It enabled him to see the light at the end of the tunnel. He could not let them down. He had to survive and emerge a better man. But he is the same funny, quick-tempered person he was as a kid, and just as lovable. His beautiful children are model students. He committed his life to God in prison, and he continues to do the work of the Lord with gangbangers and at-risk kids. He shows them his physical scars and tells them about the psychological ones as well. His courage and honesty continue to save young lives. Like all the men in our family, he has been saved from the fire, too. God has been good to us.

My daughter Blair aspires to follow in her grandfather's footsteps. She possesses a strong inner strength, and has an exquisite voice and timbre that reminds me of my father. She sings R & B and though she hasn't been able to record in her grandfather's studio as he promised her, she is currently working on a debut CD. Note by note and song by song, she is slowly creating her own sound and repertoire. It is exactly what her grandfather did early in his career, without help from anyone. When asked what her grandfather's greatest legacy to her is, she answers promptly, "My music." I know he is watching and his spirit shall rise in her.

Both of my daughters are strong young women. They have inherited their grandmother's beauty and courage, and their grandfather's determination. Instead of running away from their feelings as I did, they have transformed the pain into strength. Blair says my failures have made her strong, and have shown her that she can stand on her own. Erin refers to herself as a warrior, a woman who has learned to fight fiercely for those she loves. They are very close, fiercely loyal to each other and to me. They are realistic about my failures as a father, but they also understand the father I wanted so much to be, the father I was some of the time. They honor my intentions and my heart instead of dwelling on my mistakes. I have learned from their forgiveness and I am humbled, and now I can forgive myself. Erin, a makeup artist, feels her grandfather's legacy not as a burden but as a support. Whenever she is tempted to back away from something that seems too difficult to achieve, she thinks of her grandfather. She reminds herself that he never allowed being blind, black, or poor to stop him from going forward. If he could achieve all that he did, she has no excuse. Both of my daughters carry their grandfather in their hearts every day. And when you mention his name, they simply smile. They remember him with joy and laughter. A fond memory for Erin and Blair is the day they did a photo shoot with him for *People*. We are blessed to have that quality time captured on film. It was special for me to watch my father spend time with the girls as he had done with me.

As for little Kennedy, her mother believes that God gave her a daughter so that I would have the chance to be the papa to Kennedy that I so much wanted to be to her and Blair. Kennedy is the apple of my eye, and I will argue with anyone who doesn't think she is one of the three most beautiful little girls I've ever seen. When my father passed away just before Erin planned to introduce him to Kennedy, Erin and I both grieved that he would never see his great-granddaughter. Now, though, we are not quite so sure. Some odd things have happened since Kennedy was born.

When Kennedy was a baby, she liked to sit on Erin's lap and look into the mirrors on the bedroom closet doors. Erin assumed Kennedy liked to look at herself, the way babies do. One day when Erin and Blair were in the bedroom, they looked over at Kennedy, who was sitting on the floor looking into the mirror as usual. As they watched, Kennedy looked intently into the mirror and then started rocking from side to side and smiling, exactly like my father did on the piano bench. Erin and Blair looked at each other. They knew Kennedy had never seen a video of my father performing, but her movements were a dead-on imitation. Just as they were about to reassure themselves it was a funny coincidence, Kennedy smiled at the mirror, stopped rocking, and said, "Bye, Papa, bye!" Erin and Blair stared in disbelief. They didn't know what to think.

About a year later, when Kennedy was a little over two years old, she was misbehaving in the living room. Erin put her in one of the dining-room chairs and told her to stay there for a time-out. Erin sat down in the chair next to Kennedy to talk to her about her behavior. Instead of focusing on what her mother was saying, however, Kennedy kept staring over the top of Erin's head. Erin began to get irritated. She turned Kennedy's face to look at hers and said, "Kennedy, what are you looking at when you should be listening to Mommy?"

Kennedy pointed over the top of Erin's head and answered, "Papa." Erin had always been puzzled that from the time Kennedy could speak, she would say "Papa" whenever she saw a picture of my father. Erin couldn't remember telling her who her grandfather was, but Kennedy clearly knew. His spirit lives.

Erin was married last summer to Demarcus James, a wonderful man. The wedding was held outdoors at a beautiful hotel in Manhattan Beach.

It was a picture-perfect California afternoon, with a slight breeze to cool the guests. Erin looked stunning in her gown. As I stood there waiting to walk my daughter down the aisle, I could see my entire family assembled for this joyous event. Kennedy was dressed like a princess in a floor-length pink gown with a tiara atop her long black curls. My mother, along with Duana, sat in the front row, glowing with happiness in her bright magenta dress so becoming. David and his wife sat in the second row with their children. At the end of the aisle, waiting to receive us, stood my brother Robert in his white robe and surplice, waiting to join his niece and her fiancé in holy matrimony. Blair, the maid of honor, smiled as she preceded her sister down the aisle. I remembered my journey to this beautiful day, as we stood together against all odds. Tears fell the moment I saw Erin approach me in her wedding dress, and the first thing she said to me as we prepared to walk down the aisle together was, "Dad, please don't cry."

Only one person was missing that evening.

The bridesmaids' processional music faded to a conclusion, and I stepped onto the end of the black-and-white runner with my daughter holding tightly to my arm. As we took our first step down the aisle, my father's voice, as though from the heavens, filled the air. He was singing "Over the Rainbow." Tears filled the eyes of almost everyone watching. In that moment I knew that my father was there with us, seeing his granddaughter walk down the aisle, her heart filled with his voice that lingered in the air. He could see her. *See* her. He could see us all, completely, as he had never been able to see us in life. I knew he could finally see us as I had always longed for him to. And at last, I could see him with the vision that only God could give me.

This September, shortly after my third sobriety birthday, Kennedy started kindergarten at the same school I took her mother and Blair to on their first days of kindergarten. It is the same place I played with my friends during the long summer afternoons so many years ago. As I sit on the bench in front of the auditorium, waiting for her, the breeze rises from the ocean not too far away. When Kennedy walked through the gate, my eyes filled with tears, that strange mixture of joy and sorrow that pierces my heart at such moments. God has given me another chance. Kennedy and I will walk together, I will listen to her little thoughts, I will laugh with her and nurture her.

TO KENNEDY

Kennedy, I will be there to love you.
I will be there to protect you.
I will be there to pick you up when you fall.
I will be there if you need me to hold you.
I will be here, right here to watch you grow.
I will be here for your kisses and hugs.
I promise, I love you, little girl.
—*Paw Paw*

By being there to watch Kennedy grow and by being a part of her life, I am born again. I pray that the painful memories fade with time for my daughters. I want Erin and Blair to know that I love them very much and God does, too.

Ray Charles lives, his blood shall continue to flow in his children, grandchildren, and great-grandchildren.

That is our legacy.

Poems for My Father

I Searched for You

Dad, I'm searching for you and now you are gone
You and I were like two ships sailing in the
Night. Just missing each other, each searching
For the light in the other. Seeking each other for love, seeking each
    other for strength.

Wishing you were here to bump into, to feel your hands cup my
    face, running your hands over my shoulders to my waist, to the
    top of my head, and to you I have grown all over again.

Wishing I could kiss your forehead and tell you not to worry, I
    crossed my own boundaries, my trials were necessary.

Though the rain shall come again, I promise to follow the sun.
    When I see you again in the light of God, His will shall be done
    and you shall smile to see I have found my way to the light.

In the light there shall be no more past, no disappointment or
 reliving the pain, only love.

You shall see me for the first time as I shall you. We shall walk and
 talk together about all we can look forward to in life eternal.

Dad, please tell Grandmother Aretha, Grandfather Bailey,
 Granddaddy, Uncle George, Mary Jane, Grams, Aunt Sadie,
 Mama Lee, Elaine Bailey, and Elaine Chenier hello. Also say
 hello to Hank, "Fathead," and Leroy. Please let them know
 they are missed, too.

Dad, do not forget to touch me in my dreams, so I can continue to
 follow life's beautiful schemes.
Until we see each other again, you can rest now.

I love you, Dad.

Inside the Music

Dad, inside the music was where you belong,
Your first love, your beginning, and your ending.
Your music was the experience and your dreams
At work. It was all of the words and your feelings
You could not express.

Inside the music was your private world, your gift, and your
 journey.
It's where the requiem of your thoughts and
Dreams could be heard
All in real time to be deferred.

Inside the music was our common ground,
It was our sanctuary to search our thoughts,
Souls, and dreams to abound in
Those beautiful life schemes.

Inside the music was life in all its splendor
With all of its sunshine and rain. Yet we survived to remain, no one
    to blame. With all of the love meant, Dad, life with you was
    still as beautiful as the dream.
It is here in the midst where they shall find you and me, inside the
    music.

It's a New Day

I have witnessed the injustice and civil unrest during the 60s in
    America,
And I watched the assassination of an American president.

I remember the disappointment and the fear of the Watts riots,
    "Burn Baby Burn,"
And I remember feeling the hopelessness the day Dr. Martin
    Luther King Jr. was assassinated.

I watched a man walk in space,
And I remember how the balance of scale tipped with the Voting
    Rights Act of 1965 for our race.

I remember voting for change in 2008, America's status quo was
    rearranged
And the result was our first African American president, Barack

Obama, the forty-fourth president of the United States of America.

With great strides taken in the twenty-first century, God bless our president and God bless America.

My father would have been surprised, oh say can you see, it's a new day for you and me.

ACKNOWLEDGMENTS

I would like to express my gratitude to my agent, Alan Nevins, and his staff. Thank you so much for working tirelessly and believing in my story to get it published. With great appreciation and gratitude, I would like to thank my editor, Julia Pastore of Harmony Books, and her staff. As well, I would like to thank my cowriter, Mary Jane Ross, for her tireless effort and bringing her own perspective to my story. I want to thank all of you for your patience, understanding, and the way you handle the sensitive nature of my family's personal lives. I could have not asked for a better team.

I would like to extend a special thanks to our close family friends who helped fill in the gaps of my life in echoing my father's thoughts and words, and clarified some of the events in our lives. I would like to thank Herbert Miller, David Braithwaite, Reverend Mable John, Duke Wade, and Mr. "T" Terry Howard. I know by telling my own story, you were reliving your own lives with RC as well. Thank you for sharing your lives with my father with me; your input was vital and forthcoming.

I would like to express my love and appreciation to Rhonda Bailey for her patience, love, and encouragement. Thank you to Lisa Nkonoki, who gave me the inspiration and the courage to write this book. Also a special thanks to all of my close friends who have encouraged me during my trials over the years: thanks to Paul, Shed, Gary, Les H., John T., Al M., Jeru, Randall, Holder, Emile, Larry, Renard, James W., Tolly and Billy Harris, Jack S., Malcolm, and D. Brown.

Once again, I cannot express enough gratitude for the men who took their valuable time to help nurture and mentor me during my formative years. I shall never forget what values and joy you brought into my life. Thank you, General Titus Hall, John Williams, Mr. Kaiser, Mr. Ramirez, Mr. Hill, and Jonathan Leonard.

As well, I would like to express my gratitute to Universal Studios for an impeccable job of promoting and distributing *Ray*.

And congratulations to Concord Records for *Genius Loves Company*.

Finally, I would like to express my love and gratitude to my family for their unfailing support and understanding. I thank my brothers, David and Robert, for their willingness to share their own trials and temptations. I am grateful to my daughters, Erin and Blair, for sharing their memories with love and forgiveness. Thanks to my uncle James for his love and encouragement; you have always been there for me. With love and appreciation to my mother, Della B. Robinson, for the many hours she spent recounting her life memories, filling in the gaps in my family history, and sorting through our family photos and memorabilia. Your courage and honesty in sharing our family's journey made this book possible. I love you, Mom.

In Memoriam: Peace and Love to Terry Howard,
who passed away on February 26, 2010.

INDEX

ABOUT THE AUTHOR

RAY CHARLES ROBINSON JR. is the oldest son of music icon Ray Charles Robinson and Della B. Robinson. Ray grew up in Los Angeles, California, in a home filled with music and frequented by great musicians like Hank Crawford, David "Fathead" Newman, Quincy Jones, Milt Jackson, Marcus Belgrave, Gerald Wilson, and arranger Sid Feller. He is an alumnus of Whittier College and the Lancer Society of Whittier College. He majored in business and minored in economics.

Ray is an independent film producer. He co–executive produced *Ray Charles: 50 Years of Music*; co-produced the concert DVD *Ray Charles Celebrates Christmas with the Voices of Jubilation*; produced and appeared in *Black Prince*, a Grand Jury Prize award winner of the New York International Independent Film Festival in 2005; co-produced *Ray*, a Taylor Hackford film with Crusader Entertainment/Walden Media; and co-produced *Hotel California* with Alliance Group Entertainment, among many other projects. Ray is currently in the process of financing two independent films as an executive producer and transitioning his experience to the real-estate finance market.

He currently resides in Los Angeles with his girlfriend, Rhonda Bailey, and spends as much time as possible with his daughters, Erin and Blair, and his granddaughter, Kennedy. He is committed to helping those in need in his community, especially those struggling with addiction. His personal mission is to continue to be the best person, parent, and grandfather he can be.